ICE
CAPADES

ICE
CAPADES

A MEMOIR OF FAST LIVING
AND TOUGH HOCKEY

SEAN AVERY

with Michael McKinley

BLUE RIDER PRESS

NEW YORK

blue
rider
press

An imprint of Penguin Random House LLC
375 Hudson Street
New York, New York 10014

ISBN 9780399575754
Ebook ISBN 9780399575761

Printed in the United States of America
1   3   5   7   9   10   8   6   4   2

BOOK DESIGN BY MEIGHAN CAVANAUGH

Penguin is committed to publishing works of quality and integrity.
In that spirit, we are proud to offer this book to our readers;
however, the story, the experiences, and the words
are the author's alone.

To the sixth-grade kid who hates sitting still,
to the high school junior bored to death by class,
to the new intern on Broadway:

"Every now and then, say, 'What the fuck.' 'What the fuck' gives you
freedom. Freedom brings opportunity. Opportunity makes your future. . . .
'What the fuck.' If you can't say it, you can't do it."

—Miles Dalby, *Risky Business*, 1983

CONTENTS

PROLOGUE

I loved playing hockey. More than anything, really, from the age of five, when I first saw *Hockey Night in Canada* on TV. I knew at that moment that I wanted to wear an NHL jersey and have thousands of fans cheer for me. But if you're here for stories of me growing up under starry winter skies playing hockey on frozen ponds with a hot chocolate chaser, you're in the wrong place.

I was an NHL player for thirteen seasons, and I played to win. I wanted to be great. I mean, why do anything if you don't want to be great? But I didn't lie awake at night tossing and turning, hoping that one day I'd be in the Hall of Fame. I just wanted to get everything I could out of the game. Sure, I was playing for the money, just like everyone else. But I was also playing for the opportunities. A lot of doors open for millionaire pro athletes, though most guys never look to see what's behind them. Don't get me wrong, I also played for fun. No one can say that a Gordie Howe Hat Trick (goal, assist, fight) doesn't put you in a great mood. One of the few improvements I can think of is the Sean Avery Hat Trick: playing a great game, going to a club afterward and getting wasted, then taking a supermodel home for a nightcap that lasts till sunrise.

That doesn't sound so terrible, does it?

People have offered up some pretty strong opinions about me over the years. It's hard for me to say whether they're fair or not—and no one is going to care about my self-justifications anyway. I'm certainly not going to claim to be perfect. I'm not even going to claim to be a good guy. It's not my business to tell anyone what to think of me. I will say this, though. The guy you may have seen on the ice? The hate-filled wrecking ball? That's not *exactly* who I am. It's probably ridiculous to think we can know anyone from the way they play a game on TV. And in my case I played to the camera, and the crowd, and the press box. I made sure everyone was watching. That wasn't me being myself. That was me being who everyone thought I was.

I loved having the bull's eye on my back. Anyone who thought they were hurting my feelings by talking about me had me all wrong. So did every guy who got red in the face and tried to take my head off. If someone was writing about me or taking runs at me I was *winning*. I was making my team better, yes (that was my job), but I was also making myself richer and more famous. Name me a more famous third-liner in NHL history.

Not that it was all an act. Scoring a goal in Madison Square Garden is a feeling I think anyone would enjoy. I have to say, though, I enjoyed kicking the shit out of Mike Richards at center ice at Madison Square Garden even more. That may sound awful, but trust me, it was fun. I also did quite a lot of other things, and if I had the chance to do them all again, I'd take it.

And yes, I miss the game since I walked away from it. I miss the roar of the crowd. I miss the sheer speed of life. There are some days when I feel like nothing will ever be that good again, but those days are fewer and farther between now. So don't expect me to get nostalgic about how I miss hanging out with the guys in the dressing room. I met some great guys over the years, but I also wasted a lot of time on planes and buses with some truly boring people, and even more time playing by other people's rules. I don't miss that at all.

I'm not 100 percent sure what motivated me—and you need plenty of motivation to be one of the fittest guys in one of the toughest leagues in the world. I do know one thing, though. If you tell me I can't do something, I can pretty much guarantee I'll do it. So thanks, by the way, to all the people who told me I'd never make it. Without you, it's entirely possible I might never have put in the hours of work it took to play in the NHL.

Maybe you thought I didn't play the game the right way. But try to imagine having 20,000 people chanting your name after you've scored a goal, won a fight, or taken down the best guy on the other team, and then tell me you'd act any differently. On the other hand, I'd be almost as happy having 20,000 people absolutely hating me (hello, Philadelphia). I'd much rather be hated than ignored.

Sometimes getting a rise out of the crowd was a way to entertain myself. The NHL season is long, and there are some nights when it's hard to skate like nothing else matters. Because other things start to matter, and you can't win all eighty-two games. So sometimes I went out and turned the world upside down just to get through the game. Other guys took drugs.

Once upon a time the great Steve Yzerman told me that I should think about shutting up and just playing hockey. He said I had the talent, and that was good enough, and who wouldn't be flattered by having a Hall of Famer like Stevie Y tell you that?

I didn't take Steve's advice because talent wasn't enough for me. I needed the adrenaline that constant conflict—and sometimes chaos—gave me. I went on a thirteen-season tear by playing the game by my own rules and learning more and more about who I was. Along the way I met so many interesting people and forged so many life-changing relationships that I think I might have had more fun than any guy who ever played in the NHL.

1

LAST CHANCE

I've wanted this since I was five years old. I'm now twenty-one, and time is running out.

Of course, looking back I realize I had lots of time, but in September 2001, all I knew was that playing the game I loved more than anything in the NHL was the only option. There was no Plan B.

My heart is pounding. I am here to earn a spot on the Detroit Red Wings of the National Hockey League. The fact that people are already talking about this as one of the best teams in history isn't going to make things any easier. I am going to have to take a job away from someone the Red Wings actually want on the roster. And they've already told me in several ways that they don't want me. This is my third crack at making the NHL—I've already played two seasons in the minors. Every year, a new bunch of rookies shows up, diminishing my odds. When I look around at the guys in camp, or when lying awake in bed last night, I have to ask whether I am good enough. I'm not an idiot. I know most people would say no. The Red Wings already said no.

I had been good enough once. As a kid, I played for an All-Ontario rep team. (By the way, that's a big deal.) In my last year of junior hockey, I had twenty-eight goals and fifty-six assists for eighty-five points in fifty-five games. To put it in perspective, my fellow OHL player, Jason Spezza, had thirty-six goals and fifty assists and eighty-six points for the Windsor Spitfires in his best junior season. Spezza was chosen second overall in the first round of the 2001 NHL Entry Draft. He was beaten out by Ilya Kovalchuk, who was drafted first, and tore up the NHL for a while before walking away from $77 million and twelve years on his contract with New Jersey to play in Russia. Being drafted by the NHL doesn't guarantee anything.

I know this too well as I wasn't drafted at all. On draft day in 2001, part of me believed that there was at least one NHL general manager out there who would see what I could bring to a team, and another part of me believed that getting drafted was too good to be true. I wasn't going to sit by the phone—I spent draft day at a pool party. When I came home, neither of my parents even mentioned the draft, and I didn't ask if anyone had called. It was as if we had all moved on to the next plan of attack. I'd go to training camp as a free agent.

But still, it hurt. No one wanted me. Nearly 300 guys were taken, and not one GM wanted to use a ninth-round pick on me.

Well, I know why. The knock on me was that I was a "bad teammate." Did this mean that I stole other players' girlfriends? That I was an arrogant puck hog? That I put Tiger Balm in guys' jockstraps and thought it was the funniest thing ever when they tried to extinguish the three-alarm fire burning up the family jewels?

No, none of the above. What it meant was that I played to win on every shift, and some other players don't see the game that way. So I would let them know that they could do better. Since no one likes to be called out for dogging it, the rap landed on me that I was "bad in the room," which in hockey-speak means you're not one of the guys. Maybe it's the same in other sports, but in hockey being one of the guys goes a long way. What it won't do, though, is win you a puck battle in the corner. And it's certainly not going to win you a fight.

So if I wasn't going to make it as everyone's best friend and all-round good guy, well, I'd have to make it as the opposite.

I did have one friend in Detroit, though. I knew Kris Draper from growing up in the same town that he did, Scarborough, Ontario, which is part of Toronto but so far from the city center that it's known as "Scarberia." In 1997–98, when Draper was then in his fifth season with the Red Wings (the one in which he'd win the second of his four Stanley Cups), we worked out at the same gym. I was playing for the Ontario under-17 team, which fell under the umbrella of the Canadian national hockey program, so as "elite players" we trained at the same facility as pros like Drapes.

He had success, money, and a lovely wife, he was a good husband, and he took care of everyone around him. He was close with his dad, he had friends, and when he let loose he could put any frat boy to shame. He was the best guy. Drapes also had the Red Wing workout gear, which was sponsored by Nike and which was very foreign to a Canadian kid—we had Bauer and that was it. Draper would show up in this gear and hand it out to guys like me. I saw how organized and disciplined and dedicated he was, and at that moment, I was the most in awe of anyone that I had ever been.

Draper was physically a specimen. He was not big, and that was important because neither was I. He was five-nine—and some days when he was feeling supreme he was five-ten—and 180 pounds of lean, cut muscle. He was one of the first guys to make being in top shape a cool thing. Spend any time in the gym with a guy like Drapes, and all you want is to be as chiseled as he is.

Drapes liked me because I pushed him hard and wanted to beat him at everything. So every day he showed up at the gym he had a hungry dog on his ass who reminded him that I wanted to take his job. He later told me that I added years onto his career, but at that point I was just working as hard as I could to keep up with him.

One of Detroit's scouts, Joe McDonnell, helped me, too. McDonnell had been a minor-league defenseman who played a few games in the NHL for Vancouver and Pittsburgh. He'd moved on to coaching in the Ontario Hockey League, and he knew I could play. Mac was not a suit-and-tie guy, he was a players' guy, a real hockey man—he loved the game and wasn't interested in playing politics, so when he said that I had a shot in Detroit, I believed him. He wasn't the kind of guy to flatter a no-hoper. I had a reputation as bad as they come and Mac's job was to have good judgment. In my mind, he'd put his job on the line by taking a chance on me, and I wouldn't let him down.

But even with Drapes and McDonnell in my corner at that training camp in September 2001, I needed to do more than just play. Everyone in camp could play hockey at an elite level, otherwise they wouldn't be there. And they all know me, because I'd played against most of them in junior. There will be times later in my career when I will most definitely wish I could take a break from my reputation, but now it's the thing that makes me stand out and I am going to use it to my advantage. I'm here to get noticed, and a bad reputation makes that a lot easier.

I've pretty much been working on this problem of finding advantage since I was twelve years old. That was when everyone around me seemed to have a growth spurt, and I did not, and the "you're too small" stuff really got aimed at me. That dismissal, combined with the onset of puberty, was a pretty potent motivator. So while all the other players were getting bigger, I was getting smarter. I had to find a way to stay competitive until the day when I was their size. By the way, that day never came.

Hockey is a game of unwritten rules so complicated and subjective that no two people can agree on what they are. Some people call these rules the "code"; other people deny that there is a code. But everybody thinks there is a "right" way to play hockey (especially Canadians, who feel they should be able to tell everyone what the right way is). Who you're allowed to hit and how hard, depending on the score and how much time is left on the clock and how many games are left in the season—everyone thinks they have the algorithm to answer these questions, and they take it very seriously. They also know exactly how much you're allowed to celebrate, and even how you should dress. Personally, I don't care. But these things are important to me because they're important to other people. Break these rules and people will lose their minds. And when they lose their minds, a guy like me wins.

I'm no different. If another player gets under my skin, I want to punch his face in. But if I'm chasing him around trying to hurt him, I'm not doing my job. Better to get *him* chasing me, and then he's not doing his job. That makes me an agitator.

My template for success had three parts: identifying my opponent's best player, their tough guy, and their agitator.

The best player was easy to pick out because of the way he wore his uniform, or his hair. Remember Gretzky with his jersey tucked into his pants? Or Tony Amonte's flowing locks? The best player would put white tape on his stick blades or roll his sleeves up so you could see a bit of skin between his gloves and jersey. It was all designed to say "Look at me, I'm different because I'm better." Hockey players are trained to stick up for the guys with the soft hands. If you want to sucker the other team into a penalty, at some point you're going to have to target their leading scorer.

You don't have to be a scout to spot the tough guy. A true tough guy has a kind of aura about him. Watch a bunch of dogs in the park. They all know which one not to mess with, even if he's just trotting along with his tail in the air. The thing is, teams love their tough guys. Fans love their tough guys. If you disrespect a tough guy and get away with it, the whole hockey world is off its axis. He can be counted on to take a stupid penalty. It's money in the bank.

And the agitators, my species, are the most fun. You can smell their need to prove themselves. They're always small and they always have more energy than everyone else. You could see it in warm-up, when the agitators would go harder, just excited to be there. And often they would have a black eye or stitches, from bugging the wrong guy at the wrong time. Pissing off hockey players can be a dangerous line of work.

Anyway, I'd identify my three targets and systematically go after them in different ways. I'd run the best player, or take a cheap shot at him during the play. A glove in the face, or a whack to the ankles, for instance. My way of saying hello. Now he's unhappy, and his whole team is unhappy. (You know how hockey players are always talking about going out there and having fun? Not when I'm on the ice.)

As for the tough guy, I'd take a wicked two-hander against the back of his legs after a whistle (no pads, right?), and what could he do? Drop the gloves? Sure, if he really wanted to take a penalty when I leave mine on. Remember, my job is to piss people off. And nothing pisses off a hockey player more than a guy who turns down an invitation to dance. In other words, it was often my job *not* to fight.

And as for the agitator, my advantage was that I was pretty much always a better player than he was, so I would get power play time which was useful in calling out the other guy's total meathead uselessness. I would score a goal, or set one up, and then let the other agitator know that he could do that too if he had the hockey goods to be out on the ice at critical times in the game. If you can agitate the agitator, you're doing all right.

NHL teams actually have two training camps—a rookie camp first, followed by the main camp. Detroit's rookie camp in 2001 was like none that either players or management had ever seen before. I played like it was the Stanley Cup. By the time the main camp starts, I've pretty much turned rookie camp upside down. I ran goalie Andrew Raycroft, which triggered a line brawl. It's all on the edge of "out of control," but this is part of my master plan. The big club needs to realize that they need what I bring to the game—an ability to jolt a team awake, or get an opponent so mad at me that they do stupid things that cost them.

The Red Wings don't have a first-round pick that year, but they have a good crop of rookies, led by this Russian kid named Pavel Datsyuk. He's insanely talented. I know he's going to make the team, so I'm not too worried about him. But his gifts piss me off just enough to motivate me to go after the guys who think they can make it just because they're there.

And it works. I'm off to the main camp.

The first thing that happens is that we get our envelopes with our training camp per diems—eighty-six dollars a day to keep you fed and watered. The envelopes are filled not only with money, but also with meaning. The first round of cuts is in four days. So if the contents of your per diem envelope are significantly higher than four-times-eighty-six dollars, then you know you're not going anywhere. Team captain Steve Yzerman gets a per diem envelope for his entire time in camp.

My per diem envelope is four-times-eighty-six dollars.

This means that I have enough to get me to the first "Red and White" game, which is what the Wings call the intra-squad game, and which could be my last chance to show the management what this undrafted twenty-one-year-old kid can do for a team on the hunt for its third Stanley Cup in five years.

One thing I can show them is my work ethic. The NHL is becoming size-obsessed right about now, and because I'm not six-three and 220 pounds (I'm five-ten, 195), I had to try to compensate. Which is why I always aimed to be one of the five fittest guys at camp.

One of the conditioning things we do is the one-mile test, which means running four laps of a track as fast as you can. Usually the top goal scorer of any team I've been on was at the bottom of the pile with a pretty sorry time of seventeen minutes-plus. So I'd go out of my way to tell the guys I was competing against that I was feeling great—so very great that I was going to break eleven minutes. I wasn't blowing smoke, either—my best time was eleven minutes, thirteen seconds.

Back in June, I'd puked on the track running quarter-miles with Kris Draper. I was dry-heaving on the last two laps of the run, and Drapes said he couldn't stop laughing and that's why he beat me. I was twenty-one and Drapes was twenty-nine and on his way to hitting his prime. I don't think a hockey player hits his prime until around age thirty-one, because that is when body and mind are at their strongest point together, the key concept being "together." If your mind works and your body doesn't or vice versa, it's game over. I vowed to myself that I would retire from the NHL before that happened. But I have to make the NHL before I can retire.

Our training camp roster is split into four teams. Two teams practice together, and then we go into our respective locker rooms. The rink guys do a clean of the ice, and we come out and play each other. My mind is totally switched on to go full tilt, and my intense summer workouts mean that I am in game shape as we play these intra-squad mini-games up until the Day of Reckoning, which is ninety-six hours from now.

It's like my entire life has converged on this day. If I screw it up, if I get injured and need a long rehab, if I piss off the wrong person on the Wings' management, my dream is done. I'm not exaggerating. I've been a hockey player for three-quarters of my life. What else am I going to do? So I tell myself that the only way I can fail is if they beat me at my game, and I will not let them beat me.

I'm glad the hotel has such a full breakfast menu because today I need the fuel. I have eggs, bacon, hash browns, and toast. I'm going to hit the ice at full speed, though I'm sure that a veteran guy like the Wings' right-winger Darren McCarty rolled out of bed at maybe 7:45 A.M. to catch the 8 o'clock bus to the rink, and he probably downed a power bar for breakfast.

I have my eye on McCarty because he's the kind of player I want to model my game after. Mac was a guy who walked with the swagger of a 1970s drug dealer from one of those old TV cop shows, like *Starsky & Hutch*. And he dressed like it was the '70s as well, with bling and plaid and more noise than style. Sure, he was a second-round pick who's been a Red Wing since 1993, but he plays what they call a "gritty game" (he hits, he fights, he can score), and so do I. My strategy was to go sandpaper-to-sandpaper against Mac. And he's in my practice group, so I have a feeling I'll get to show the bosses how I stack up.

As a veteran, McCarty was here just to get through camp and get on with the season. He's got nothing to prove. Also, remember all those unwritten rules? One of them stipulates that rookies (and especially undrafted rookies) don't mess with veterans in camp. Now, I don't want to say that I took a run at Darren McCarty in that first scrimmage, but I definitely finished my check on him. He didn't go down (he's bigger than me, six-one and 215 pounds), but he certainly noticed. No one had hit him like that in training camp in years.

I was making a statement that I would and could play with anyone. No one was off-limits. Mac came back at me with some pushing and shoving. I know now that he wouldn't have fought me. The real danger was that he would have just smashed his stick over my head. He was smart enough to send a rookie a message without breaking his hand.

So McCarty figured out who I was pretty early because I knocked on his door, so to speak. I remember after the scrimmage that my pal Kris Draper talked to me about it in the locker room. He was very close to Mac, and played on the Grind Line with him and Kirk Maltby. On any other team, they'd have been the top line. Now Drapes was chuckling—with me, and at me. "You really picked the right guy to go after. You're going to wake up the sleeping bear and you better be ready."

I was ready. I wasn't so stupid and reckless to think that if I went after a guy like Mac I wouldn't need to keep my head up. And I wasn't going after him because I thought he'd never have any interest in mixing it up with me. I was just trying to get a job in the NHL.

Mac wasn't going to let that go and got me back. He'd make me fill up his water bottle with Gatorade during practice, or ask me to go start his car after it. At training camp the following season, he took a run at me. I understood why he was doing it, and it never affected me. It was all part of the game. And if Darren McCarty held a grudge against me for the next ten years because of the way I played against him that day back in September 2001, I don't blame him. But I wouldn't change a thing. Because it worked.

2

CINCINNATI KID

On October 12, 2001, I was sent back to Cincinnati. I think now that the Red Wings initially had no plans for me to be on their team, but I changed that at training camp, and now they had to do the math and work me in. So getting sent down was part of the numbers game that is professional sports. There are more than a few guys who "coulda, shoulda" made it, but the math just didn't work out.

I went back to the Cincinnati Mighty Ducks full of confidence. I'd proven that I could play in the NHL, and I'd also made $40,000, which was almost as much as I'd make all year in the AHL, where my salary was $48,500. Usually it was the assistant GM who delivered the news that a guy was going down, but Kenny Holland, the Wings GM, did it himself because he wanted to assure me that this Cincinnati assignment was temporary. I would be back with the big club soon, he said, and I believed him.

The Cincinnati Mighty Ducks are an oddity: half the guys on it are Anaheim prospects, hence the team name. The other half are Detroit guys. Not a lot of teams were splitting farm teams in those days, and it definitely affected chemistry. If a guy scored and he was in the Anaheim organization and you were a Red Wing, it didn't fire you up as much as if he was a Detroit player. You could also see the difference in the directions of the teams. Anaheim had a lot of Russians in Cincinnati, while Detroit left their Europeans at home and put the North American kids on the farm team. Detroit was smarter than everyone else and didn't buy into the theory that Europeans had to learn the grittier NHL game in the minors.

There are twenty-three guys on the team, and twenty of us are under the age of twenty-two. We all live in the same apartment complex, and my roommate is John Wikström, from Lulea, Sweden. He's a giant—a six-foot-five defenseman who can actually skate. He's also a great guy: he can party like a Hall of Famer, and he's single, so he likes talking to the ladies, and they like talking to him.

Our routine is hard, hard living. You wake up, you practice, you work out, and by noon you've banged out four or five hours of work. Then you eat, nap, and go out and pretty much be a college kid, even though I had never been to college—except as the guest of some hockey-loving college girl.

I have a girlfriend back in Canada. Her name is Sarah Schill, and she's a tall, athletic beauty from Kitchener, Ontario. Her brother Jonathan was my line-mate in Kingston, a very talented player who just didn't have the desire to make the NHL. While I'm in the U.S.A., Sarah is living with my parents, Al and Marlene, in Toronto. She's doing a physio degree at Ryerson, and with my schedule here—we practice all day, every day, except Monday, we're on the bus Thursday for a road trip, then we're back Sunday—I don't get to see her much at all. We talk on the phone—remember kids, no FaceTime or Skype yet—and I miss her, but I can't do anything about that except quit and go home, and that's not in the cards.

Sarah was my first love, really. But I'd never seen anything of the world, and I knew that I wanted to experience as much as I could and that the NHL was my best shot at doing that. I was a guy from suburban Ontario who was good at hockey, who met a nice girl from a good family, and I was with her until the moment my life started to change. By that I mean that my aspirations started to change. I no longer just wanted to be a good

NHL player. I wanted to live the good life. I wanted to take advantage of the world that being a professional athlete offered.

And I don't mean by going on some kind of sexual rampage. I mean, the distance from Sarah made me understand the DNA of a relationship, and as I was going forward as a pro I realized that I wasn't the kind of guy to get married at twenty-one and settle down. My priority is to have the best NHL career I possibly can, and Sarah knew it, too.

Cincinnati is a rough town, a hard-drinking place with a pretty stark racial divide. It's right on the Kentucky border, so it's where the South begins. We'd go to the casinos in the Bluegrass State and I'd see that segregation was alive and well in the U.S.A., with black people and white people living on opposite sides of an invisible line. Cincinnati is a football town, not a hockey town, and we'd be lucky to seat 2,500 fans in our arena which could hold 11,000—hard-core *Slapshot* type fans. There were nice booster-club ladies making us Rice Krispie squares for road trips. The college girls in Cincinnati didn't know who we were, but we were young white guys who had some money, and so they gave us the time of day (or night). I didn't enjoy my stay there as much as some guys did, because I was focused on getting back to Detroit. The guys who enjoyed it too much remained AHL Mighty Ducks a lot longer than they would have liked.

Chris O'Sullivan was one of those AHL lifers. He had elite-level skill and could have easily been an NHL defenseman if he had wanted to be one. I mean, he played some in the NHL, but he was pulling down $250,000 a year in the minors playing hockey and having a good time. Not exactly a life of misery. Chris was a great guy, and good for him, but that wasn't the life for me.

There is one very good thing about Cincinnati and that is our coach, Mike Babcock. No one knew then that he would go on to be a superstar in his own right, winning Stanley Cups and World Cups and Olympic gold medals. We just knew he was a no-nonsense Saskatchewan boy who could play the game well enough to know his way around the minors. Babcock is not a giant—six feet, about 220 pounds—but he has a gigantic presence, and during my time in Cincinnati he was like a lunatic compared to what any of us had been used to. I had never seen a coach like him before, had never seen players respond to or fear a coach like they did Babs. We were mesmerized by him as a group, because while his professional hockey résumé wasn't anything to humble us, his coaching ascent was incredible. I don't think anyone has risen so fast to the top as Babs did, and that's because he knew what he wanted and he had the talent to get it out of his players. He was focused on bringing it every single day, and he was as hard as he wanted to be on us, because he was just as hard on himself. He was being judged not just on his coaching but on his development of us, on making sure that the big club's investment in us would pay off. I really liked him, and saw my time in Cincinnati as a kind of blessing.

Mike Babcock was a great teacher. We listened to him, even if we didn't always understand him. He'd speak of "tracking through the middle," and we'd be scratching our heads. Then he'd explain. "Think of yourselves as a laser beaming in on the puck—you attack it and steal it back, like a thief." The possession game was his baby, and he made you see it in your mind's eye so you could do it on the ice. He wasn't trying to teach us to be like Gretzky; he was trying to teach us to see the game like Gretzky saw it. He walked us through visualizing the whole game before we played it. He was brilliant.

Babs was also a kind of pioneer, since he was at the beginning of the wave of young coaches coming from the American League to the NHL. Before that, NHL teams who had fired their coach and needed another one would just recycle some old crony they'd played with back in the days of black-and-white TVs.

And the reason players feared Babs was that he coached us all on level ice. By that I mean he didn't care if you were a first-round pick or not drafted at all. What he cared about was how serious you were about being the best that you could be, and if you dogged it, he'd bury you deep in the minors. He was coaching to win.

I think Babcock took his AHL responsibilities more seriously than any other AHL coach did. He was thinking big things. Of course, I wasn't thinking that he'd be a great NHL coach someday because I didn't know what a great NHL coach was at that point. But I was going to learn soon enough. One day after a practice in Cincinnati, as I'm heading off the ice sweaty and exhausted, Mike Babcock pulls me aside. "You're going back to Detroit, Aves," he says, as if this is a regular thing. I found Babs's timing hilarious, as he ground me through an AHL practice first, when clearly he already knew I was going up to the NHL. He was putting his stamp on the product that he was sending up to the big leagues. He was trying to make me a better player, and also, to protect his own reputation. That's classic Babs.

All I knew at that moment was that I was going back up to where I believed I belonged and was never planning on coming back to Cincinnati.

3

SHOWTIME

It's December 19, 2001, when I make my NHL debut. Sixteen years after I first decided I would be an NHL player I am pulling on Detroit's famous jersey and skating out as part of the team for a home game against Vancouver.

So you might think that I'm floating on the pure joy of having made my goal. Well, yes and no. I felt excitement, to be sure, but I would describe it as "controlled nerves." I knew I didn't need to put all my hopes and dreams into the first game, because that was way too much pressure. I needed to stay focused, to do something that made sure Detroit wouldn't send me back to Cincinnati. I think most guys embrace that first NHL game as if it's the end of the journey—a "now I can die happy" kind of thing. I didn't have that mentality because I had no plans to die, and to be honest I don't even know that any accomplishment would have kept me happy for long.

The lights were brighter because the game was on TV, the rink was immaculate, and the jerseys and our gear were perfectly laid out as though we were in some kind of magic temple. It was like arriving in hockey utopia.

I needed to throw everything out there, no feeling it out, no playing a little bit nervous, no staring awestruck into the stands thinking, "Hey there, Detroit fans, you who have seen more Hall of Famers than I have seen years, look at me—I am an NHLer!" Nope. I played my first game in the NHL just like I played my 200th. OK, maybe once in the warm-up I let myself think how cool this is that I'm finally here, but then it was back to the job at hand: now that I'm here, I'm staying.

My NHL debut is also made, not so much easier, but more comfortable because I know many of the guys on the team from my previous training camps with the Wings. Hull, Yzerman, Chelios, and Shanahan are like my wicked uncles and start grinding on me right away. They joked that Scotty Bowman talked me up before I arrived, saying, "We've got this guy who scored thirty goals in peewee and he's going to add something to the lineup." And I laughed, too. I would have laughed at anything. Because Brett Hull was my teammate. I was sitting in the dressing room with a guy who I'd previously only seen on a poster on my bedroom wall.

Of course, Scotty never said a word to me before my first game. But the fact that all these Hall of Famers were hearing about me before my debut seemed like a pretty good sign. I would come to learn that Scotty would talk crazy like that, but it was never because he liked to hear himself speak. Scotty, who'd fractured his skull when he got whacked in the head while playing junior (it ended his hockey career), always looked as if he were communing with invisible forces, his gaze shifting from you to the superior intelligence of the aliens he was exploring hockey strategies with. Part of it was the head injury, part of it was the radio waves from the Mothership.

There were a lot of guys they could have brought up or traded for at that point in the season to a team with nine future Hall of Famers on it, and so the fact that they chose me told me that the Red Wings' brain trust—and it was a brain trust, with Kenny Holland and Jimmy Devellano and Scotty Bowman three of the smartest guys I've ever met—thought I was one of those chemicals in the Red Wings potion that could keep the magic going.

Jimmy D also created a very strong support system for the big team. He would identify the young prospects, and then come down to Cincinnati a few times a year to see us. He also talked to us in training camp. He would take us out for breakfast before the morning skate, and the conversation would be aimed more at finding out what makes this kid tick than what kind of skates I liked. "What do you like to do away from the game?" he asked me. "Prepare for the next one," is what I told him. There is really no point in being completely honest with management.

I think Devellano was ultimately the decision-maker on whether a certain player was going to fit into the organization's big plan, whether the player was going to represent the team and fall into line with what they were doing. I would also learn, with gratitude, that while Jimmy D didn't tolerate fools, he believed in second chances. The Red Wings would give me more than a few.

And now they were giving me my big chance. It wasn't like they were desperate. We are at the top of the NHL at this point in the season, with sixty-five points, though on a bit of a slide. In the ten games before I'm called up, the Wings have three wins, two ties, and five losses.

You don't get to be a dynasty with lazy thinking, and Scotty Bowman was not only a great thinker, but a great psychologist. He could read people and situations and use the data however he needed to use it. He must have felt a crash coming, and so he brought me up.

One of the best things about my first NHL game was that my parents, Al and Marlene, got to be there. For years they'd hauled me all over the country to pursue my hockey dreams, but we didn't have any kind of Hallmark conversation about how great it was to be playing my first NHL game. I know that they were nervous, too, though. I mean, I'm still their little boy, who they suffered with when I was told I'd never make it and encouraged when I said that I would. Never, ever, did they doubt me. So they know how much this means. Nothing to be said, really, until it's done.

I had seventeen shifts and ten minutes of ice time in that first game, which was just fine with me. I could have had one shift and I would have been happy. While I didn't score—hell, I didn't even get a shot on net— I knew when it was over that I could play in the NHL. And we beat Vancouver 4–1.

After the game, I met up with my parents, who definitely played it cool, even though I know they were pretty pumped up. They were feeling my mood, and my mood after the game was that I wanted to play another one. But I was concerned about whether I would get the chance. I could be sent down, depending on what plans the Wizard Bowman had up his sleeve.

But I was not sent down, and with me in the lineup, the Wings had seven wins, one tie, and one loss before we met Vancouver again. It was in this game that I think I showed the Red Wings just what I could do for the team in the run to the playoffs.

We were losing 3–0 to Vancouver before the first period was out, so with just over a minute left in the period, Scotty puts me out on the ice. Why does Bowman send out a guy like me? He doesn't have to tell me. He just taps me on the shoulder. The Canucks' captain, Trevor Linden, is also out there.

I had no plans to fight Linden before that game. I mean, I was way too nervous. Hockey fights may look like good clean fun, but trust me, picking a fight with an elite athlete is not for the faint of heart. Later in my career I would look at the schedule in September and know who I was going to be fighting in a game in February. But not that night. And no one really ever planned to fight Trevor Linden anyway.

I had followed him as a kid, and thought of him as Captain Canada, even though I didn't model myself after him or his game. Chelly thought he was soft, but Linden had been chosen second overall in the 1988 NHL Entry Draft and had quickly become the darling of the Canucks and their fans. He was a great member of the Vancouver community, doing charity stuff and being nice to kids and old ladies and dogs. The guy even had dimples.

That was the perfect climate for me to strike. I must have rubbed every single player on Vancouver the wrong way during that first period. This is exactly the kind of thing I was good at in junior, and it was working here. I was a motormouth from the minute the game started. I was yapping at everybody, from the bench, on the ice. I definitely did research before the game—I mean, I was a fan of the NHL. I knew who I was playing against. For instance, the Canucks had Matt Cooke in their lineup, and I had played against him in junior. He was the same chickenshit player in the NHL as he was in junior and I was all over him.

"You have seriously bad shit running in your blood!" is what I kept yelling at Cooke, because I did think the guy was more than an agitator—I thought he was downright dirty. (See what I mean about unwritten rules? I have my own.) I remember the Canucks' Ed Jovanovski laughing about me with Kirk Maltby after a whistle, as in "Where the fuck did you find this kid Avery?"

Most fans think that opposing NHLers are at war from the anthem to the final buzzer, and I guess it's true that there's pretty much no one you wouldn't run over if you caught him with his head down. There's a whole list of guys who've dropped the gloves with their own brothers. But the guys all know each other from junior or from playing together over the years. When we're yapping at each other on the ice it's not always trash-talking. I've heard everything on the ice from guys doing deals to buy boats off each other to asking if they could get the hot cousin's phone number. Or planning to meet up for a drink after the game at a peeler bar if the visiting team's travel sked allows.

But I was not inviting Linden out for a beer. I took a run at him and whacked him a few times. Linden, as captain, decides to put me in my place. Now this is almost unheard of, the team captain fighting a rookie like me. Veterans actually consider it a favor to the younger guy to do him the honor of punching him in the face. I'm serious. But the captain sets the tone for the team. I guess Linden thought the Canucks had heard enough from me, but I was actually surprised when he dropped the gloves. He caught me off guard at first and I had to scramble to get traction in this tilt.

Linden may seem to be a bit of a choirboy, but he's six-four and when he gets a fistful of my sweater and starts in on me, I know I'm in a real fight. We went back and forth pretty good, and then when he missed with a right, his momentum pitched him forward and I yanked him down and threw another right for good measure. The fight ended with Linden on the ice and me being hauled away by the linesman and the Detroit fans in the Joe Louis Arena cheering as if I was the Brown Bomber himself. The Fox Sports guys calling the game said this was exactly what the Wings needed, and that "Sean Avery knew that."

They were right, because my fight with Linden woke us all up. Chelios, Shanahan, Hull, and Yzerman are all slapping me on the back and yelling at the team to follow my lead and take it up a level, and we won that game 4–3 in overtime. I didn't put the puck in the net but I have no doubt that my six minutes and eleven seconds of ice time made a difference. I could only hope that Scotty Bowman and Ken Holland were saying that this kid has something that most don't.

I stayed with the Wings for a month, but I had been called up because of injuries to other guys. A dirty little secret of professional sports is that guys in the minors don't mind when guys on the big team get hurt because it means we get a chance. And then kaboom, I got sent down again to Cincinnati because Igor Larionov and Darren McCarty came back and there wasn't much I could do about that. To be honest, I wouldn't have been unhappy if McCarty had been hurt for the entire season—not to wish him ill, but so I could have cemented my spot on the Grind Line with Drapes and Maltby. You do your best, and you're even good enough to stay up with the big club, but the math and the medics get in your way when a guy comes back from injury.

It was a punch in the gut to get sent down, but I returned to the Wings for the last three months of the 2001–02 season and, by the way, we won the Stanley Cup.

I would not be sent down again. By March 2002, I've been with the team for three months and am getting comfortable with the rhythms of the big time—everything taken care of, from the best coaching and equipment to player maintenance, to pre-game and post-game meals, to luxurious charter flights and swank hotels. I am still this kid from Scarborough, Ontario, who has to pinch himself to make sure it's not a dream.

On any given day you would walk into the dressing room and a Red Wing legend like Ted Lindsay would be working out. I'd ride the bike beside Lindsay for half an hour, and then spot him on the bench press. He had to have been seventy-five years old then, but he was in great shape.

The traditional rules that were part of other organizations—rules saying that nobody could hang around the team at any point and that the dressing room was off-limits—were not in play in Hockeytown. Detroit was an organization that understood what it really took to win.

Scotty Bowman and Steve Yzerman weren't concerned on any level that Terrible Ted Lindsay was in the weight room on the day of a game. It wasn't even a question, because they knew it wasn't going to make a difference in how we played. As a player, I was starting to understand what the league was about, as taught to me by the Red Wings. When you've played in Detroit and you move on to other places you have to bury your knowledge deep, because when you see the bullshit these other organizations pretend to worry about and how petty it becomes, you know a good team doesn't care about stuff like that. Because you've been on one and seen it work.

On March 2, 2002, a Saturday afternoon game in Pittsburgh that was being beamed out to millions on NBC, we were leading 2–1 with five minutes on the clock. In a situation like that, every bounce seems to go to the other team. But this one went my way. The Penguins were trying to carry the puck out of their zone when we came in hard on the forecheck—three of us on two Penguins—and Tomas Holmström digs the puck out from a scrum.

It pops onto my stick just about even with the dot in the face-off circle to the goalie's right, and I take a couple of strides, but my shooting angle is one for magicians—because now I'm on the goal line. Even so, the mantra that *"you can't score if you don't shoot"* has been drilled into my head since I was a little kid, so I shoot, from the goal line, about fifteen feet to the right of the Penguins' goalie, Jean-Sébastien Aubin. And amazingly, he's drifting away to his left, assuming that I'm going to pass, and the puck hits him and bounces in the net.

I have my first NHL goal. I celebrate it like I'm eight years old, because I've imagined this moment since I *was* eight years old and played my first hockey game. It's not a meaningless goal, either, as it puts the game into the safe zone for us, and it gives me street cred with fans in Canada and the U.S.A. who are watching and who maybe now think that yes, Sean Avery can play in the NHL.

And yes, we pay attention to fans. Not only in the arena, but those watching on TV. On that Saturday afternoon in March there is no Google yet, no livestreaming of games on Twitter, no watching on demand. We were definitely aware when a game was going to be aired across the country on TV, and we'd let our friends and family know. I'd called my grandmother in Florida and told her to tune in to see her grandson do what he always told her he would, and when I score, I think of her, cheering at her television, cheering for me. I know how proud she is, and that's even better than the goal.

The guys on the team are very happy for me, and when we land back in Detroit they have a special treat for me: we're going to the Flight Club.

The Flight Club is a self-described gentleman's club on Michigan Avenue, about a fifteen-minute drive from the airport. It's huge—10,000 square feet on two levels, with a purple 1967 Corvette that drops out of the ceiling (that would be the flight part of the club . . .) when any one of the 300 dancers is onstage getting into her birthday suit.

So me and my first NHL goal puck and the Red Wings are frolicking about in this massive peeler bar and I'm on the stage with three naked ladies blowing bubbles out of a bubble gun and singing along to "Celebration" by Madonna (perfect, right?) when Joey Kocur tells me to follow him as fast as I can move. So I do, and we run smack into the district attorney, who has come into the Flight Club to get us the hell out of there before the cops raid it.

We make it out, and it's all over the news the next day that twenty-two people were arrested by Wayne County sheriff's deputies who "found the club in violation of state liquor laws and a judicial order that prohibited lap dancing and other sex acts." But there's not a word about the Red Wings being on the premises.

A week later, on Saturday, March 9, we're on ABC for another afternoon game, this one at the Scottrade Center in St. Louis. People are saying that the 2002 Detroit Red Wings could be the most talented team since the 1984 Oilers—the team that iced Wayne Gretzky, Mark Messier, Grant Fuhr, and Paul Coffey, and were coached by Glen Sather—or even the 1972 Canadiens—who had Ken Dryden, Guy Lafleur, Jacques Lemaire, and Larry Robinson, and were coached by Scotty Bowman. Both of those coaches would have a huge influence on me and my career.

There's a reason an undrafted twenty-one-year-old kid is on this team of superstars. I worked harder than anyone to get here, and my job is to keep the seasoned vets on their toes when an eighty-two-game season gets boring and they need a little energy. Which is exactly what is called for when we find ourselves in a 2–2 tie early in the second period and somehow Sean Avery and Tyson Nash are lining up against each other at center ice.

Nash has become the most hated player in the NHL because he's good at what he does, which is getting under the skin of his opponents, who then retaliate and wind up in the penalty box. You can't do that job if people don't hate you. Nash ends up in the box too, but he's shrewd about it and usually brings someone whose ice presence is more valuable than his is into the box with him. But there's a new kid in town, and I am about to introduce myself to the NHL's reigning agitator.

I want to fight this guy. Yapping at him isn't enough. I would lose credibility if I didn't fight him in that game. So I say hello to Mr. Nash, and we drop our gloves.

I have my right hand tied up so I drop my chin into my right shoulder, unleash a six-pack of quick lefts, and down goes Nash. When Hull and Chelios and Shanahan and Federov and Maltby and Draper and Hašek and six other superstars tell me "Great fight!" at the end of the game it makes me feel like I'm getting closer to being a true NHLer.

I can't remember my first hockey fight. There have been quite a few of them. It was certainly when I was a kid, and we swiped at each other's face masks until we eventually figured out how to pry them off. And it just went on from there. You play hard and fast, you collide, you have weapons in your hands, things happen. And sometimes in a game, you need a tilt to make things happen.

When I think about fighting in hockey, I think about the five-division world boxing champion Floyd Mayweather. By no means am I comparing myself to "Money" Mayweather, even though we're about the same size and weight, but I always agreed with his fighting approach and tried to run my hockey fights the same way. I made the decision early on that I wasn't going to stand there and get punched. In the best-case scenario, I was going to win without ever having to throw or take a punch by getting inside their heads. But if you have to hit, then hit first, hit hard, and don't fight battles you have zero chance of winning.

Why do hockey players fight? Well, partly because you see the pros do it when you're a kid, and partly because sometimes you get hit so hard or a guy says something so foul that you just want to smack him. Your adrenaline is on overdrive, and it unleashes its power through your fists.

And why is hockey the only sport that allows players to fight without kicking them out of the arena? Fair question. I've never seen a fan leave the rink in the middle of a fight, so that's probably the answer. Fans love it, so owners love it, and I can tell you that players love it. There are plenty of good arguments against fighting, and I'm not saying they're wrong. But players will do anything to get a bit of jump in their game. You see guys on the bench take smelling salts to wake them up and clear their heads. Watching your teammate put it all on the line is an even more powerful rush than that. Fighting is like a drug.

Scotty Bowman pulled me aside one day in practice and said, "Don't ever fight when we're winning games. That's the moment you put yourself at risk of hurting us." I had never really heard that idea before and I readily agreed. I don't know a time that I ever fought when we were winning a game. As an agitator, being in the lead gave me leverage, because guys on the other team would want to fight and I would say no, then give them a poke with my stick and try to draw them into taking a penalty. Fighting is all about feel—the physical feel of anticipation and delivery, and the feel of deciding when and who to fight. In theory, you can't lose a fight if you fight a bigger guy, but theory is no good when you're on the receiving end of a thumping. You don't get applause from the crowd for getting the shit beat out of you by a guy that's bigger. I always picked guys that I knew I could beat.

I do know some players who actually enjoy the feeling of getting punched in the face by a man who has superhuman strength, though I am not one of them. Colton Orr used to say that he liked getting hit early because it woke him up. I can assure you that even with all the adrenaline pumping through you as you do the war dance, it feels like you are getting hit with a baseball that you did not see coming.

And when a fight ends on the ice it's really just the beginning for the fighter. An hour after the game is done is when you really start to feel the fight, and the pain of taking a right cross to the jaw or grappling for a full minute with your opponent until it feels like you're underwater, wearing sand bags instead of skates. When you wake up in the middle of the night to piss and your pillow is covered in blood, and getting on your feet feels like you're taking the last steps before you reach the top of Everest, you have to ask yourself if you ever want to do this again. Then you say yes.

Eighty percent of the time you don't hate the person you're fighting. I was trying to swing momentum when I fought, so I would have to make myself mad at a guy to get ready for a fight. You have to keep it all balanced. Anytime I was fighting out of real anger I didn't do as well as when I had controlled, or manufactured, anger. Sometimes you wind up fighting friends. I fought Rob DiMaio, and we used to train together and I would hang out with him and his wife. He was a tough guy and we split the fight down the middle. We would laugh about it afterward, and in fact, we still do, every time I see him.

My strategy is to be tactical and to not actually get hit, but to show patience until BOOM you can catch your opponent with a solid punch after he's thrown four or five wild ones and is starting to get tired. Then I roll my head under his arm and come over the top and BOOM! and another. I throw a quick left to surprise him, then tie him up.

As long as you can keep a fight going for twenty seconds—which is a fucking eternity when you're actually in one—and you can land on top of the other guy when you both go down to the ice, then you've won the fight and maybe saved your life from being a clouded fog of shit when you hang up your skates. I used to laugh to myself when I'd watch two guys stand there and feed each other punches to the face until they couldn't see straight. It was such a waste.

But while I believe fighting can bring as much to a team as a goal, and while I brought everything to the Red Wings that I had in my hockey tool kit, the one thing I did not want to do was fight Bob Probert. There was no way I was going to win against him. He was six-three and 225 pounds and one of the most fearsome physical specimens that I've ever seen, while I was the kid who was supposedly too small to even play the game. Also, it was my job to draw penalties, and it was his job to take them. But for guys like that, time in the penalty box is an investment. Everyone on the other team felt a little bit smaller after Probert had rag-dolled their toughest guy. This doesn't show up in any stat line, because you can't measure it. But the Proberts of the world make their teams better just by existing. No one actually says "Don't touch the goalie, because Probert's in the lineup," but if you're crashing the net, you might find a reason to veer off at the last moment. And while no hockey player would admit to being afraid to hit Probert, I guarantee most guys would take a little off their bodychecks on him.

Which is, of course, why I took a run at him at the end of the second period in a game in Chicago in late December 2001. And when the scrum got going after the whistle, I went over the top of the pile of players and sucker-punched him in the side of his head with my glove still on.

I knew he'd be pissed off, of course. You don't punch a hockey player in the face unless you're prepared to tangle. But there is such a thing as biting off more than you can chew when you're young and stupid, and Probert was arguably the scariest guy ever to wear skates. There were enough bodies between us that he couldn't lay a hand on me, which only pissed him off more. He's yelling to Scotty Bowman that Bowman better not put me on the ice again or he's going to kill me. Everyone who heard it believed it. I certainly did.

It was the only time I've ever been truly afraid to go out onto the ice. Scotty Bowman saved my life that night by benching me for the third period. I'll never be able to thank Scotty enough for that gesture and realized then that he must have liked me just a little bit. We also won 5–0.

4

MONEY, SEX, AND
FUN IN THE SUN

I signed my first professional contract in 1999. It was for three years, worth $1.275 million, and included a $125,000 signing bonus. I was rich.

In truth, I was anything but rich. Now don't get me wrong—it was a lot of money, but the NHL doesn't just hand it out because they like the shine on your shoes, so I figured that they figured I was going to be worth it. Or what was left of it.

I learned that my big $125K bonus shrank awfully fast (the Feds took their taste first, so that I saw $50,000 of the signing bonus go pffft! into the pockets of Uncle Sam). My agent took another three percent for getting me the bonus. That left me with $71,250. The wildly irresponsible thing to do would have been to go out and buy a GMC Denali—everyone was buying those stud-sized, fully loaded SUVs that would set a guy back $70,000 (and leave me without enough money to insure the damn thing).

No, I was not that guy. I bought a Ford Bronco for $28,000. Did I need a Ford Bronco that wiped out more than a third of my remaining bonus? No, I did not. I should have bought a used Ford Bronco for half that price, but what did I know? There was no one around to tell me what to do, and

I probably wouldn't have listened anyway. The NHL does not give guys money advice, and neither does my agent. He just takes his cut.

After getting my bonus and my Bronco I played in the minors in Cincinnati for two years before I finally made it permanently to the NHL with Detroit. My first NHL paycheck was for $14,500. And what did I do with that? I bought a Jeep Cherokee.

No, I leased it, because I couldn't afford to buy a Jeep Cherokee. I might not be playing in the NHL the following week, but I figured that I couldn't park my Bronco next to the rides of the twelve future Hall of Famers on my NHL team. I know now that they would have liked it because it would have said humility, and hard work, and honesty, and all those things that are good in the world. But all I knew at the time was that I was now an NHL hockey player, even if I didn't really know how to be one.

On my first road trip to Chicago I went with my teammates to this men's fashion joint called Zegna (pronounced Zeh-nyah). I found a pair of pants I wanted to buy, and the nice saleslady told me I owed $750. I thought she meant seventy-five dollars, but no, she did not, and this was not the kind of place where you bargained. I was too choked to ask the guys if we could go to Banana Republic so I could buy what I could afford, and more importantly, what I wanted.

So I paid more than five percent of my first NHL paycheck on a pair of pants.

My fashion sense was, shall we say, getting an expensive education. I was certainly interested in how money would allow me to express my personal style, but the guys around me were like almost all hockey players—running with the herd when it came to clothes. I could learn how to spend money on clothes that I didn't want from them, but I wasn't going to learn how to dress. That was going to be a lesson I would pick up from seeing as much of the world as I could.

I was paid $2,500 to go to a shopping mall in suburban Detroit to sign autographs for one hour. That's easily the best hourly wage I've ever earned, and I felt a little bit shocked. Getting paid well to play hockey—and make money for the owners and the league while doing so—is one thing, but getting a fat chunk of cash for signing my name is quite another. I would have paid more attention to perfecting my signature if I'd known it was going to be a money spinner. Even so, I sat at a table and signed pictures for people who'd paid probably fifty dollars a picture (I was paid twenty dollars per photo so you see the type of margins), and before and after this event a player would sign a minimum of fifty to 100 pucks and another 100 pictures that would be sold online. You weren't able to raise your rate or have another signing until the majority of the inventory had been sold.

It was a supply-and-demand type of industry and the demand was completely in your hands—play well, get a following, then you get demand. At this point in my baby NHL career I'm starting to have my own little following of fans in Hockeytown, and it's giving me a little bit of swagger. I'd been signing autographs since junior in Kingston, when people would come up to guys on the team in restaurants and bars and have us sign anything they had on them (though I did not sign body parts, despite being asked). I always signed for fans in the NHL, too, though backed off the professional autograph seekers. They could pay for it, since they were going to sell my signature anyway.

After I made the NHL and saw someone wearing a jersey with my name on the back, it made me feel like I was a superstar. I went out of my way to give those people a stick or a puck, and let them know how happy I was that they were on my team.

Meanwhile I lived downtown, in the Marriott Hotel at the Renaissance Center. A hotel room, even if it's a nice one, is still a hotel room, and even though room service is tasty, you get tired of pizza and burgers and it's all a bit lonely. Whenever I have time I get in the car and drive to Windsor, back in Canada, to have dinner at some of my favorite Canadian restaurant chains, like the Keg, which sits on Riverside and overlooks the Detroit

River and the city's skyline. Sometimes I would drive across just for a Harvey's hamburger.

The tallest building in view across the river is the one I live in at the Ren Center, so I can eat dinner and look at the place I'm escaping from. I have made the NHL, but I'm looking at it from a distance. On my own. Thinking of the future, and where I wanted to be in ten years. Still playing in the NHL was always the answer because now that I had a taste of the big time, I was like a glutton at an all-you-can-eat joint. Keep going for as long as you can.

On game days we would eat at Roma Café, which is about a ten-minute drive from the Joe Louis Arena. The place is on the site of the original restaurant that opened in 1890, and it's a family business that looks like it could have been the location for some bad action in *Goodfellas*. We always ate in a back room, and the oil-and-vinegar salad they serve is hands-down the best salad I've ever had, and you'd eat it along with your broiled chicken and spaghetti Bolognese.

The team gives you an eighty-dollar per diem when you are a call-up and living out of a hotel. The dry-cleaning and room service bills become a bit high but it's all now relative as my take-home pay is around $14,000 every two weeks, which still surprises me each time I see my name and the amount on the check. I start to put $8,500 from each paycheck into my savings account because I have no idea what I could spend this money on. Not yet, anyway, but that will soon change.

One of the perks of being an NHLer in a real hockey city like Detroit is that you have a kind of golden key to the place. And yet the Red Wings, true to their fans and their own sense of cool, liked to hang out at the Post Bar. The place was a legendary hockey watering hole in Detroit that was like the city itself—not glamorous, but a ton of fun. It was right next to the Joe, and both players and fans went there after a game. It was so crazy with Red Wings fans that the players would stand behind the bar all night, and we'd even wind up serving drinks to fans. The bar didn't count how many drinks went out—they would just tally the till at the end of the night and if it all tallied up, then great. If not, then great.

The Wings did not pay for any drinks of course, and I would marvel at guys like goalie Manny Legace downing a case of Bud Light like it was apple juice. Joey Kocur wouldn't even smile until he'd downed a six-pack. "Where's my fucking beer?" he'd holler and beer would appear.

You would see Kocur playing pool with the crazy guy who danced in the stands at the Joe. Steve Yzerman would come in occasionally and have a beer in the staff office. When he popped out to use the bathroom, fans would say, "Hey Steve, great game," because what else could they say to Yzerman? But everybody respected his space. If they didn't, he wouldn't have gone there.

I've never seen a bar like the Post anywhere, and on a Monday night in Detroit, when it and the casinos were the only things open, it always seemed like we had just won the Stanley Cup.

I never understood why Stevie Y only came to the Post once in a while until years later when I realized that eventually that sort of fan admiration wears thin. As I got older, the ugly-sweater team parties were not my thing, nor was the Halloween party where the guys got smashed and would stare at the wives who dressed in the kind of Halloween costumes you would not want any kid to see, costumes designed to show off the kind of body you can get when you take five Pilates classes, four spin classes, and a few private weight training sessions every week because you are a stay-at-home mom with a live-in nanny. At age twenty-two.

I give these women their due, though, because it's a full-time job trying to keep your twenty-three-year-old husband's eye focused on you and only you when there are so many distractions on the road. On most bus rides over the course of my career I'd hear some guy on the phone trying to put out a fire with his wife. You have twenty-three guys and certainly not twenty-three angels, and someone was always being careless and sloppy, or was married to a detective for a wife. I played with many guys who fell in love with a wide range of women from the beer cart girl at the golf course to the flight attendant on the team plane to the nanny. Some of them had happy endings.

But temptation is everywhere. On every team I played on in the NHL, the flight attendants from our charters would get drunk with the coaching staff at hotel bars on the road. And their memorable perfume would waft over us in practice. Just another hockey rink smell.

I have been growing further apart from my first real girlfriend, Sarah, and she is from me as I have been away. I think I saw her all of three times last year, and our phone conversations are marked by longer periods of silence. Some guys' girlfriends make them call them when they go out on the town and when they get home, but not Sarah. She is her own person, which is why I fell for her, but it's also why we're falling away. She doesn't define herself through me, which is what I loved, and I don't define myself through her, and now that we're in different places, doing different things, the distance emphasizes this reality of our relationship. After getting called up to Detroit, to be honest, I wanted to see more of the world I was in, and so I think less and less about a life back in Canada, married to Sarah, raising kids in the suburbs. I was still a kid myself, and best of all, I knew that. Sarah had left my parents' place and was commuting to college from Kitchener, so it all just kind of came undone naturally. When we formally broke up in December of 2001 it had been over for some time.

NHL rookies' relationships go one of two ways. Most often, the player moves his teenage girlfriend to whatever shitty AHL city he's playing in. Then the guy buys her a dog for company because he's away playing hockey all the time and she doesn't know a soul. Or he pays for online university courses and takes her shopping a few times a month and buys her a gym membership and leaves her in an apartment complex with eight other girls who have identical résumés to hers. Then when he gets called up to the NHL he either takes her with him or sends her back to whatever small town in Canada she's from, and gives her enough money to pay for school and live for a year, which probably costs him one two-week NHL paycheck.

It can be painful all around because some of these girls have put all their eggs in one basket. She feels so much pressure to make the relationship work that both she and the player wind up living a life of misery when they should be having the time of their lives, being together on their own and raising a dog.

What she really should say is, *"You had better start putting in more time at the rink because if I'm going to subject myself to this misery you better become really rich so I can start having babies and eventually send nude photos to your former teammate while I'm taking half your fortune in the divorce."*

The usual way hockey relationships roll is that the player tells his girlfriend to pack up the truck because "we" have been called up, and just like that "she" has also made it. All the people back home who told her it was dangerous to commit to a fickle hockey player will be eating their words now because next summer, these kids will be house hunting for some new digs and hosting the family birthdays and Canada Day or Fourth of July parties. I would love to see a statistic on the percentage of NHL players under the age of twenty-five who have two kids.

The reason these guys marry Jen from Owen Sound is that they can't handle the lonely nights that come with being a professional athlete—all those Friday nights when you need to be in bed by 10:30 P.M. because you have a game or a practice or an early flight, or those nights when you're ordering room service in a hotel room on New Year's Eve after being minus-two in a 3–2 loss.

Hockey players have *huge* emotional swings on a daily basis. In Tuesday's game you are on the second line, and you score the first goal of the game, but by the end of the second period in Wednesday's game you are minus-one and on the fourth line. Having someone you can come home to or call after that game who tells you the dog had a great day at the park and she just finished having some wine with the girls and she thought you had a great game and the defense played like shit is why guys don't go at it alone. It's why they don't wait to get married until toward the end of their career when they have grown up into men and are over the groupies and jock sniffers.

The groupies are a constant presence, from junior hockey onward. Athletes, and hockey players in particular, are creatures of habit. It's what we learn from an early age—repetition creates perfection. Or something close. And so that carries over into our personal lives, and makes the groupies' job much easier.

When the Wings would go to Chicago we'd always stay in the Drake Hotel. The lobby bar is full of groupies, who don't take money for sex, and hookers, who do. I think sometimes guys would rather take the hooker for a ride because it's easier, and safer. Groupies knew where we ate and drank and would show up in bars and restaurants to make their pitch, and I've never seen a guy get upset with a groupie. I've also never seen a player judge another guy because he goes off with a groupie. It's not like the Hollywood cliché where the dumb jock has to chase the girl for two years to get her attention. Quite the opposite. And sometimes a groupie ends up marrying a player. Many an NHL superstar has wound up happily married to a groupie. And the more that I think about it, marrying a woman who loves the game is a bonus.

Marriage, no matter how you get there—high school sweetheart, groupie—is a job, and you need to work hard at it. I didn't want to commit my twenty-two-year-old self to a job that stopped me from being free to do the job I wanted more, which was playing in the NHL. But it didn't mean that I was a monk, either.

The other thing I really started to enjoy about this big new world I'd entered was the chance to travel to places I'd only dreamed of being able to afford, and I discovered that I was a pretty adventurous traveler. In February 2002 the Red Wings went on a road trip to Florida, and for some insane reason that still escapes me—maybe the guys let me run with the idea as a test, I don't really know—I came up with the idea of organizing a road trip to Miami Beach for the night.

The Panthers played out of Sunrise, Florida, which is fifty-five miles up the road and a planet away from the sand, surf, and sexiness of Miami Beach. By 12:30 P.M. on the day of the game against the Panthers I already had seventeen guys committed to the adventure, and I was chartering a bus and booking hotel rooms at the Delano South Beach in the Art Deco district. I cold-called bars and clubs until I was connected to the manager, and I told them that the Red Wings would be in town and would like to visit. Surprisingly often, the person on the other end would be from Detroit or some other NHL city and would be a hockey fan, and so now I'm reserving our tables at clubs like Mansion. I was as far from Scarborough as I had ever been, and I realized that the success of this trip would further my status among the Hall of Fame crew in Detroit. Most of these guys would just go to some industrial chain hotel and then to a hockey bar. I wanted to show them the kind I life that I wanted to lead. And I wanted to belong.

Brendan Shanahan wouldn't commit, though, and I was upset with him, because I wanted Shanny's approval. I wanted to show him what I could do. However, I was just learning the subtle ways of Shanny.

After a big night out in Miami Beach and a long spell staring at my breakfast because I was too hungover to eat it, we settled by the iconic Delano poolside with its cool white cabanas. We were soaking up some restorative vitamin D before we got back on the grind, with our next game three days away in Pittsburgh. At first I thought it could have been a hangover hallucination, but through the blue Miami Beach haze I saw Shanny walking toward the pool. The Red Wings' best-dressed guy was wearing the hotel's room slippers and a bathing suit that was not a certified Prada along with a very un-Shanny T-shirt featuring the famous smiley face logo on the front and the words "don't worry be happy" on the back.

It was no hallucination. Shanny told me that because he'd played well the night before he decided to hail a cab and make the run to South Beach. He hadn't packed a bag, hence the generic bathing suit and awful T-shirt, bought in a gift shop because he didn't think people would appreciate him strolling naked into the pool. Shanny always did things on the down low and was very cool about his execution. He had a dark, cynical side to him that he hid in this man-of-the-world suit, and it amused him greatly that people bought him as an urban sophisticate, because essentially he was a goofy suburban Canadian.

It was a great two days off, and as I didn't even have a credit card, I never got stuck with the bill. Nick Lidström would often spring for it, and Lidström putting a $7,500 bill on his credit card when he was making about $400,000 every two weeks is the equivalent of a guy who makes $5,000 every two weeks spending $100. And since we only went to LA or had a two-day layover in Miami once a year, guys were more than up for it. I soon became the team's Maestro of Fun because these rich hockey players trusted my taste and imagination. It was that kind of thing that made the veterans look upon me as something more than just a rookie, and it made me realize that I had a talent for life beyond the walls of the arena.

5

THAT CHAMPIONSHIP SEASON

Of course, Detroit has possibly the greatest coach in the history of the game, and Scotty Bowman is not like anyone I have ever met. One day in mid-season I had a steam bath with him and Chris Chelios and boy, was that weird—I would have said you need to adjust your meds if you'd pitched that scenario to me a year ago. Cheli and I had stayed after practice to do some extra skating because Cheli didn't lift weights during the season, he just skated and rode the bike. A lot of guys didn't do weights— Shanny only went into the weight room if he was pissed off about something, and I don't think he worked out much at all compared to other NHL players. He didn't need to, really. But Cheli was a bike hound. He rode a hole into the ground.

The hockey body—and Chelios had a perfect one—is all about the legs. From the waist up it can range from a six-pack like Cheli has to the physique of a plumber. A hockey player's going to have skinny calves, guaranteed, but if you want to play the game at a high level, you need thighs as big as tree trunks, and a superhuman ass. There's no way a serious hockey player can fit that ass and quads into anything off the rack. I've seen guys jump five feet straight up in the air in the gym—that requires an unholy amount of power. Ziggy Pálffy had the worst body I've ever seen on a hockey player. His chest was almost indented, he had no muscle on it at all, it seemed, and he had skinny little arms. But from his knees to his torso, he had thighs like torpedoes.

So Cheli was pounding out a "desert storm ride" inside the sauna. A desert storm ride was when Cheli would wheel an exercise bike into the sauna and ride the shit out of it in order to sweat out every drop of the toxic fluids inside his body. Now it's 108 degrees in there and sometimes it gets up to 115 and this fucking animal is pounding intervals on the bike. And then Scotty wanders into the sauna and has suddenly become a student of Sean Avery. He wants to know what my parents did for work (my mom works for the Canadian government, helping immigrants, and my dad teaches special education), and about where I grew up, and what I liked to do for fun. I couldn't really come clean on that without sticking Cheli in it, though I'm pretty sure Bowman knew that his three-time Norris Trophy–winning defenseman was also a superstar at debauch. Cheli is single-handedly the most badass motherfucker I have met to date in my time on this planet. And I have met a lot of badass people.

There were times when I was in Cheli's bar at 3:30 in the morning watching him count out the take after we'd already had a very full night. The guy would count shoe boxes full of cash and then load them into the trunk of his car (Cheli had a landline installed in the Wings' sauna in case "Bulldog," the manager of his Cheli Chili Bars, had to get hold of him urgently). He'd give this bar cash to his wife, to run the house and feed the kids. No matter how late, or how much we'd had to drink, Cheli would drive home, and if he was earlier than 4 A.M., we'd sit outside his house and wait. I asked him why and he said, "If I get home any earlier than four then Tracee will think I'm screwing around." As I said, hockey players are creatures of habit, and so Cheli kept a regular time to his late nights, and would always be there the next day at practice, going foot-to-the-gas, or taking one of his four kids to their sports practices. He was always the first guy at the rink and the last guy to leave, and he never had a bad game because he was too hungover or too tired.

I thought Cheli was a god, and believe me, hero worship wears off quickly in the NHL when you spend six solid months with guys—and longer if you go deep in the playoffs. I was one of the only guys who could keep up with Cheli—who is thirty-nine years old at this point—partly because I was twenty-one and partly because I had the "go hard" gene. What I learned in Detroit was that part of being a pro is being able to go hard on and off the ice and never letting it get the best of you. Some guys can go hard at night and come back and play harder the next day, and some guys need ten hours' sleep a night with five meals a day. Not me. And not Cheli.

Now, I think swagger is both good and bad and needs to be controlled, but the reality is I was a little out of control when I was twenty-one. There was too much drinking, too much sitting in bars until 5 A.M., too much chasing women, and then trying to go to practice and play at an NHL level. But you know, all of that "out of control" stuff made me ornery on the ice, and so I'm sure that living like that actually helped me. I took after Cheli and made sure that nobody knew I was hungover or hurting (though they knew at times, I'm sure). The Sean Avery you think you know was a character I started to play right about now, and he was born from my desire to succeed in this league, and also from the fact that I frequently felt like shit.

I am beginning to find some chemistry on a line with Boyd Devereaux and Tomas Holmström. Homer is very similar to Nick Lidström, but a grittier "meat and spuds" version. They are best friends, and while some people might think that athletes have professional friendships because we wear the same jersey, it's much more than that. You go through wins and losses and injuries and late nights and early mornings with these guys, and you do become a band of brothers. Sure, sometimes one of those brothers is annoying as hell, and sometimes I was that guy. But the friendships were real.

Holmström is a fun, happy guy—a great teammate, everybody likes him, and he's a superb player. Homer uses a straight stick, which I have never seen anyone use before. I actually think his stick is curved a little bit in the opposite direction, which would make sense for his astonishing ability to tip pucks. And he can stickhandle faster than anybody I'd ever seen. He sweeps the puck toward the net, because he couldn't snap it or it would just slide off his stick. Homer scored 243 goals in the regular season and another forty-six in the playoffs. He played fifteen seasons.

Boyd is a very interesting guy, a center who comes from a small town in Ontario, about a two-hour drive west of Toronto. He's one of the most die-hard music fans I have ever met, he goes to as many concerts a week as he can, and he especially loves Leonard Cohen. Boyd Devereaux, a straight arrow and great guy, would have a puff on a Bob Marley to enhance his musical experience.

Boyd is truly one of the nicest guys I have ever met. He has a beautiful wife, Leah, who doesn't try to fit into the very narrow NHL wife box. She could come across as grumpy, but looking back now, I think she was quite a bit smarter than most NHL wives and didn't have as much interest in playing "the game," which really just means not doing or saying or even thinking anything that will embarrass your husband and his team. It's kind of like being a political wife, though your husband can get tossed out of office not by the voters but by management.

Boyd is teaching me about music and has got me into this band called Dashboard Confessional and another called Sparta, a Texas band whose members used to play at the Drive-In. I went to see Sparta at State Theatre in Detroit, and I was amazed when I saw the crappy van in which they were traveling around the country. You really have no idea how lucky you are to be a professional athlete in one of the four major professional sports leagues. Most rock stars do not get treated as well as an NHL player does.

I've also met a group of girls that plays soccer at a local college and I've gone to some parties on campus and in the dorms, which I like, even though I feel self-conscious about not quite having finished high school. Not that I feel stupid or anything, but just that I missed out on an important part of life. It's why I'm so keen to learn things, and why I ask so many questions.

I wasn't thinking about going to university or anything like that, but I was curious about their world at Oakland College. I met them all at a bar in Royal Oak, a district of Detroit where a lot of college students hang out, and they invited me back to their dorm. It was a chance to hang out with girls and guys my own age, and they'd ask me about the NHL and I'd ask them about college, and we'd just be normal twenty-one-year-olds together.

One of the girls bartends at a Rick's in Ann Arbor, home of the University of Michigan Wolverines. The Big Blue are a religion in this state (unless you went to Michigan State, the other college-ball religion). So I drove down to Ann Arbor to watch a college football game with the mighty Chris Chelios and the subtle future superstar Henrik Zetterberg—you know, teach the Swede some American culture—and shall we say that it was a very long day? Cheli, as I mentioned, can run social marathons on just a short nap, so after the game—and fuck me, there were a lot of people at that football game, more than 100,000—we go to Rick's and do shots of tequila from this amazing ice sculpture that looked like that castle in *Beauty and the Beast* (I still can't figure out how they built it), and then we go to a party at a sorority house, and then suddenly it's 6 A.M. That feels like a long time ago, but I seem to remember that when you're twenty-one, there aren't a lot of things more fun than being a professional athlete in a sorority house.

I wonder to myself on the car ride back to the Joe if anyone is going to notice that I have the same clothes on that I wore yesterday, and I also wonder why I have more money in my pocket now than I did when we left yesterday. I can't remember going to a bank machine; maybe I won a bet. I certainly didn't win the tequila shooters contest. Cheli won that. To this day, I have no idea how that cash got there. Or how I made it through practice, but somehow I did.

It feels like I am unstoppable.

Less than a week after I turned twenty-two, we finished the season as the best team in the NHL and received the Presidents' Trophy following our final game, a 5–3 loss to St. Louis at the Joe. With our 116 points, we finished eighteen points better than the Blues, and fifteen better than the next best team, Boston.

The Presidents' Trophy has been handed out to the NHL's best team— i.e., the one with the most points at the end of the regular season—since 1985–86, and if you don't go on to win the Stanley Cup after winning the league, the Presidents' Trophy is no consolation prize whatsoever. Some guys say it's a curse, as only eight teams that have won it have gone on to win Lord Stanley's jug. Twenty-three have not.

Winning the Presidents' Trophy just means we have even more pressure on us as we get ready to chase those sixteen post-season Ws that allow you to hold the one trophy that you really want to raise to the hockey gods in thanksgiving, the Stanley Cup.

We're at the end of practice and we're working on our front net tips. This usually consists of a defenseman taking shots from the blue line while a guy stands in front of the net attempting to screen the goalie while you tip the puck. You need all kinds of jam to do this at all, let alone do it well. The puck is traveling at nearly 100 miles an hour, so you have a split second to connect with it in just the right way so that it deflects past the goalie, who you can't see because he's behind you, while the opposing defensemen are pounding on you.

This is one of the hardest things to do in sport and probably takes the most balls. Imagine trying to hit a fastball with a hockey stick while an MMA fighter pummels you in the back, and you get the idea. Thomas Holmström is the master of deflecting pucks. Holmström would take a beating as he fought to remain on the arch of the crease, screening the goalie until he could slice pucks out of the air like a chef dicing tomatoes into the stew pot. Get it wrong, though, and you end up with a puck in the face, which you only realize when you wake up on the ice choking on a mouthful of blood and broken teeth.

(I know the feeling firsthand, because it's happened to me twice. When the puck hits you in the face it's more of a shock than a blast of pain. The pain comes later when they put in the stitches, which have left me with two of what I now consider my most distinguished scars. It looks like I was bitten by a pit bull and he took part of my face with him to snack on later. Still, if given the choice today to be hit or not to be hit, I would say go ahead and take your best shot because it's a very effective way of telling people that I've paid some dues in my professional life. And to be honest, the ladies have always liked it. So did *People* magazine, which named me Sexiest Scar of 2007.)

So today at practice, I'm in front of the net trying to tip pucks when Mathieu Dandeneault tees up a slap shot that catches me off guard. It hits the bone just above my skate boot and just below my shin pads. The one place where there is absolutely zero padding.

I know the moment it hits me that I'm fucked and I immediately start hobbling toward the bench. For the first time in my career I shriek in pain, a kind of wounded animal howl which gets everyone's attention. The buzz-saw of pain is now followed by a terrible wave of nausea. Three seconds after impact an entire season flashes through my head as I puke all over the ice in front of the door that leads from the ice to the team bench. I continue vomiting as I hobble down the hallway and into the dressing room.

It was a few days before an X-ray revealed a hairline fracture of the non-weight-bearing bone in my fibula, which means I can walk without pain but it feels like a red-hot knife is skewering my leg when any pressure is applied.

I actually practiced for two days after my leg was broken. I was pretending that nothing was wrong, because I wanted to be in the lineup heading into the playoffs. How do you go from pain so intense you're puking to pain manageable enough that you can fake your way through an NHL practice? Part of it is mental (I'm hardly the first guy to play on a broken leg). But a big part of it is pharmaceutical.

I'd already been in the minors for two years, remember, so I knew a thing or two about solutions that come in pill form. The medical staff isn't there to ensure that hockey players live long and satisfying lives—their job is to help guys play. If you've ever gone from excruciating pain to mere discomfort, you know how gloriously welcome a Vicodin or a Percocet can be.

Well, Vicodin kept me out there on the ice, though it didn't heal me, of course. Finally, Scotty Bowman came over and told me to hit the showers and get that leg taken care of because he was going to need me.

Being told by hockey wizard Scotty Bowman that he needs you is a lot better than the warm glow of a Percocet, I can tell you, and a lot harder to come by. Suddenly, the pain in my leg morphed into a kind of ecstasy, because I felt, finally, like I belonged. It's a feeling, I would learn, that can change in a shift, but for now, I was needed.

I watched the first two playoff games from the box, and by the end of them, we're down two games to zip at the hands of the Canucks. The Presidents' Trophy winners have lost their first two games at home. Two more losses and we're golfing, and I'll believe in that curse.

We land in Vancouver for Game 3 around 3 A.M., and on the drive from YVR to the hotel downtown there are dozens of cars—as many as forty of them—full of Canuckleheads driving alongside our bus holding brooms out the windows to remind us we're two games away from being swept from the playoffs. Popping out of the cars' sunroofs are ladies who've yanked up their tops to show us they're braless, and have "sweep" painted across their tits. Just in case we'd missed the message with the brooms. I have to admit I preferred the ladies' way of delivering it.

Only in Canada would fans stay up all night waiting for the opponent to land so they could fuck with them. During the playoffs, visiting teams usually rent out an entire floor of a hotel to keep the players away from that kind of fan. Not to mention puck bunnies and autograph seekers.

Seekers are the norm in pro sports these days, and while most guys always have time for starry-eyed kids, they cringe at the seekers. There are guys who wait outside the team hotel twenty-four hours a day like paparazzi, trying to get players to sign every type of card or iron-on jersey number or fathead picture or anything else that could decorate the wall of fame in a man cave. Autographs that they then sell for a sweet profit.

I learned about this game from the best: Stevie Y, and Shanahan, and the king of autographs, Brett Hull. These guys could make $250K a year just by selling autographs, so they were very smart about setting prices and not flooding the market.

After they won their first Stanley Cup together in 1997, they would only sign team pictures as part of prearranged deals done directly with the autograph dealers. The guys would also sometimes personalize their signatures so the dealers couldn't resell them. Brett Hull told me my autograph was horrible and so on a road trip we sat together on the plane and he helped me find the signature that I still use today. "All you really need is the first and last initial and the rest is just scribble," he told me. This lets you sign fast and easy.

I'd mailed Brett Hull a hockey card to sign ten years earlier, and he told me that a family friend had probably done it. In return for all those "Brett Hull" signatures, he paid for her college education. I felt like Santa Claus had just been busted but was also impressed at his business sense. Of course he could never have signed all those cards and letters. I know that most of the greats had a similar situation set up with either a stick boy or assistant trainer who was more than happy to make the extra cash and could have signed a few dozen cards while sitting on the toilet, if they really wanted.

You could also make money just by being in the playoffs, when players are not actually being paid, but when there are bonuses and cash bumps for doing well.

At the beginning of the 2002 Stanley Cup Playoffs we were each given a form to fill out with the number of additional tickets (beyond the two given to every player) that we wanted to purchase. I'm sure the haters are going to see this as proof of what a terrible man I am, but I bought these extra tickets to sell to a broker I'd become friends with, and who was a great contact for tickets to shows in Vegas and NYC. If the face value of the ticket was $100 then he gave me $200, and this sale price would increase game by game and round by round. I bought six tickets for each round and by the finals I was making around $2,000 profit per game, so let's call it roughly a $15K profit over the four rounds.

It's absolutely laughable to me that anyone should object to this. But it's so typical of the old-school sports mentality that you're vilified for what you say rather than what you do. Keep your mouth shut, and you can do whatever you want. I'm not like that. I wouldn't do something that I wouldn't own up to. The way I saw it, I was taking advantage of an opportunity presented to me because of years of hard work.

And then, it looked for a horrifying few minutes as if that opportunity was going to vanish forever.

On our first morning in Vancouver for Game 3 I get a call at 9:30 from the Wings' GM, Ken Holland, telling me to meet him in the restaurant downstairs ASAP. I think "Holy shit! They're putting me in for Game 3!"

"Hi Mr. Holland," I say, greeting the guy with the ultimate power over my career, to which he quickly replies, "Cut the shit, you know the guys call me Kenny."

Ken Holland had a great relationship with almost every single player who's been part of the Red Wings core over the years, and one of the reasons for this was that he didn't lie or bullshit them. This is a rare trait among NHL general managers, who would lie to their own mothers about being their sons if it meant they could keep their jobs. So many of them had permanently chapped lips because of all the ass they'd kissed along the way.

So just as I'm thinking that good guy Ken is going to tell me I'm dressing for Game 3, he surprises the hell out of me by barking, "What the fuck did you do last night?"

"I was in my room as soon as we got to the hotel," I reply, suddenly feeling not like the game buster I imagined I would be but some sniveling kid in the principal's office. For a moment I even think to myself, "Jesus did I go out last night and just can't remember?"

Holland looks like he's already sentenced me to death. "I got a call from the owner of your complex in Detroit who said your motherfucking buddies broke your front door down and proceeded to destroy everything in sight, and were running around naked with a bunch of broads." (Note: All NHL GMs refer to any women their players are fucking—except for their wives—as broads.)

I told him I had no idea what happened and I would kick my friends out immediately and pay for any damage. At this point my eyes are starting to fill with tears. I've never been this scared in my entire life, and there's also the gut-punch feeling that I've let down the guy who's given me the thing I've put every ounce of my soul into achieving since I was eight years old. I'm wondering if I just ruined my life.

Holland told me it was the last time anything like this could happen, or else I'd be finished. I believed every word that came out of his mouth that morning. And I could have wept with relief that I wasn't finished yet. He'd given me a second chance.

Game 3 did not include me leading the team to a glorious comeback in the famous winged wheel sweater, and honestly, that was fine, as I was still too hurt to play. But the way things turned out in that quarterfinal series against Vancouver shows what big-time veterans we had on that team, guys who played even better in big-time situations.

We won Game 3 in Vancouver because of one of the flukiest plays I've ever seen. It was at a point in the series where if we'd lost the game, we were probably done. We were tied at one goal apiece with thirty seconds left in the second period when Nick Lidström skated the puck out of our zone and just before he hit center ice, fired it toward the Vancouver goal. It was a knuckler, and it dipped right underneath Canuck goalie Dan Cloutier's glove. You could hear the wind being sucked out of the arena, and the Canuckleheads, and their team. We won 3–1, and the Canucks never won another game in that series.

I ended up playing with Dan Cloutier toward the end of his career in LA. I'd always heard rumors that he was tough, and for a goalie to be tough is like a baseball pitcher being a great hitter. But it was true. Dan Cloutier had three fights in the NHL and one in the AHL, and for a goalie, that's like being a rabid dog. He had crystal blue eyes and Clark Kent looks, but he was really a fucking savage inside.

That goal he let in was something that could happen to anyone, and a good team shrugs it off and comes out harder. It was largely Dan's play that got the Canucks into the playoffs in the first place. He won thirty-one games that season, posted seven shutouts, and went 7-0-1 down the stretch. So they'd definitely overachieved going up two zip on us, and when that fluky goal went in, the Canucks looked in the mirror and we looked forward, to our next opponent, the St. Louis Blues. We knocked the Blues off in five games. We'd won eight of our last nine. I can feel the momentum rising in the room, and now we're halfway to the sixteen wins needed for the Cup. Standing in our way to the final are the evil Colorado Avalanche.

Because I looked up so much to the guys on Detroit, I inherited their hate-on for Colorado, which started with Claude Lemieux's nasty, nasty hit on Kris Draper in the 1996 Western Conference Final. Lemieux checked Draper face-first into the dasher boards and got five and a two-game suspension while Drapes—who had a concussion, a broken jaw, broken nose, and broken cheekbone—got a new face, as the medics pretty much had to rebuild it.

The Wings also hated Lemieux because he was hard to play against. He was a very smart defensive player—you could always feel him breathing down your neck and you knew he was going to finish his check. He was unusual because French-Canadian guys played a skill game and left the tough stuff to others, but not Claude Lemieux.

I tried to do my part both times I played against Colorado in 2002. The first game was on February 4, 2002. I was sitting on the bench doing my usual routine of giving every guy on the other team who skated by a piece of my mind about how they should just resign from humanity.

I soon learned there were guys in the league that my Hall of Fame teammates wouldn't allow me to unleash on. Standing at the end of the bench was something I did till the end of my career because I knew it was annoying to my own team if I was constantly shit-talking while moving up and down the bench until my name was called to hop over the boards.

Brett Hull sometimes would stay at the end of the bench when he was pissed off at his line-mates for not seeing the play open sixteen seconds before it happened, the way he could see it happening. In my first game against the Avalanche, with Hully right next to me, I leaned over to tell Joe Sakic that I'd seen him walking into the arena before the game and that he should sue the blind thief who sold him his sports coat and that I wondered how a guy making $8 million a year could dress that badly.

I threw in the intel that if our shifts overlapped, I was going to follow him like a Scud missile and blindside his old ass. As those words came out of my mouth I felt a hand the size of a baseball mitt attached to a wrist the size of a ham pull the back of my jersey onto the bench. I turned to my right and was shocked to realize that it was Brett Hull grabbing me, and then he told me, loud enough for Sakic to hear, "You are never to speak with or to Mr. Sakic in that tone again."

It was the first time Brett Hull was pissed at me, and I suddenly understood that certain guys were really truly off-limits. Brett would have been the first to smile if I'd put Mr. Sakic on his ass with a clean hit between whistles, but he was not smiling at the other stuff. So the character of Sean Avery got a major adjustment at that moment. I'd have to find another way to get the future Hall of Famers off their game.

After my leg healed I resumed my daily grind as a Black Ace, which is the term we use to describe the extra players on a team's roster during the playoffs. Usually these guys get into the lineup at some point, and in Detroit there were five of us who'd spend an additional hour on the ice after the guys in the lineup were finished practicing. The Aces would do skating drills hidden inside shooting drills which would be followed by a "bag skate." This is when you start at your goal line, skate to your blue line, stop, skate back, stop, do it again, stop, skate to the center line, stop, skate back, stop, skate to the far blue line, stop, and skate back again, until you've skated your bags off. Some coaches use it as punishment, but during the playoffs conditioning is king, so they want to be sure we're game ready if we get tapped.

We'd then finish Black Aces sessions with a four-on-four game that also included the assistant coaches: Joey Kocur, Dave Lewis, and "Bug-Eyed" Barry Smith. Dave Lewis would be our coach the following year, though we didn't know it then, and Barry Smith was another one of Scotty's secret weapons. Because he had the same kind of wide-eyed stare that Marty Feldman has we called him Bug-Eyed Barry, but he didn't notice. You could always talk to Barry about Scotty and feel that he wasn't going to throw you under the Zamboni.

Joey Kocur was one of the toughest guys who'd ever played in the NHL. He was a big, strong Saskatchewan farm boy with hands so massive it looked like he could do one-handed curls with bales of hay. He was the hardest-nosed guy I'd ever played with, and had over 2,500 penalty minutes to show for it. Not to mention three Stanley Cups.

Joey had recently made the transition from playing to coaching, and he broke down video for us during the playoffs. I remember he was looking rough one morning during practice, which could only mean he'd been out late washing down our latest playoff win.

I was getting bored with the daily Black Aces grind, so I had to push through it and work extra hard, which was my way of keeping it fun. One day, I guess Joey didn't like how hard I was working, because after a goal that he buried on a rebound—one that he scored when I'd been hooking him—he turned around and open-hand punched me in the shoulder and sent me flying backwards four feet, easily, and it would have been even further on fresh ice. He hit me so hard that I lost my wind and was looking up at him gasping for air as "Bug Eyed" Barry skated by and explained, "Nobody hooks Joey when he's hungover."

The series against Colorado was long and tough, with three of the first five games decided in overtime and Colorado taking a 3–2 lead. But, again, I saw firsthand what a championship team can do when push comes to shove. One of the biggest differences between a team that knows how to win and one that doesn't is that the champions buckle down. They all understand that for two and a half months, everything shuts off—personal life, social life, your phone between periods, everything. There's total focus.

Winners also don't panic when facing adversity. They understand that it's a seven-game series and the first to win four games takes the series, so it takes as long as it takes. And championship teams are able to balance their attack so that every line can get the job done. Federov was not going to be dominant every night, but other guys would rise to the occasion. The Grind Line would step up and win the game and no one would feel that they'd stolen the superstars' chance to shine. It's very hard to play against a team like this, as Colorado found out. We shut them out the next two games, with a 7–0 emphasis in Game 7, to win the series and a place in the Stanley Cup Final, which we would go on to win in five games.

There is a story from Game 6 of the Western Conference Final, though, that I don't think has ever been told.

So we're facing elimination, and we go up 1–0 on a very strange goal by Shanahan—Patrick Roy made a showboat Statue of Liberty move after a glove save, but he didn't actually have the puck securely in his trapper as he raised his glove to the ceiling beams. The puck dropped to the ice and the ever-opportunistic Shanny poked it into the net.

Roy had a reputation of being as hard on his teammates as he was on himself. It's what drove him to be great every night. When we saw him showboating and making an ass of himself, we loved it. He wasn't as much of a superman as he thought. But even so, he did the same move again about thirty seconds after Shanny scored on him. This time, Shanny tapped him on the pads to congratulate him on not giving up another bad goal. The bench loved it. Then my old pal McCarty intercepts a pass in the defensive zone and goes in on a two-on-one. The usual play here is the pass for the tap-in, since it's pretty much impossible for any goalie to get across in time for that save. But McCarty winds up and leans into a slapper that beats Roy cleanly. It's a pretty obvious fuck-you to the guy who is supposedly the best goalie in the world. Goalies like that can get inside guys' heads, can get players missing the net or not taking shots at all since they think they have to shoot for the corners. But a shot like McCarty's says "we can score on this guy." And now it's 2–0.

So there's 2:23 left in the second period and Colorado is on a power play, trying to get back in the game and close out the series. Their coach, Bob Hartley, is holding what he thinks is an ace. He calls the ref over and asks for a measurement of our goalie Dominik Hašek's stick. Hartley thinks the goal stick is illegal, and if it is, the Avalanche will have a two-man advantage at a crucial point in the game.

Illegal sticks are very common—"illegal" meaning the blade is too wide, or has too much of a curve, or is too long. In the playoffs, everyone is trying to get an edge, and everyone knows it. So it's like an elaborate game with its own set of rules. Everybody does it—the trick is in the timing. For example, guys play with illegal sticks for most of the game, but also have a "legal" stick stored on a rack behind the bench.

Nobody would dare to make that call in the regular season—you'd be seen as a petty worm. If a team even tried it, there would probably be a bench-clearing brawl (see what I mean about unwritten rules?). But if Colorado can win this game they eliminate us, so Hartley gambles.

He never did get his five-on-three, though. At that moment, Dominik Hašek was using a perfectly legal stick. I mean, he used an illegal stick all the time. But not in that game. Cheli told me that sometime before Game 3, someone from the Avs snuck into our dressing room at the Pepsi Center in Denver with a measuring tape. He confirmed what was probably obvious to the naked eye: Dom's goal stick blade was too wide. So the intel goes into Hartley's file. But he doesn't use it in Game 3, doesn't use it in Game 4, doesn't use it in Game 5.

Game 6, though, down 2–0, he decides it's time to pull the trigger. What he doesn't know is that sometime before the game, the locker attendant assigned to our dressing room decided he didn't like this spycraft. He pulled Cheli aside and told him what was being planned.

Cheli warned Dom, and the illegal stick was left in the room when Hašek hit the ice. As hockey fans know, there's also a two-minute penalty for asking for a stick measurement if the stick turns out to be legit. Hašek got a shutout with his legal stick as we won the game 2–0. I think Cheli ended up giving the room attendant some form of paper thank-you which was "thanked but not accepted." We call that "the Love of the Game."

6

STANLEY CUP SUMMER

I never did play again that year. Did I feel sorry for myself that my leg blew up a few days before the playoffs started? Not at all. Any idea how many minor hockey players actually have a career in the NHL? About .002 percent of them. And how many of those win the Stanley Cup their first year in the league? You get the point. I wasn't moping around the Wings' dressing room. I'd just won the fucking lottery.

It was pretty much a blur from then until the Stanley Cup parade. I used to drink alcohol like most hockey players. Yeah, twenty-two-year-olds like to drink, and yeah, Canadians know how to put away some beers. That's the baseline. Pro hockey players are in another league altogether.

It seemed to me that the best players in the world are the guys who like to throw them back the most, sort of like some genius artists who need to lose themselves in booze and drugs once they've finished creating art. It's as if reality just isn't interesting enough. But despite what you might expect from me, I'm not a boozehound. True confession: I don't really like the taste of alcohol. I'm more a "dry vices" kind of guy, but firing up a joint wasn't really an option around the NHL.

I remember the afternoon before the Stanley Cup parade, when Cheli said he was coming to pick me up so that we could go out and get relaxed before the city showered us with adulation (and more booze). I have a major-league sweet tooth, so I poured myself half a glass of amaretto and half a glass of Dr. Pepper and slugged it back to get a protective little buzz going. There was absolutely no way I was going to keep up with Cheli.

Cheli was a beer guy to start, and then he'd get into tequila or Jameson, and then he'd black out. When he got really bad you'd have to carry him out of the place or he'd just sleep there. Then he'd wake up in the morning and he'd shake the dust off and go to the rink and he'd be the hardest working guy in practice. Clone his DNA and you'd have a race of supermen.

So the day before the Stanley Cup parade in 2002 we went over to Eminem's house with Lord Stanley's jug. Eminem lived in a rich suburb of Detroit in the biggest house I'd ever seen. He didn't have gold lions or a shark in the pool or anything like that, it was just this massive house and him.

I don't know how we ended up there or who set it up, but the whole thing was really awkward, actually, as Emimen didn't know anything about hockey. It was a really more like a photo-op for everyone. He'd just become famous, and he had a lot of hard-core hip hop guys hanging around. When you meet famous people it always cuts one of two ways: either they wish they were professional athletes or they don't care about sports at all. Eminem was the latter.

So I left Eminen's place to run around town with Cheli, and then Sergei Federov joined us, and we ended up at my townhouse overlooking the mighty and beautiful Detroit River. I'd moved into the condo from the hotel after I'd made the Wings for good, and my mom, Marlene, and father, Al, had come down to see their boy celebrate his team's Stanley Cup championship. Cheli's the kind of guy who could sit down and have a beer with my dad and me, and it would seem completely normal. Because it was. No one was pretending to be someone else.

I was very glad that my parents were staying with me, because I was conked out on the bathroom floor when my mother woke me up at 9 A.M.

on the day of the parade. Fortunately for both Marlene and myself, I was in my tighty whities, but I had no idea how I wound up on the bathroom floor. Well, I did, but no specific memory of what had happened.

And now I realized to my horror that I was late to the Stanley Cup parade. My head was a swamp. Just getting out the door was going to be an accomplishment.

It's not like they were going to delay the parade until I arrived, so I thought that I'd just sneak onto a float or car when I caught up with it. But the parade was running late, too, so I made it in the end. They gave us each our own car to ride in—a Thunderbird convertible—and I brought Leslie, who ran the family room for the Red Wings, along with me, because that's the kind of atmosphere the Wings created, and I thought she should be there.

Ford had launched their retro Thunderbird model earlier that year, but they put Scotty in the original car from 1955. We were all chauffeured down Woodward Avenue from "Hockeytown," a bar that the Red Wings' owner, Mike Illitch, built across from Comerica Park. It was a short parade, just the one mile down Woodward into Hart Plaza, where they had set up a stage.

I had no idea what a Stanley Cup parade was like. There were two million people in downtown Detroit, all there because of us. I'd never seen that many people in one place. The Plaza was packed and the sun was hot and I was guzzling water from a bottle just to keep myself from passing out, but when I was introduced to the crowd as one of the Black Aces by the announcer, and he said that they were going to be hearing a lot more from us, I felt as if I'd played every single playoff game for the Wings and scored the Cup winner. It was a thrill like I had never experienced, and it was also overwhelming.

The noise, the people, and the fact that the Stanley Cup was the reason for it all was just staggering to me, because I was still a fan. So you could say I was a fan at my own Stanley Cup parade, and that's what I remember most about it—watching me, watching it, all in awe. I didn't even think of all those people who told me I'd never make it. I just thought about next season, and winning this thing again. Of course, I never would win it again, but that's the nature of the beast. When you're twenty-two you think you're immortal and that the Stanley Cup is yours for the taking every season. But those seasons go by fast and that Cup is very, very hard to win. So looking back, I'm very glad that I made it to that parade because there wouldn't be any others.

A few days later, I'm working out with Drapes at a gym in Detroit when he mentions that he's going to New York to model tuxedos. Oh, and he's signed me up too. I didn't know there was such a thing as "Wedding Week" on *Good Morning America*, but suddenly I was part of it. This is so surreal on so many levels that I just say "Sure." By the way, no one minds being told that they have what it takes to be a model.

As it turned out, I was a model on TV for all of about twenty seconds on that trip. No one on set cared about Sean Avery or Kris Draper, and there was no small talk about the Stanley Cup. Why the team or the league wanted us there, I have no idea. But I learned a lot from being on the other side of the camera. Strutting around under the TV lights, I realized there was no way anyone watching *Good Morning America* would have any idea what I was thinking. You can't figure someone out by watching them on television. In that moment I understood the complete rift between what someone looks like and who they really are.

It occurred to me that models always look like they've got their shit together, but that was not how I was feeling. Even for a guy who'd spent the previous year jetting around and staying in luxury hotels, the St. Regis off Madison Ave was a cut above. It made me realize that I was still just a suburban kid figuring this world out. (Even the prostitutes were elite— not the usual suicide blonde draped in too much faux gold, but more like a hot pharmaceutical rep waiting for a meeting.) I had the same experience walking around Soho, which is the coolest part of New York with its cob-blestone streets and old loft-style buildings that rise up six stories. The people walking the streets are different here than in Detroit, or Scarborough. They just seem so confident, as if they each own a piece of this amazing city—I don't mean real estate, but the "anything is possible" sense of the place. I mean, if you walked around dressed in black from top to bottom in Scarborough or the Motor City people would offer their condolences and ask where the funeral was happening. But in New York, it looks clean and elegant. I had to admit, it was sort of intimidating.

I may have looked like a model that day, but I knew I was the same guy who had to wear two undershirts after gym class to stop the sweat from seeping out. Part of my job is to figure other people out and you can't do that if you bullshit yourself. I wasn't walking around Manhattan feeling like a big shot. I was taking notes on all I had to learn if I wanted to fit in here.

Well, maybe more than just fit in. As I walked back to the hotel from Columbus Circle after the GMA gig I see, in my mind's eye, a billboard with my face on it. I feel like I've just taken the smallest peek into the mind of New York. Now that I've glimpsed its power and passion and its massive scale of possibility, I want to come back and stay longer so that I can see how far I can push myself.

I also remember realizing that the NHL had no idea how to promote itself. No idea. We'd just been on network television, and no one even mentioned our names. Only people who already knew us would have cared. That's how the NHL is—only people who already care about it will watch it. If you want to grow—and that's what businesses are supposed to want, right?—then what you need are personalities. Heroes, villains, people for the fans to focus on. But the NHL is no good at creating character. So if I want attention, then I'll have to create a character for myself.

———

Not long after my first modeling gig I was on a plane again with Kris Draper. He and his wife, Julie, and I flew out to Los Angeles to go to Cheli's Stanley Cup party at his beachfront HQ in Malibu. Cheli and I were the same kind of social animal and were drawn to each other. He hung out with me because I was always available and I could keep the insane hours that he kept. He was energized by my energy, and I was energized by his diverse interests.

We stayed at the W Hotel in Brentwood, which was close to Luc Robitaille's house, which he'd kept after being traded to Detroit in 2001 after twelve seasons with the Kings (and a couple with the Rangers and one with Pittsburgh; Luc would go back to LA in 2004). Luc was having his Stanley Cup party on the Friday night, so we had the weekend pretty much covered.

Luc's party was a total family affair, with guys and their wives and girlfriends and parents and kids. He had an In-N-Out Burger truck in his driveway during the party.

All I knew at the time was that I'd stepped into a much bigger world than the one I knew, and Detroit was already huge compared to the world I'd come from. Jerry Bruckheimer is at Luc's party, and Bruce McNall and Chad Lowe (Rob's brother). Luc's wife, Stacia, is a former Laker Girl (cheerleader for the basketball team) and a lot of her nicely turned out girlfriends are in attendance. So I'm partying with a bunch of celebrities and NBA cheerleaders and taking it all in—because I don't fit in. Not even close. I was wearing a golf shirt, tucked in, with jeans and loafers. To all those fine SoCal babes who are there I looked like a hockey player who had some money but no idea what to do with it. If I was five years older and more experienced I'd have had the pick of the litter, but I'm still a rookie and if the lady hasn't worn a jersey to some sort of sporting event in her life, then right now I probably don't have a shot.

It's also my first time in Malibu, with the drive from Westwood down Sunset Boulevard to the ocean and then along the Pacific Coast Highway—or

"PCH" to those who know her well—feeling like it's straight out of a movie, which of course it has been, many times. It's a little like being on set again, and it gets me thinking the way I had been back in New York (another city I really only knew from movies and cop shows). Seeing yourself in a place you always kind of imagined as fake and realizing it's real gives you a whole new sense of what's possible. I mean, these gleaming beachfront homes of glass and steel—they're real. If I work hard, I can have one. My friend has one.

It's the same thing with the guest list. Rocky was at Cheli's party, as in Sly Fucking Stallone, here at the same party as Sean Avery from Scarborough, Ontario. So are Hilary Swank, and Tom Hanks, and Kid Rock, and Cuba Gooding. Wayne Gretzky is here. As I walk down to the beach, I meet two magnificent human specimens, and I recognize the incredibly beautiful five-eleven brunette—a cross between a Greek goddess and the sexiest All-American girl from small-town Oklahoma—as Gabby Reece. She is the most famous pro volleyball player in the history of the sport and she's married to the most famous big wave surfer on the planet, and probably the best-looking man I've ever seen, Laird Hamilton. They're having a conversation that's so animated and joyful it seems like they just met.

But because it was Cheli, it was a family beach party with the Stanley Cup. There were kids romping in the water, and people hanging out on lounge chairs soaking up the sun and some beers, and the vibe was very friendly and earthy, even if the star power was high. Watching the waves come in, I wasn't congratulating myself for having made it this far. Trust me, I knew I wasn't Chris Chelios. But seeing all this—seeing this world and the people in it—made me realize just how much is possible. More than ever, I wanted to figure this all out. I wanted to be part of this world.

Hard work separates those who truly rise above and stand out from those who merely get by. Not hard work as in showing up to the same job on time for twenty-seven years, which is a fine thing and absolutely an achievement (if you can find an employer that will keep you for nearly three decades without outsourcing you). I mean the kind of hard work that leaves you alone at night while your college peers are doing keg stands and your grown-up friends are taking a well-earned breather. I mean the kind of hard work that most people just won't do.

That takes desire. Raw, unstoppable desire. Driving back to the hotel in LA, I look at the Pacific Ocean lit by the moon and stretching off into forever, and I know that desire is not going to be a problem.

After Cheli's party I flew home to Toronto and used the roughly $20,000 bonus that each Red Wing received for winning the Presidents' Trophy to rent a house in the east end neighborhood of Toronto known as the Beaches. Ten years earlier, while strolling through the Beaches with my mom and dad, I told them that when I made the NHL I was going to buy a house there and have them over for dinner, but they'd have to go home afterward because I was going to be with my friends. I was twelve years old when I made this grand pronouncement.

That summer was as good as it gets for a twenty-two-year-old guy. I had two of my best friends living with me, guys I'd played junior hockey with who were hoping to land in the NHL, and from Monday through Thursday we had a fairly standard routine: 6 A.M. wake-up, followed by a track or gym workout from 7 A.M. to 11 A.M. A quarter-mile is one full lap around a track, which is also 400 meters. For twelve years, quarter-mile runs—and I mean runs, we'd do them in ninety seconds—were an integral part of my summer training. They provided me and my training partner, Kris Draper, with a tool to push ourselves and each other to become stronger and stronger year after year. We'd run a quarter, then move on to the next one, and onward until we'd done ten. When your heart rate hits 195 beats per minute the dry heaves or outright pukes would start. Drapes and I had some epic battles on the track in those summers, and that training and the pain of it were critical for me becoming a NHL player.

Of course, once the run was done, my buddies and I would hit the gym for a couple of hours to lift weights. One thing hockey players do is take a bar that you'd bench-press with and power-clean it. So you lift 145 pounds above your head, then drop the bar onto your shoulder, then jump up onto boxes three feet high, then jump back down. We'd do eight of those box jumps.

After knocking off on Thursday we'd head to Muskoka, which is Ontario's famous lake district. We'd stay either near the Kee in Bala or at the Sherwood Inn on Lake Joe, with either place soon turning into "Animal House." Bala is a tiny town on a huge lake three hours from the nearest city, but the Kee is a legend. I mean, Drake, Rush, the Ramones, Snoop Dogg, and tons of huge bands have played in this little bar. That's how good the party is.

We would go to all the local lake bars, and because Canada is Hockey Nuts I was almost guaranteed to be recognized, which meant I could get anything (within reason, though reason can have a shifty boundary). A hockey player in Canada in high summer can pretty much do whatever he wants. He can take all his clothes off and dance naked under the moon on the deck; he can fuck/drink/snort his mind out in the bedroom, on the beach, in the parking lot. You have your pick of women—married, single, in between—and if your taste runs to men, well, they're available too, though not once in my entire hockey career did I ever meet a player who was out as gay, and that's possibly because the standard insult for everything and everyone in hockey is "Fag!" I mean, you'd have no chance.

Hockey players are the hardest partying athletes of the four major league sports, hands down, and summer in Canada for a hockey player is one big buffet of sex and drugs and rock 'n' roll. At that age I also wanted to be recognized, and I came to like talking to starry-eyed Canadians (I mean, that was me in Los Angeles a couple of weeks earlier) about the NHL, and what it was like, and did I know Stevie Y?

"Yes, I know him, he's my fucking teammate."

"What's he like, as a person?"

"He's the kind of guy I'd like to be if I weren't me."

I didn't actually say that, but it was true. That summer I spent a weekend with Steve and his awesome wife, Lisa, at their incredible home in Muskoka. They lived in the compound that housed the former Hudson Bay family home and had been redone by Lisa, who has great taste, and in the world of hockey wives that means she basically created the word "taste." She could do that because she was married to the captain of the Red Wings and one of the greatest players in the history of the NHL. In other words, Steve and Lisa were allowed to stand out.

The trouble with hockey wives' taste could be nature, but a lot of it is nurture. When you walk into players' homes they look like they're a recreation of a Pottery Barn showroom. They're all the same, and even if a woman has great taste, it's dangerous to express it because then it might seem as though you think you're "better than them," which is a big taboo. The last thing the league wants is for players to become powerful, or worse, interesting. Sergei Federov, who was hardly a rebellious outsider, would go to Paris in the summer to be with his girlfriend, tennis player Anna Kournikova, and rather than see this as a guy enjoying the bigger world, other players would assume he was putting on airs.

But Lisa and Steve epitomize the concept of "happy family," and they are a rarity in pro sports. I wonder to myself during that weekend if I will ever have what they have, with the only exception being that I am starting to fantasize about meeting a woman who is powerful and successful and beautiful—and not Canadian. My reason for her not being Canadian is that I'm starting to crave exposure to the rest of the world and don't see myself on the lake every summer for the rest of my life. Of course, neither might a Canadian girl whom I could love, so the idea has a few holes in it. But the main point is that after New York and LA I am beginning to imagine my life on a much bigger stage.

That notion came home to roost at an end-of-summer party we had at the Beaches house. As the festivities rolled along, people started to complain about someone locking themselves in the washroom. When people would knock on the door all that came back were grunts. This went on for ten minutes until I'd had enough and started to bang on the door, telling this person—who I assumed was an invited guest—to wrap it up and get out of there.

All of a sudden the door opens and some girl is sitting on the toilet, weaving in and out of consciousness. I made the decision to call the cops and have them take care of it so nothing would go wrong on our end— I didn't know what she'd ingested or how seriously she was impaired, so I left it to the pros. To this day I have no idea who this girl was or where she came from, but I hope if I have a daughter, she never gets that wasted. It was a pretty stark reminder of what I wanted to leave behind and what I wanted to accomplish. It made me focus even more on making the upcoming season the best one yet.

TWO IS THE MOST
DANGEROUS LEAD IN HOCKEY

In September 2002, after what seems like the longest summer of my life (but is actually the shortest because we played until June), I go to the Red Wings' training camp. This year, I don't have to go to rookie camp. I get to report to the main camp like the rest of the guys who play for the team that just won the Stanley Cup.

Things have changed a bit. Scotty Bowman has retired, and one of our assistant coaches, Dave Lewis, is now the boss. And just before the first game of the season, I find a poem in my dressing room stall, as do all the other Red Wings. It's from Dave Lewis. It's about a page long, and it starts like this:

This is the time. This is the time when it starts.
This incredible dream, it never goes away . . .

It was something so unique that even guys who'd been playing for fifteen years had never seen it done before. And since Dave left the poem in our stalls just before a game, we didn't sit back and talk about it. But maybe that was the point. He'd coached for so long with Scotty, who used to do things to distract guys from thinking so that they could just play, so maybe this was Dave's way of doing the same thing, literally getting us on the same page as him from the start of the season.

Later in my career, when I was with LA, Andy Murray would put quotes in his daily notes to us, and you'd pay zero respect to them because you knew Andy was just ripping them from some quote website. It was his way of trying to motivate a bunch of guys he had no idea how to motivate because he'd never been in our shoes. Dave Lewis played fifteen years in the NHL and he wrote a poem for us. We paid attention.

Dave Lewis had a tough job because not only was he taking over from Scotty Bowman but he'd been an assistant coach with the Wings since 1988, after retiring from the NHL. The assistant coach's job, among other things, is to bridge the relationship between the head coach and the players. When you move from assistant to head coach, you have to adjust your friendship with the players because now you're not the bridge, you're the boss.

Dave was an outgoing man of few words. He was pleasant and personable, but he didn't yammer at you with nonsense. He knew the game, he knew how players thought, and he knew he didn't need to give us endless tutorials. He just needed to bring out our best, and the Wings were a team that wanted to be the best, so it was a smooth transition between the legend that was Bowman to Dave Lewis.

My training camp in 2002 was very similar to the others I'd attended in that it usually consisted of me playing three games with a goal and a couple of assists, a couple of fights, and a ten-minute misconduct penalty for driving the opposing squad so crazy that they were thinking more about how to kill me and less about how to win the game.

I am feeling very confident as the season starts because I know I've raised the level of my game, which is what any player wants to do going into a new season. Now I'd like to raise the amount of my paycheck, too.

And I hope that the agency representing me does as well. Newport

Sports Management is the biggest and most powerful in the sport, and my agent, Pat Morris, did a good job of getting me out of some tough situations I'd put myself in during the course of my career. I certainly made him work for his money. Pat Morris was one of the biggest agents at Newport, which, as the largest hockey agency on the planet, is actually a hockey player factory—they sign a lot of players to their stable, from superstars to grinders, and the amount of money you make dictates the amount of time you get from your agent. Morris was close with Chris Pronger, Brad Richards, and the Primeau brothers—they were his core group. I wouldn't hear from Pat for months, and then he'd pop up when it was contract time. There were times when I couldn't get Pat on the phone for a few days.

He wasn't a former player but a lawyer. He was a very nice guy, and I honestly believed that he cared about the players, but it was in a "business first" kind of way. I'm sure he did stuff for me behind the scenes when I got into my various jams, but I wasn't a member of Pat's inner circle, so we didn't spend a lot of time talking about anything other than money.

The only time you ever heard guys talking about their agents was when they were bitching because they couldn't get their agent on the phone. Or because they hadn't heard from them in years, if a guy had a long contract.

The agency game is a racket, run by the good old boys who have so many side deals with NHL general managers that it puts a sports book to shame. And while I get that it's good business in the big picture to keep the GMs friendly, players can't help but wonder when they get traded or have to go to salary arbitration whether their own agent is sacrificing them to keep some other more lucrative situation in play. That said, agents don't really give a shit what happens to their players, apart from the guys who make in excess of $60 million. They're all very motivated by an extra zero or three before the decimal point.

There's so much that agents could be doing for players to help them make the transition after their careers are done, but mostly they choose to do things that fatten their wallets. For example, Newport had a financial division where they opened bank accounts and credit cards for players, and set up your car insurance and bought bullshit mutual funds that made you a fraction of what a proper family office would. A family office—which is a boutique service tailored to manage the financial life of a high-net-worth person or family—would also help a player with estate planning and creating a diversified portfolio, the stuff a guy needs when the game is done.

Newport took 3 percent of the gross contract and then players could pay an additional 2 percent of assets under management—so a player who had stashed $10 million with them would pay $200,000 for the privilege. They would also charge 20 percent gross on endorsements.

Another example of the greed and laziness of these guys lies in disability insurance. Some players take out this kind of insurance to make sure their contracts don't evaporate should some goon cross-check them head-first into the boards. Sports agents often obtain this insurance through a broker, who may, coincidentally, be a former player and who adds a percentage to what you'd pay an established insurance agency. What does the agent get out of this? Don't know. Just asking. I found out that all you have to do is call Lloyd's of London directly and buy your own insurance at a cheaper rate from them, because that's what my friend Adam Campbell did when he started managing my money and that of other players.

Newport Sports is the last place I'd allow my son to be represented. It's a tough call when you're starting out because you need the professional help—but with agencies like Newport, when you really need help, it's not there. If I had a son, I'd send him to Ryan Barnes, who became an agent after his NHL career. I know that if he had fifty players on his roster, each and every one of them would get his full, honest attention. He knows the game, and he was the best of teammates. And he understands better than anyone that a player never really knows how long the ride is going to last until it's all over. Most players don't see the end coming, and most don't have any help planning that transition. I know that Ryan does because he's been through it. There were times I got frustrated enough to think I should go into the sports management business when I'm done playing.

Which is another way of saying be careful what you wish for because I got sent down to fucking Cincinnati again shortly after the 2002–03 season started.

Did I see this one coming? Nope. It was like I'd just poked my head up to look at my second season as a secure NHLer and the Wings had whack-a-moled me. It hurt, but I had to look at it like a professional. Plus, it wasn't really a big surprise. Not when you looked at the lineup the Wings were dressing in October 2002:

Chris Chelios

Mathieu Dandenault

Pavel Datsyuk

Kris Draper

Sergei Fedorov

Jiří Fischer

Tomas Holmström

Brett Hull

Igor Larionov

Nicklas Lidström

Kirk Maltby

Darren McCarty

Luc Robitaille

Brendan Shanahan

Henrik Zetterberg

If I'm Dave Lewis looking down the bench to see who goes on the ice next, I'd be embarrassed by the richness of choice. Lewis was a very good coach, but even John Tortorella would have to work awfully hard not to win with this crew (still, he could manage it). And while I was very, very disappointed to be back in Cincinnati again, I knew it was just a matter of time. The Red Wings sent me down to get in some games while they got rid of some bodies and contracts. And sure enough, I was called back up at the end of October, and then the Wings told me the magic words: "Find a place to live."

I was ecstatic. This meant I was going to be around on a more permanent basis, although at this point in my career there were never any guarantees. So I kept a travel bag packed, just in case.

One day in the dressing room before practice, Brett Hull asked me where I planned to live. I told him I didn't know, so he said, "Why don't I ask Darcie if can live in the apartment above my garage?" I accepted on the spot.

Brett rented a house behind the Blockbuster Video in downtown Birmingham, which was a hip and fancy suburb of Detroit. Everybody called his place "the Jukebox" because that's what it looked like. I mean, it had fluorescent lighting around the border. There were certainly occasions when we made the place rock.

The daily routine was fairly consistent. In the morning I'd always pull either the Firebird or the Navigator out of the garage into the driveway and turn the heat on so it was warm when Mr. Hull was ready to go. We'd make a quick stop at Starbucks and then we were off to the rink, always being among the first to arrive, just after the trainers and Cheli. We'd practice, work out, and then have lunch with some of the guys. We'd drive home for a nap, and then meet for dinner in whatever joint Brett and his girlfriend (now wife), Darcie, were craving that night—usually Mexican or sushi. We'd then hit a movie or head back home to settle in and watch TV.

Hully rarely watched sports, with the exception of golf or football. I don't ever remember watching a hockey game with him.

One of our morning drives to the rink was memorable because of the wretched state Brett was in. Darcie told me before we left for practice that he'd been up all night rolling around on the floor, moaning and clutching his stomach, and when he could speak, was strongly of the opinion that he was dying.

During the thirty-minute drive to the rink Brett was drinking his coffee and trying to figure out what was wrong with him. "Jesus, Aves, I feel rough," he said to me. "Don't know if I can survive a practice without puking my guts out. Think I should just sit in the sauna and sweat out whatever the fuck this is." Hully was always game to go, and seeing him like this made me worry.

In the end, he decided to battle through practice, and told me to hustle up afterward so we could get on the road home. It was obvious he needed some sleep. As we walked out to the car I checked my phone and saw that I had fourteen missed calls from one of my best buddies, who'd made the drive from Toronto the day before to watch the game and do a little partying afterward.

When the boys had arrived in Detroit they'd swung by the Jukebox around 5 P.M. to drop their bags before the game. They also dropped some cookies in the fridge and then headed to the Joe. After the game, we had the usual Friday night adventure of wine, women, and general mayhem.

Brett had gone home after dinner that night and was delighted to find those cookies my friends had left in the fridge. Well, it turned out those cookies were packed with weed, and Brett ate two of them, which means he ate enough weed to put a guy in the hospital. When he was rolling around on the floor in the middle of the night he must have truly believed he was dying. I can't fathom what getting that stoned, without even knowing you're stoned, must feel like.

I waited a few days to tell him, until after he'd buried two goals and notched one assist in a game and was feeling pretty good. Brett was untouchable after a game like that and you could tell him pretty much anything. When I revealed the source of his near-death experience, he was so happy to know what had happened to him. He'd thought he had some awful disease that hadn't been diagnosed. He laughed about it, even. "I didn't expect cookies would be the way I'd get high on pot for the first time in seventeen years." And thank goodness he still had the touch—700 goals and counting. I could have fucked everything up for him—and for the history of hockey—thanks to my cookie-baking buddies from the north.

I was becoming really good friends with Boyd Devereaux, and one day he asks me before practice if I want to go see a Canadian band called Our Lady Peace. I've been a fan of theirs since I was seventeen. Instant yes. Boyd is one of the smartest guys I've ever met, and he's really well-versed in culture—from literature to music to world affairs. He's a far cry from your average puck-chaser and I'm flattered that he thinks me worthy of his company. I also want to learn what he knows.

The OLP show was brilliant, as expected, and after the encore we got to go backstage, which was a big thrill but also a little daunting. I felt like a groupie waiting to meet a stranger whose performance you loved. That can go one of two ways: they could be a total asshole, which would instantly change my perception of their music, or they could be the kind of person you were glad you knew.

That night I got lucky and met a lifelong friend in OLP drummer Jeremy Taggart who, aside from having music instead of blood in his veins, is one of the most fun humans I have ever had the pleasure of knowing and taught me more about music than I could ever dream of.

My first real Rock Star Party was courtesy of Bob Ritchie, aka Kid Rock, and it began as a team bonding exercise, organized by Cheli, who was pretty much the team's chief executive of fun. I'd first met Kid Rock at Cheli's Chili Bar after a game, and despite his rock star snarl and American Badass persona, I couldn't believe how normal and nice he was in person. At this point, Kid Rock, or "Bobby" as he was introduced to me, has a few Grammy nominations and is a very fast-rising star in the music world. I find it amazing that I get to meet him just because I play a little hockey, even though I'm no different from most of his twenty-two-year-old fans who like to drink and screw. "American Badass" is not an act, and what you see is what you get.

The Wings were an older team and a lot of the guys had families, so Cheli put something together for those of us who weren't at home with the wife and kids. We had a few days off between games, including a rare Sunday of rest, so after practice on Saturday Cheli rounded up about ten single guys and we loaded onto a party bus. We drove around to our favorite bars, picking up a few people from each of them as we cruised through the outskirts of Detroit, with the final stop being Rock's house in Oakland County, which is about a half-hour drive north of where I was living with Brett and Darcie.

Detroit gives way to the countryside pretty quickly, and Bob's house was a beautiful old redone farmhouse with a barn. He also had a guest house in which he'd built a studio, as well as multiple bedrooms and kitchens on the ground floor and in the basement. When we rolled into the driveway, I knew this was going to be a big one. Now, difficult though it may be for some readers to believe, in 2002 there is no Twitter, Instagram, Snapchat, or iPhone. Despite these primitive conditions, word had ricocheted around Detroit that Rock was throwing a shake down and the place was crawling with strippers and singers and hippies and roadies and every hanger-on in between.

Rock's party marked the first time I had seen cocaine and it was a few of the local dancers who were leading the revolution, so to speak. Even though I was at a party that America's Badass was throwing, I was certainly a little bit shocked. And also curious. This was like a party you'd see in the movies, with couples drifting off into bedrooms, and more coke appearing. It was like the Mark Wahlberg movie *Rock Star*. Bobby ended up jamming and playing a few songs which Cheli jumped in to sing along with him. As I've mentioned, Cheli was an Olympic-class drinker, and so was Rock, and so were a lot of the Red Wings.

I couldn't drink like these titans so by 3:30 A.M. I was in better shape than most of them, and that's when I usually did my best work with whatever babe with whom I was planning my immediate future. Remember, I was twenty-two years old and single, and I was hanging with a bunch of legends. Plus I had solid credentials of my own—young and single. I was not going to dismiss such cosmic generosity, and enjoyed the bounty bestowed upon me.

Of course, bounty goes both ways and I soon got my chance to give back to the cosmos at one of the more beloved NHL traditions: the Rookies Dinner. It's beloved only by those who are not NHL rookies, because they don't have to pay for it. The Rookies Dinner is a chance for the team's veterans to get blind drunk on the most extravagant food and wine known to mankind while the rookies pay the freight. And when you're a rookie on the 2002 Red Wings, you're buying dinner for a team of superstars with very expensive tastes. I didn't really mind my NHL initiation, though, because, after all, it was an NHL initiation and not some hazing into a college fraternity.

My Rookies Dinner happened in Vancouver in November 2002, when I was technically no longer a rookie, but it would have been dickish to dwell on that, so I sucked it up. We all went to a restaurant called Gotham in the city's funky Yaletown district and they gave us a room to ourselves downstairs. I can't remember what I ate, but I do remember the bill: $22,000. By the time we'd finished, my teammates had bought everything in the restaurant including the fucking steak knives. And here's the problem: we only had two rookies, me and Jason Williams.

And Jason Williams was my roommate—the roommate from hell.

When I entered the NHL, only guys who'd played 600 NHL games or logged ten years in the league could get their own room on the road. After the 2012 collective bargaining agreement, only kids on entry-level contracts got roommates, and the rest of the team could dance naked to MTV in the middle of the night in a five-star room of their own if they wanted. But back then, pretty much everyone was bunking up.

I had roommates on the road when I started out, and for a while they were a rotating cast, but then I got saddled with Jason. On the surface, we had a bit in common. We played against each other in junior in the Ontario Hockey League, me with Owen Sound and then Kingston, and him with the Peterborough Petes. He also signed with Detroit as a undrafted free agent, just like I did, which is unique. He was a highly skilled center with a huge shot, and at this point in my life, I can't stand him.

I can honestly say that I would not have shed a tear if Jason Williams choked on a bone at the Rookies Dinner and we lost him. Yes, I know, that is a terrible thing to say, but I thought he was a kiss-ass one-dimensional automaton. Jason Williams was the type of guy playing on a team all by himself who rubbed pretty much everyone the wrong way, and I know something about that. "Williams is a weird dude" was something I heard many times that season, but on this night what I heard from him when the bill arrived was, "How much can you pay?"

I had an upper limit of $8,500 on my credit card, and it was already carrying some charges, and Williams was in the same deep hole, so between us the best we could do was put up $16,000. A difference of $6,000 between what you have and what they want is a little more than you can work off by hosing down plates in the kitchen.

But we got bailed out by one of the veterans, who quietly paid the difference. No one ever stepped up to claim it, but I'm almost positive it was Nick Lidström. The dinner was also notable for the fact that midway through it some beautiful Vancouver women showed up to join in the festivities. They had crossed paths with some of the guys, who'd been out sampling Vancouver's waters in the afternoon, and showed up at the Rookies Dinner in time for the dessert course.

After dinner the guys wanted to have a nightcap, and there were two expeditions in search of two very different pleasures. A bunch of us went to a sports bar on Robson Street for a drink, while others went to a legendary Vancouver spot—a place that has swallowed hundreds of per diem envelopes over the years—called the Swedish Touch.

They don't have any actual Swedes working at the Swedish Touch, which is on the fifth floor of a building on Hornby Street. It billed itself as a massage parlor, but its services are rumored to be more comprehensive.

Back in 2002 I was too young to even understand what this place really was, and besides, I had just maxed out my credit card. Plus, I preferred the excitement of going to a bar filled with people who'd be impressed to see the Detroit Red Wings roll in as opposed to a small private room with Ilsa. Some players preferred to have their hangovers massaged out with a trip to the Swedish Touch to standing in a crowded bar with all these adoring people—and working on a new hangover. Even so, at that point in my NHL career I wondered why they hadn't wanted to come with us and get all that attention. To think that the guys had the balls to go there is mind-blowing, especially these days when even thinking about walking in would somehow result in a photo of your thought on Instagram or Twitter.

It was a great night, though, and the only NHL Rookies Dinner I ever had to pay for. As a measure of how good it was, we got shit-kicked the next night by the Vancouver Canucks 4–1.

I realized that my identity in the NHL was coming into focus when I heard that GM Kenny Holland had told one of the kids in the system, Nik

Kronwall, to stay away from Sean Avery. Kronwall wanted to hang out with me, but the Red Wings didn't want me to mentor anyone. I took it as a point of honor, as it meant there was only one me, and I couldn't teach me to anyone.

Of course, it could have also meant not to get too close to me because I wasn't going to be around for long. I played thirty-nine games for the Red Wings in my second season, but in March 2003, Darren McCarty came back from an injury and I got hit again by hockey math. I was sent down to Cincinnati because we had too many healthy bodies.

I was pissed off, because even though I've known since December that I'm an NHLer, I'm still the kid on a roster of stars. Hully said "See you in a few days" when I packed up my gear, and that made me feel better. I went back down and played my ass off. It was actually fun, because I got a lot more ice time, got on the power play, and was able to show off my NHL pedigree in the AHL, confident that I wouldn't be down there for long.

And I wasn't. After practice, Danton Cole, who is now the Cincinnati coach, calls me into his office and tells me something shocking: I'm not going back to Detroit. I've been traded. I had no idea—no one had told me I was on the trade block, no coach, not my agent, nobody. And even if you know it's coming, "You've been traded" are scary words for any player at any level to hear, because it means your life can get much better—or much worse. And right now, I don't want to leave Detroit, I want to get the hell back to Detroit. And yet . . .

I crave the chance to get a real shot with an up-and-coming team, but I hope to hell it's not Carolina or Columbus, because I don't really see my world expanding by playing in either town. But no, I hear three magic words as to where I'm going: Los Angeles Kings. And they're sending Mathieu Schneider, one of the highest-scoring American defensemen in history, along with a first-round pick, back the other way. It was clear that the Wings were going for another Cup, and so traded my promise for a proven veteran, and I was going to a team that would give me lots of space to shine. Suddenly, I feel like my stock in the NHL has shot way up. Actually, my reaction was more like: Holy shit! Buckle up! I'm returning by invitation to that crazy world I tasted at Cheli's beach house party, and now it's going to be mine. All my hard work is about to pay off in the SoCal sun.

8

BECOMING A KING

The LA Kings give me a few hours to drive to Detroit and pack up the rest of my gear. Cheli and Hully and the guys are happy for me, saying "You lucky fucker, you're going to LA." They wanted me to succeed, and recognized that I was getting my shot with a young team in a great city. I then caught a flight to meet the Kings in Tampa Bay for a game the next day. I landed late that night, and when I checked in to the team hotel and opened my room's door, I meet my new roommate: the captain, Mattias Norström.

Now you might wonder what GM would have the balls to room his captain with a twenty-two-year-old he'd just traded for. It was a numbers game. At that time in the NHL, players didn't get their own rooms, so when I landed, Matty Norström was without a roommate. Matty's a very cool guy and didn't seem to be bothered that they were putting him with the new guy, but I couldn't imagine Detroit doing that to Stevie Y.

It was pretty clear that I was going from a culture of winning in Detroit, with a team of veteran superstars who will do whatever they need to do to win, to a culture of well, not winning yet. Even so, I was excited to be there because I was going to get a chance to play.

Now, here's a strange thing. You would think that when you change job locations, the new office would welcome you to the fold and introduce you to everyone. I mean, that's what would happen in pretty much any job you could name. It's not what happens in the NHL. Trades happen so routinely, and guys get called up all the time, so there's not any kind of welcoming committee on any team because players and coaches would be distracted from the job at hand. When I walked into the LA Kings dressing room for the first time, we were on the road, and everyone was busy, so I did what all players do: I went and found the trainer and told him how I liked my skates sharpened, what sticks I used, and so on. It was all very businesslike. Then I said hello to the guys passing by me, and then I put on the uniform and played. As I had not played against the LA Kings before, there was no one on the team who wanted to kill me. Yet.

After the first game in Tampa I go out with my new teammates to a local bar around the corner from the team hotel, just like I'd done a hundred times before—hockey players having fun after a game we'd won, 4–2. I wound up pulling one of the waitresses back to the hotel and we start out in the hot tub outside by the pool before eventually making our way upstairs to the room, where we go straight into the bathroom so I don't wake up the captain, who I'm sure thinks I'm a total fucking nut by now. But he never says a word to me about it. In fact, all he says to me the next day is, "Pass me the black tape." This is three hours after I was fucking the barmaid on our bathroom vanity.

When I land in Los Angeles, I check in to the Hilton Garden suites beside the practice rink in El Segundo, which is between Manhattan Beach and Venice Beach and beside LAX airport. I immediately start looking for a short-term rental as well as a rental car so that I can dig in to the LA lifestyle. I need a Porsche, but I can't afford a Porsche. I can afford shorts and flip-flops, and love the feeling of strolling into practice like I'm going to a day at the beach.

I wore No. 16 when I was growing up, but I'm not going to get that number with the Kings because it belonged to the great Marcel Dionne and it's hanging from the rafters of the Staples Center, never to be worn again. Hockey players generally want to keep the same number, and I've always worn 16 because that was Brett Hull's number. In fact, you don't usually have a choice about your number until later in your career, or unless you're a high draft pick. I get lucky because No. 19 is available, and that was Steve Yzerman's number, and I loved him.

You can't pick your coaches either. My new coach, Andy Murray, is one very strange dude. It's as if he's an alien impersonating a human, and not doing a great job of it. And that's just my first impression. He seems to think I just wandered in off the street. He has no interest in how I'm settling in. He just tells me to talk to the trainer, and to see assistant coaches Mark Hardy and John Van Boxmeer to go over the power play and penalty kill. And that's it.

I find a place to live right on the ocean on the border between Venice and Santa Monica. It's a fully furnished short-term rental that I can pay month-to-month. I also rent a Cadillac Escalade, which—I know, I know—is not the best car for Cali because it's a real gas guzzler and you have to drive everywhere in LA, even to get a jug of milk. But I need something to drive, and I realize very quickly that this town is all about the show and that the valet parking game is where it starts.

This means that the vehicle in which you pull up to the club or restaurant usually dictates how long you wait for your table or if you even get past the velvet rope which lets the chosen enter the magic kingdom—and I don't mean Disneyland. This kind of social management would not fly in small-town Ontario, but here it's the cost of doing business.

In LA, I connect with some of my oldest friends, guys I grew up playing hockey with and against since I was eight years old, and I meet some new ones, Canadian guys working the LA game. Many of them had recently moved to LA to build their respective careers in the music/movie/agent game. Almost everyone started as an assistant and was learning the ropes from grizzled Hollywood vets who had the boys versed in the art of the hooker and coke dealer before their new California tans had even set in.

There was Cody Leibel, whose dad, a real estate guy in Ontario, had created a travel team for Cody to play on with good players who were Toronto kids, including me. If we had a big win, he would come into the locker room and peel off crisp $100 bills for us. We were twelve years old. Cody was in LA making his way as a professional money spender.

Joey Scoleri was another Toronto guy, a VJ known in his Toronto life as Joey Vendetta and now a music executive, and I met him when I got traded to LA. Same with Matt Budman—his father Michael created Roots Canada. He's become a big-shot film producer.

Blake Leibel was Cody's brother, and I lived with him for a couple of months in LA while I was waiting to close the deal on my own house. He became a film and TV director and in the summer of 2016 he was charged with torturing and killing his girlfriend, who had just given birth to their child. (At the time of writing, the trial is still pending.) I'm relieved to say that he seemed totally normal when I bunked with him, but apparently he was anything but.

And then there was Lawrence "Larry" Longo, who I'd played hockey with for most of my life. He'd quit playing when we were teenagers because he liked food and girls too much, and he became my best friend in Los Angeles. Larry was the guy who was game for anything and who lit up any social situation. Very rarely would he not be there when I walked out after a game, and we'd go and have dinner, or to a party, or a concert, or whatever LA had to offer. I didn't live in the Kings' compound in Manhattan Beach (Luc Robitaille was the only other guy who didn't live there), and would venture outside the herd as I got to know my new hometown. I was here because I played hockey, but I knew that I wanted to be much more than a hockey player.

It looks like success was going to happen on the ice for sure. With ten games to go in the season, I am truly focused on helping this team make the playoffs because that will mean they made the right choice in dealing for me. I want to give everything I have to the Kings, so when any of my teammates score a goal I stand up and cheer with 100 percent authenticity, which I can promise you is a rarity in the NHL. You may want the team to do well, but you don't necessarily want your teammates to do well.

In the NHL, you get paid first and foremost for putting up good numbers. The other thing you get paid for are the intangibles—drawing penalties, winning a well-timed fight, or making a big hit that shifts momentum. Let's just say you make a lot more for tangibles than intangibles. So a player like me is never going to be fully happy when a fellow third- or fourth-liner scores a goal, because that just made him more valuable than me. And when you hang 'em up at the end of your career, it's all about how much money you can make during that career, one that can end in one quick moment in a game or even in a practice when you get that injury from which you never come back. So yes, hockey was a game I loved when I was eight, and it's a game I love still, except now I can make—or lose—my living by how I play it.

Don't get me wrong. To be paid handsomely for playing a game I love is no bad thing. Only the most selfish players make this seem like a chore, and that reality usually catches up with them when they stop producing and become dispensable. The best pros are the guys who figure out the balance of wanting personal success versus wanting team success. I don't think my teammates ever questioned my desire to win, and I honestly think it hurt me on occasion with some guys because I was hard on them for not playing hard enough or for bailing on taking a big hit to make a play.

I suppose that I'd have been better off in the eyes of many if I'd bit my tongue and played the constant cheerleader role, but that would have been dishonest. Just because you're pulling down more money in a month than most people make in a year doesn't give you the right to consider everything you do to be beyond criticism. I was there to win, and I was not cool with a teammate letting me down. The more I won, the more money I'd make, the more opportunities I'd have to explore life, and the more women I would have in bed—for a night, for a week, and one day, forever.

Andy Murray, my coach in Los Angeles, was, as I mentioned, a puzzle—to put it mildly. I don't really know where to begin to explain this guy, so I'll start by saying that he was fired on March 21, 2006, even though our team was 37-28-5 and poised to make the playoffs. Why fire a winning coach? I have no idea.

He was the most prepared coach I've ever seen. He created these detailed scouting sheets that he'd slide under hotel-room doors the night before a game, and they were so annoying and mind-numbing that guys would stuff towels under their door to keep them out.

Andy had a very deep voice that became very high when he got angry, so he sounded like a girl when he was yelling at us. He was five-eight and maybe 130 pounds, and he was so pale that he was almost translucent. He always wore an LA Kings golf shirt and slacks. He looked like an elementary school math teacher who was looking for his compass and pencils to draw up pretty plays. (Scotty Bowman, on the other hand, looked like an MIT math professor.)

Andy would have had a tough time playing in a beer league because he could barely skate or handle a puck, so it was pretty rich to have him yelling at us for making a bad play or not skating hard enough. You don't have to be a hockey superstar to be a coach—in fact, it's probably better if you're not, because superstars don't have to think about how they play—but you'd better have some sense of your own strengths and weaknesses.

The Kings' GM, Dave Taylor, hired Andy after he won a championship with Shattuck-St. Mary's, the best high school hockey team in the U.S.A. Taylor was a mild-mannered guy who had a serious stammer that vanished only when he gave a speech. Between him and Andy, the Kings didn't present the players with anything to fear, and players sometimes need to be a little bit afraid to motivate them to find the next gear.

The LA Kings drafted Andy Murray's son Brady in the 2003 NHL Entry Draft while Andy was the coach of the team. Talk about awkward. Did Andy and Dave Taylor actually think people were going to believe them when they said Brady Murray was the best player available when the Kings were called to the podium to make their sixth pick of the draft? I mean, Dustin Byfuglien, Brian Elliott, Jaroslav Halák, Joe Pavelski, and Tobias Enström, all NHL All-Stars, were still available, and Brady Murray played four games for the Kings and then wound up playing somewhere in Switzerland.

I never saw Andy in the weight room, and I never saw him with his shirt off or naked in the steam room or shower, like you'd see other coaches. I'm pretty sure I never saw him drink a beer or a glass of wine or smoke a cigar with the other coaches around a fancy fire pit at a hotel on the road. It was very difficult for Andy to say the word "fuck" and that alone was probably enough to prevent guys from taking him seriously.

In fact, he never swore. He was a Bible thumper, though he never thumped it at me. If we ever saw him in a restaurant it was extremely uncomfortable for both parties, because we assumed he was counting our beers or glasses of wine. But because he rarely went beyond the rink or the hotel, it wasn't a common occurrence.

Andy lived in a suite at the Hilton Garden Inn beside our practice rink, which is beyond weird when you have a wife and family, but his wife lived back in Minnesota. I don't remember seeing her in LA at any point, which doesn't mean that she was never there, but if she'd been around even a little bit we would have known.

As much as Andy Murray and I were complete opposites, he must have seen that I could be an effective player because I found a nice spot playing on the left wing with Éric "Belly" Bélanger at center and right-winger Ian "Lappy" Laperrière on the third line. They were both from Quebec, but really polar opposites. Lappy was charged with looking after Belly, because Bélanger was very easily distracted, shall we say. He liked to have a very good time off the ice. Lappy's job was to make sure that Belly's extracurricular fun wasn't going to land him in the kind of trouble that would screw up the game of his linemate and babysitter.

Belly was also a bit of a sulker at times, because he had been a great offensive center and now he was being asked to play a defensive game. But he was a great two-way player. Laperrière played a very similar game to mine, full out, so we were a hard line to play against, but I also think Lappy didn't like me for that very same reason. I was younger, and a challenger. That said, he would be the first guy into the scrum to back me up if I started something, and vice versa.

We are the Kings' checking line, which means we're tasked with playing against the opposing team's top line, and if we do a successful job at keeping them off the score sheet then that will almost always give our guys a much better shot of skating away after sixty minutes with a W. But we're more than clock killers. We also generate offense, and I like playing with these guys. Belly is a very good face-off man, one of the best, and so is Lappy, and when they're not fighting with each other in French—on the ice, on the bench, in the locker room—we do very good work on the ice. We were a very good line, and that was new to me because I'd found myself an NHL role—we were on the ice during the last minutes of the game to protect our lead, and people could see that I was actually an NHL player of value. I'm getting attention.

I'm also doing a fairly good job at pretending that I'm not starry-eyed as I drive around Hollywood, but the truth is I'm still so green in Cali and all that comes with it. It was a step moving from small-town Ontario to Detroit, but this is like moving to another planet, where the rules are all about how you're seen. So I decide to make myself as visible as possible, off the ice as well as on it.

I've taken measures to fit in, starting with something I always recommend when you're new to a city or country: make the most of your wardrobe, with whatever budget you have. Your wardrobe is a big piece of your confidence, and looking good feels good. In LA, I need something efficient but stylish in an all-purpose kind of way. I'm now past the tucked-in golf shirt and slacks, which made me look like some small-town tourist. I think I'll go for a James Dean look, which is retro Hollywood, but new to me. So I buy fourteen white T-shirts (seven V-neck/seven crew neck) in a snug size medium, four pairs of AG soft-washed denim jeans (two dark-washed, one light-washed, one black-washed), a pair of black Hugo Boss military boots, and a black leather motorcycle jacket. It didn't cost me the moon and this uniform was actually good enough to get me into and through every single LA situation with the exception of a funeral or the Oscars.

I had read about Sunset Strip's famous club the Viper Room, which at the time was partly owned by Johnny Depp, so I wanted to check it out for myself. I drove solo into West Hollywood in my Cadillac and pulled into the back parking lot behind the Viper Room, which despite its fame is a brick slab of a building with everything painted black, including the bricks and the awning above the black door, though the club's name is in white letters. I threw on my jacket, lit a Marlboro Red, and posted up across the street to the side entrance where the doorman was manning the velvet rope.

I would always scope out a new joint before attempting to get inside because in those early days I didn't know anyone and was still unrecognizable on the LA scene. I made the call to wait it out in the line, and when I got to the front I'd tell the doorman I was new in town playing for the Kings and wanted to hear some music. I was alone and humble and this would be a lock for access.

As I'm standing there I see a tall guy with long blond curly hair walking toward the door from the back parking lot. He's wearing tight black jeans and the classic rocker black ankle boot and he has two women, a brunette and a redhead, walking beside him who have some miles on them but still look good because this is LA. They have tight frames and the mandatory augmented C-cups because a big firm C is the new D.

This guy steps to the side to let the girls pass through the velvet rope and then he looks at me and does a double take. "Are you Sean Avery?" he asks, surprising the hell out of me. "Yes, I am," I manage to admit. He asks what I'm doing waiting in line in a tone you'd use to ask someone if they were crazy. I told him I was new in town and didn't know anyone but wanted to hear some music. And all of a sudden I'm walking into the Viper Room with Bobby Carlton and his friends, past all the other people in line who are looking at me with a mixture of loathing and awe.

Bobby Carlton is an LA legend who happens to be a season ticket-holder of the LA Kings. He's originally from New York, and that's where he learned hockey. He started going to Kings games when Gretzky landed in LA, because that was the cool place to be. The Forum Club was a venue at the old LA Forum and it was a genuine LA destination for the rich and the famous. There was more excess back then, and LA team owners like Bruce McNall of the Kings and Jerry Buss of the Lakers were fast and loose in ways that let sex and drugs flourish because they were living that wild life themselves. The Staples Center was not like that. But Bobby Carlton is only there for the hockey, and here, at the Viper Room, he's about to change the course of my life.

The Viper Room is a music venue with two floors and bands going on both. The downstairs is more of a square box bar with tables. They're not private tables, so anyone can sit anywhere. I sit downstairs, which has a pretty small stage and also these leather banquettes in green and red and blue that look even brighter under the lights. I'm not listening to the band.

I'm totally transfixed by Bobby as he tells me about his life as a recovering addict who made his money in the late '80s and early '90s as an A&R (artist and repertoire) manager for rock bands.

Bobby knows everyone in the Hollywood scene. Eventually I'll figure out that it's really pretty much a town full of empty relationships, but to me, Bobby makes every handshake and air kiss a little bit more authentic. He introduces me to all the people running the velvet ropes of the city's hot spots, and this is like gold in Los Angeles.

These introductions to the gatekeepers mean that I can valet the car then open my date's door and waltz her up to the velvet rope to see those friendly hands raise it up like a perfect sunrise. It makes me feel for all those guys who are left standing there holding their valet ticket with their disappointed dates, making other plans for how the evening is going to end when they're told "not tonight" by the gatekeepers. I know, it's superficial as fuck, but if you're young and in the spotlight—as an athlete, musician, actor, mover and shaker—it's the way the LA game is played.

All the hot spots in LA have women running the velvet ropes, and getting to know them is a lesson in power, albeit one that is particular to Los Angeles. These girls work for the men who own these clubs and bars, and the good ones probably make $125K a year in salary and another $100K in tips. They build relationships with the stars, and often celebrities will only go to the clubs that "their" girl is running that night because you certainly don't want to run the risk of getting turned away by a stranger. LA insecurity is what fuels the whole circus.

The door girls of LA control everything from who gets on the covers of US Weekly to who ends up marrying and divorcing each other, according to their introductions of male and female celebrities. I mastered the art of taking care of these girls, starting with "Pantera Sarah," who was kind of the den mother to all the velvet rope girls in LA. (We eventually had a falling out because Justin Timberlake was in her Rolodex, and when I ended up falling for Justin's best friend's fiancée and she for me, that was the end of me in Sarah's clubs.)

I'd always slide a $100 bill into the girl's leather jacket when she lifted that velvet rope for me and my date, and sometimes I'd make it a gift certificate to Barney's or a massage at Sunset Tower Spa, both much appreciated in the "how you look is who you are" world of LA. I did not spend money to snag a choice table, but would sometimes be given a nice one to sit at with a few friends. I'd normally have a two-top (bar lingo which describes a small round table with two chairs) no matter what, so I wouldn't need to sit at someone's table like an annoying mooch. I also rarely brought anyone other than my date, along with the infamous Larry Longo, and this discretion in numbers was part of why the door girls respected me, because I never tried to take advantage of them.

LA back then was a town built on cocaine. Doing cocaine in LA was as common as having a coffee in the morning for the rest of America. Asking for blow was as common as asking someone if you could bum a smoke. To this day I've never done a line of cocaine, and this isn't because I was fearful of failing a drug test, because nothing would have happened to me in the NHL even if my test showed cocaine in it. The league's drug policy at the time was the same as a Stanley Cup Championship in Toronto— nonexistent. That changed in 2005, but when I started with the Kings, you could do any drug you wanted.

I never wanted to try cocaine because I was afraid I'd like it. Although I don't have any addiction issues, I do know that sometimes I'm excessive, even if it's just too much dessert. This means that if I have that extra helping of German chocolate cake then I do an extra thirty minutes on the exercise bike. If I smoke a few too many cigs at a party, then I can't have a cigarette for two days afterward and I have to do extra wind sprints until then.

This counterbalance strategy for dealing with an excess of vice is common to most hard-core athletes, and it's dangerous because you're pushing your body one way and then pulling it another. You can get away with it for a while, but not if you want a long career.

My desire to have a long career is another reason I never tried cocaine. I was also deterred by how stupidly people can act when they've done a few lines. What they don't show in the movies when they depict glamorous people doing coke is how dull it is to listen to them repeating the same story over and over and over again.

Not that guys don't use other drugs.

The best feeling in the world is when the needle plunges through the skin of your ass and you feel a burst of Toradol rushing into your blood. You take it after the warm-up, fifteen minutes before the game. Toradol is an anti-inflammatory drug used to counter severe pain, and once it gets in your system you feel its magic move from the tip of your toes to the top of your ears. It's the same vibe as the scene in *Iron Man* when Tony Stark turns the suit on and suddenly his body is covered by this indestructible armor. You feel indestructible. While having a continuous orgasm. There's nothing better.

That said, it's terrible for your liver, and so during the regular season you take it in pill form. It's the playoff injection in your butt that presents the liver damage risk, but hey, it's the playoffs. You take a lot of risks.

I chuckle when I read all these stories about Toradol abuse in the NFL. The NHL makes the NFL look like amateurs in the Toradol department. My cocktail of choice during the eighty-two-game regular season was one Toradol pill and one 30 mg Adderall tablet, split in half. Adderall is what doctors prescribe for people with ADHD to help them focus. I'd take half with the Toradol and half between the second and third periods. The Toradol makes me feel like I can skate through a brick wall, and the Adderall acts as a stimulant, giving me that extra gear and dialing me right into the zone. Adderall is prohibited by the NHL, that is, you are allowed to take it only if you have a TUE (which means "therapeutic use exemption"). Coming out of the 2004 lockout, the list of prohibited substances was a lot longer, but guys still loved their Adderall.

Guys also used Sudafed, which is also a stimulant, though one that was a lot more alarming to see in action than the Toradol-Adderall combo. Lots of guys on the Kings used Sudafed, and I saw some so jacked up on it that they lost their hearing. They were so wired and so shaky that they couldn't understand what you were saying to them. Toradol was the exact opposite.

In Detroit they used this thing called Power Orange, which worked like Sudafed. Even after the FDA pulled it, it could still be found in the Red Wings' locker room.

The NHL did drug testing at the time, but the only thing you could get suspended for was an anabolic steroid. They tested for recreational drugs, but didn't suspend you for it. There was no advance warning, and they tested us all at the same time. So you showed up to practice and there would be signs posted directing you to the WADA (World Anti-Doping Association) people who would take your details, give you a little bottle to pee into, and direct you to a stall. You'd give them your full bottle of piss and then they would test it. You could do it before or after practice. Sometimes there were guys who stayed two or three hours after practice just drinking liters of water in order to be able to pee.

The tests were anonymous in the sense that only if something got flagged would WADA check whose urine was in violation of league policy. If they found a guy with a load of cocaine in his system, he'd get a call from the NHLPA doctor, who'd talk to him about his recreational drug use, and if need be, strongly suggest that he needed rehab. But between the Toradol, Sudafed, Adderall, Vicodin, Percocet, and other PKs (painkillers), you didn't really need to buy street drugs. You could find the right state of mind right in the trainer's room.

9

SUMMER SCHOOLING

We miss the playoffs my first year in LA, which doesn't feel great after staggering through a Stanley Cup parade less than a year before. But despite the fact that the Kings send me down to the minors for a bit of playoff experience, I feel pretty good. I feel like I'm in the league for good. I've decided to stay in my old room in my parents' basement in Pickering, Ontario. I want to live like a normal person and train my ass off during the week so that when I go to the Kings' training camp in September I'll blow the other guys out of the water.

Of course, I also have to drive down to Detroit to pick up my stuff from Brett Hull's place. And while I'm back in town it wouldn't be right not to throw one last rager in that house.

By the time I get to Detroit, Hull has packed up to head home to Dallas for the summer. The Red Wings ended up losing in the first round of the playoffs after the deadline deal which sent me to LA. To make my party one to remember, I round up some old friends and a couple of strangers at a bar. It was closing time, so I asked if anyone wanted to party at Brett Hull's place. "Yes" was the answer.

Around 4 A.M. we'd reached that terrible abyss feared by all ragers—we'd run out of booze. Or almost run out. There was that magnum of champagne sitting on proud display on top of the Jukebox bar. After we polished that off and the cabs had arrived to take away the last guests, I retired upstairs with a friend who taught some of the Red Wings' kids at the local private school. Being old enough to hook up with the hot high school teacher but young enough to still pinch myself about it was the kind of cosmic synergy that made the night perfect.

But not quite.

That magnum of champagne was the only thing Brett had that was signed by the entire 2002 Stanley Cup champion Detroit Red Wings. Now the seal had been broken and the bubbly consumed by his twenty-three-year-old former roommate who'd lived above the garage, along with his merry band of guests, some of whom he didn't quite know.

There was only one thing to do. I filled the magnum with 1.5 liters of water and pushed the cork back inside, which is no easy feat, I can tell you that. I still have no idea if Brett knows, though now I guess he will.

I go back to Detroit twice more over the summer of 2003, and each trip has an incident that makes my departure from Motown a little ugly.

The first began as a golf tournament in Sarnia, Ontario, which is about an hour from Detroit. I stay at Kris Draper's home on Friday night and we get up early on Saturday morning to drive to Sarnia to play in this charity tournament, which has a bunch of Detroit Red Wings alumni playing. I specifically ask Drapes to find out if Bob Probert is attending because of that sucker punch I hit him with a year earlier in Chicago—I don't really feel like getting my face caved in on the nineteenth hole. Good news: Probert isn't attending.

After the golf tourney there's a banquet, and then the bar opens and the real party begins. Local talent in the form of a group of divorced women in their early thirties arrive, and these gals are hungry. Hockey players refer to women who make it very clear that they want to sleep with a hockey player (or with any man for that matter) as "hungry."

Toward the end of the night I'm in a white stretch limo (at this point in my career I only travel in white limos . . .) with some of these hungry ladies, and we're getting ready to head back to the hotel we're staying at when suddenly former Red Wing Dino Ciccarelli sticks his head inside the limo and asks to speak with me. I say "no problem" and step outside. Dino Ciccarelli has always been one of my heroes, and Sarnia is his hometown. Maybe he wants me to come back to a party at his place.

No, he does not. In a matter of seconds we're in an argument about whether the ladies in the limo want to go back to the party I'm throwing at my hotel or not. They do. Dino wants them to come back inside the banquet, and after he calls me a "rookie" I file how much I loved Dino as a player in a safe place in my head and get ready to defend myself.

Dino now takes a step toward me with a hand up like he's going to grab my shirt and then push me back—which is a classic hockey fight move— or pull me closer to give me an ear full of well-lubricated advice. Either outcome is not what I want, so with one quick move with my right hand I slap his incoming hand down, and see the blood rush to his head. Then we both push each other at the exact same moment, which moves us both back a step away from each other.

Fuck it, here we go, outside a stretch limo in beautiful downtown Sarnia. We both have our hands up and we square off to fight when thankfully my real-life guardian angel Kris Draper comes to the rescue to break it up, and saves both of us the painful Sunday morning embarrassment that would have followed.

The next and pretty much final weekend I've ever spent in Detroit began on the Fourth of July, 2003. I went to a Tigers game with Cheli, Kid Rock, and John Cusack, along with some legendary guys from Cheli's Chicago crew. After the game we piled into a rented tour bus and headed to Cheli's Chili Bar in Dearborn for a surprise Kid Rock concert. This is what made Cheli and Rock such fucking legends.

Halfway through Rock's set I go out to the bus with two girlfriends I've rolled with for a few years in Detroit (and who are truly just friends) to smoke a joint. Yes, it's true, though I hardly drink these days I like to burn a joint and listen to the music. The bus is deluxe—a multimillion-dollar Prevost that rock stars tour in. I once smoked a joint inside Willie Nelson's Prevost, which actually has a gigantic portrait of Willie smoking a joint painted on the entire back portion of the bus. Cheli is already on the bus, taking a breather.

Then this guy walks on the bus and sits down beside one of Kid Rock's buddies.

The buddy politely asks the kid to leave, but the kid—he's maybe a bit younger than me, but not much—doesn't budge. So I stand up from the kitchen table and tell him it's a private bus and he needs to get off right now, but this guy tells us he's going to stay and hang out and asks if we're going to smoke a joint. I can't believe it.

The guy then stands up like he's going to walk to the back of the bus, so I move toward the front. We're just about face-to-face when the guy drops his shoulder, which means a punch is coming. Before he can get one off, my right hand goes from hanging beside my waist to the dead center of his face and instantly I can feel a sharp pain shoot up my forearm.

The guy is flat on his back, sucking air through his mouth loudly, deeply, and fast, but he's definitely out cold. It was the longest thirty seconds of my life before he came to and we got him off the bus and had one of the doormen put him in a cab with a fifty-dollar bill in his pocket.

I woke up the next morning before my drive back to Toronto and read a text from Cheli saying that his actor buddy John "Platoon–Wall Street" McGinley had found the guy's front tooth, root and all. I hit that guy as hard and as perfectly as possible, and it was the most expensive punch of my life because although the cops wouldn't charge me, the kid sued me in civil court—my first lawsuit, by the way. We settled on a $26,000 lump-sum payment. But I was so pissed off by the whole incident that I made the guy wait—$200 a month until he tried to garnish my wages. Then I cut the guy a check.

I know from experience how expensive dental bills can be, so hopefully replacing his front teeth didn't leave much for him to take a vacation to Myrtle Beach. Anyway, lesson learned: when you have money, the bull's eye on your back is real and you need to be careful.

Imagine this. You're living in your parents' basement in a Toronto suburb and Brad Norton—NHL heavyweight, master of sarcasm, barroom charmer, and all-round fucking savage—invites you to LA to go to the ESPYs. By the way, he's your roommate. You go, right? Brad is my kind of guy.

The thing is, though, it means you're living in two very different worlds. This is probably true for most athletes. Most of us come from small towns, or poor neighborhoods, or poorer countries. Then we end up in chartered planes and luxury hotels and clothing stores where pants cost $750. Every big-league athlete goes through it. But big-league athletes who end up in LA experience culture shock of a different order of magnitude.

I mean, when I head back to LA from my parents' basement, I stay at the Chateau Marmont. The place looks like a Bavarian castle sitting on a hill overlooking Sunset Boulevard. From its Gothic cloisters to its poolside bungalows, it's a magical spot where celebrities live out all the excesses they desire. When I open the patio door of my room, I look out on a garden restaurant where it's almost impossible to secure a reservation because from 8 A.M. to 2 A.M. it's filled with every major director/ movie star/producer/agent/musician in town, meeting to discuss upcoming projects.

In those days they let you smoke at the fucking table. Actually, they sold cigarettes like a side dish on the menu. Joaquin Phoenix is sitting poolside drinking a Diet Coke and chain-smoking while reading what I assume is a script.

At one end of the pool are a couple of guys who play in a band hanging out with LA party girls. One of the ladies orders her Diet Coke with three lemons and smokes a pack of American Spirit yellows. Over there, a middle-aged balding man who has a stack of scripts on the table talks on the phone the entire day so loudly that everyone within a 200-foot radius can hear his bullshit. (He's the same guy you always see in the boarding area at airports who treats the entire captive audience to his stupefying speeches to some poor minion on the other end of the line.) There's a supermodel drinking bottled water and also smoking a pack of cigarettes, this time Marlboro Lights. And there's an English or Australian couple who are in dire need of a few days' sun and can't stop staring at everyone and wondering if they're "someone."

So, yeah, LA is not like anything life has prepared me for. In Detroit I'd hear people talking about Michigan football and jobs in the auto industry. I may not care about football, or have anything to do with auto unions, but I got it. They were talking about the same world I grew up in. In LA, they're talking about themselves, about their summer plans and their winter vacations, and about how to burnish their image. I definitely have some insecurities when I hear people talking about places like Paris and New York and Aspen, but I've decided that the best way to deal with this sort of thing is to be honest and ask questions when I need to. I lived in West Hollywood, which is well stocked with men and women of the world who have resources and style, and I ran up against it all the time. I won't pretend to be something that I'm not, which at this point is a globe-trotting hotshot who's been around the world several times. I've only flown in first class once, to model tuxedos on *Good Morning America*, and while that's not the measurement of success, it just goes to show you how wide-eyed I am.

Still, I'm starting to feel very comfortable in my life beyond the rink. Day in and day out I meet a lot of agents from alphabet-soup agencies like CAA and UTA and WME. I meet a lot of "floaters," which is a term describing a celebrity's or star athlete's "friend," someone who somehow has a schedule allowing them to be by their famous friend's side at most social events. It's a very LA species, and a floater sticks out like, well, a floater in the toilet. The thing is, there's so much money sloshing around that there's a whole ecosystem of losers who thrive just by hanging around and living off handouts. Let's just say I didn't meet a lot of floaters where I grew up.

But then, I didn't want to stay where I grew up, did I? I love this place more than any place I've ever been in my obviously boring life to date.

Back to the ESPYs for a second. Remember who won Best Athlete that year? I'll give you a clue: he was later outed as an epic steroid user (along with a cocktail of other performance-enhancing drugs). Yes, it was Lance Armstrong. It was roughly around this time that people started wondering whether NHL players were on steroids, and figured they should test us. But they shouldn't have bothered. Steroids work for sports where you need bulk and muscle, not for the ones where you need speed and agility. No hockey player I know has any interest in steroids.

When you look at pro hockey players stripped of their gear, it's surprising to many people how lithe we are. Hockey players need to be able to skate. When some TV analyst says that a player isn't a strong skater, it's all relative. A guy isn't going to make the NHL if he's not an elite skater. That's as much about agility and balance as it is about performing one movement more powerfully than the next guy. Carrying around a few extra pounds of beef, or being able to bench some ridiculous amount, is only going to slow you down and make you a worse hockey player. So, no, there's no steroid problem in the NHL.

But life in LA is not just smoking cigarettes by the pool or walking the red carpet with Lance Armstrong. Before I go to the ESPYs with Norty, I head to Runyon Canyon Park, which is 160 acres of lush and rugged parkland between Hollywood Boulevard and Mulholland Drive, to run "vertical sprints"—a fancy term for running up a hill.

The first three steps you take from a dead stop to surging forward during a hockey game are the most important. Having a bomb like Shea Weber or being able to stickhandle like Connor McDavid would be nice, but that's not what makes you a good hockey player. Lots of guys have great careers with those weapons. But no one sticks around if he can't control the most important thing: how far away you are from the other guy. If he's got the puck, you need to close the gap fast. If you've got it, you need to pull away before he closes the gap. If you can't do that, you're not in the NHL. Because if you can't do that, you don't have time to do anything out there. I bet most guys would trade just about anything for an explosive three strides.

It's all about that gap. The moment that you know the pass is coming until the moment it hits your stick is less than two seconds. You've got a few fractions of a second to make an important decision. By the way, you're also skating at full speed, aware that if you're looking at the puck, there's a guy who hates you just out of your field of vision making a decision of his own: can he run you over before you've got control of the puck? So you have to decide whether you stay wide on the defenseman or need to cut in the moment the puck hits your stick.

Let's say I'm staying wide. I'm going to protect the puck by getting my inside shoulder in front of the D-man who himself has pivoted from backwards to forwards and is now skating beside me, trying to get his stick in front of the shot I'm about to take. That shot is probably less than two seconds away. Meanwhile, I'm trying to figure out where to put the puck. My eyes are up, looking to see whether the goalie is guessing that I'm going to cut across, whether he's tight to the post, or whether he's hedging his bets and opening up his legs to be ready either way.

The game's great goal scorers can make it look slow and easy when they drop their shoulder at the goalie to freeze him, then calmly put the puck wherever he's not. But trust me, it's neither of those things. If you can't explode into open ice to take that pass, maybe you don't have the body position you need to get the shot off. Or if you arrive a fraction of a second later, maybe that defenseman has stepped up and smoked you. The difference between a guy who almost made it and a star who makes millions and hangs out in LA art galleries is a fraction of a second.

This is why I run fifteen five-second, then twelve ten-second, and then ten fifteen-second sprints up a serious hill at 5:45 P.M. on a Friday in the heat of LA in July. I also do it because if I don't push myself up that hill then what should be the best weekend of my life will now be a three-day guilt trip with me unable to dodge the shadow of shame for not putting in the work. But if I survive the run, I get to head to a party at the Mondrian hotel with Norty.

10

THE KING OF LA

I truly believe what kicked off my 2003–04 season was getting into it with Laird Hamilton at Cheli's place in Malibu in July. Just a couple of years earlier when I first saw him standing on the beach with his wife, Gabby Reese, I was in awe of their majesty. But I'd gained a lot more confidence in those two years, and now I was finding Laird's swagger to be a little much.

Me and Cheli and Laird and a few other guys had worked out, and we were having beers on the beach. Laird was always the alpha of the pack, and had to make sure that any guy in his vicinity knew it. I'd heard enough so I just started laying into him like I'd do if we were on the ice. "Your wife is way more famous than you," I said. "She's way more successful. She makes tons more money." And so on. It drove him fucking nuts, and because he couldn't trash-talk me back, he wanted to wrestle me.

So we had a wrestling match and I put him on his ass. He underestimated me. He was a strong guy, but come on, he's a surfer. He's not a brawler. Even when I beat him he said he'd lost because I was sweating so much that he couldn't get a proper grip on me. Cheli just smiled.

I felt that tussle on the beach with a guy whom I'd hero-worshiped was another milepost. The hero had become a hot-air balloon, and so I punctured it. Because I was now feeling like an equal.

I took that feeling into the Kings' 2003–04 training camp, and I'm once again at the top of the fitness class along with Matty Norström, who understood fitness and took it seriously, and Kip Brennan, our resident tough guy, who looked like he'd been pulled from the pages of a fitness magazine. (God help Laird Hamilton if he were ever to have a disagreement with Kip on a beach somewhere.) On the other hand, Luc Robitaille wasn't in great shape, but that's not what he did. He got by on talent. But younger guys were starting to figure out that if they wanted a long ride at the top of their game, then they had to look after the machine they were riding.

At this point in my career I will still fight in training camp, which is a rarity among proven NHL players, but I feel that I'm not a proven player yet. In the 2003 camp I don't remember who I fought, but it would have been some no-name East Coast Hockey League player who was trying to play like me. At the time, this guy wasn't modeling his game after me— he was just trying to do what I did. As my career went on and more guys played like me, I didn't have to fight in training camp because they'd modeled their games on mine, and they didn't want to mess with me.

I've started training camp on the same line that I ended the previous season. Belly and Lappy still yell at each other in French, which I found funny last season and annoying now, because I really don't know if they're talking shit about me. Lappy isn't a very good skater, but he's fearless—except when it comes to me. He's afraid I'm going to take his job, and it creates tension between us. We're similar players but Lappy has six years on me, and along with that he has an old-school hockey mentality which emphasizes that young players should know their place and not bring much attention to themselves, which is obviously the opposite of everything I'm about. By the way, I did end up taking his job a couple of seasons later, so he had more of a problem with me than I did with him.

So yeah, there was sometimes a bit of tension on that team. But tension is not necessarily a bad thing. Tension keeps a team on its toes and motivated. Tension holds us all accountable, and it's an important ingredient in teams that win. This means that teams are not always one big happy family, because when you create team chemistry, you get chemical reactions.

I think teams do need to police themselves, and if the leadership group thinks a player is a problem then they have every right to go to management and tell them about the problem. It has to be done by the leadership group and not by one guy, because then you can get jealousy and revenge as the motivators. Personally, I'd just air it out in the room. I like to win, I hate to lose, and I don't like it when guys don't work hard. I'm also impulsive and not great at thinking things through before I say them, which has landed me in trouble a few times. But that also means that I expect guys to say things to me if I'm not pulling my weight. That doesn't happen much, though. The majority of professional hockey players leave it to the coaches, whereas I would call guys out myself. Again, not always the best idea, but it's who I am.

I've been called a bad teammate over the years. I didn't hang out with the Kings a lot. I didn't enjoy going to the same fucking hockey bar—Harry O's in Manhattan Beach—after every game. I didn't dislike the guys, and I don't think they disliked me. I just didn't want to hang out in the same bar every night.

One rumor that came out of the "bad teammate" narrative is that I made fun of Dustin Brown's lisp. But I never made fun of Dustin Brown's lisp. I *did* make fun of Dustin Brown's girlfriend (now wife), Nicole, and told him to maybe wait a bit before he committed his entire rich, successful life to his teenage girlfriend, considering that at the time he was a teenager playing for the LA Kings in the land of beautiful California girls. Maybe my delivery needed some work, but I swear my intentions were good, and isn't that what teammates are for?

In September, the league sent the Kings to play a pre-season game in Las Vegas. The NHL had been flirting with putting a team there for a while now, and we are part of the flirtation.

Vegas is probably the single worst place an NHL pre-season game could be played, and I should know. It's not because the fans and players don't love it—they do. It's not because the atmosphere wasn't awesome—it was. It's because veteran NHL players don't take pre-season games that seriously. A veteran NHL player under contract for the upcoming NHL season would take full advantage of three days in Las Vegas to attend to any secret desire he hadn't yet fulfilled so that he could leave Las Vegas regretting something. That, I promise you, is true.

I'd never been to Vegas, so I was curious to see if what they said about Sin City was true. We check in to the MGM Casino and Hotel and I see that they've doubled me up with a roomie, Brad Chartrand, a pretty strait-laced guy who wasn't a fellow traveler in my pursuit of fun. I immediately go back to the front desk and explain to the woman that I'm here with "The Hockey Team" (the term we'd use in places that didn't really know hockey) and I wanted my own room so that I could have some privacy during the next couple days.

This lady knows exactly what I'm looking for, so after a quick conference with her manager she asks how I'd like to pay for my room, and I gladly hand over my American Express Green Card—something I'm very proud of because it means I'm a successful adult.

We don't have a practice until the next morning and we don't have a team dinner or any other bonding BS, so tonight is a go for freelancing fun. I head to dinner with Matty Norström and Big Bad Brad Norton. Matty is a great guy who comes from the School of Cheli when it comes to partying: all in. He can sit down and drink a bottle dry, and then he's the first guy on the ice the next day. Same with Brad Norton. Norty Norton is six-four and 240 pounds of pure muscle, and it was pretty much a guarantee that by midnight Norty would either have the bar or the party chanting his name and/or we'd be trying to defuse some DEFCON 1 situation. We have dinner at Wolfgang Puck's. As we walk in, some nearly naked models— who'd be completely naked but for the rose petals they're wearing—splash around in bathtubs. So far, Vegas is living up to the hype.

I'm not a big strip club guy, but the strip clubs in Vegas are like shows on Broadway. So we climb into a white limo (as I said, that's my ride . . .) and make the ten-minute journey from MGM to a legendary peeler palace.

We walk up to the club and a six-foot-five bouncer—I know this because he's about an inch taller than Brad Norton—tells us to step inside where the table hostess will seat us and to enjoy our time in paradise. By the time we sit down and thank the hostess, we're all $80 lighter. I should have known trouble was coming.

The waitress then sashays up and asks us for a credit card. For some reason that remains high in my Greatest Hits of Stupidity, I offer my prized green Amex to hold our tab for the night.

Spoiler Alert: The lesson I learn tonight is the birth of a rule I live by still and have never broken. I will never, ever hand my card to a waitress in any club till the day I die, because that guy always gets stuck with the bill and he never gets paid back. Or worse.

The waitress comes back with our drinks and a credit card authorization form for me to sign. This heavy-handed bit of bureaucracy is done by strip clubs so guys can't say their card was stolen and that it was not them, no way, no how, who spent that $14,000 on lap dances in the champagne room.

Because this is not a cool story I will speed it up.

Twenty minutes after signing the form, I was face-down in a full-body sweat, puking out Mr. Puck's culinary delicacies onto the floor of the strip club. Matty Norström had to carry me out of the club and then he got me back to the MGM. I could barely stand, let alone walk, so the hotel got me a wheelchair and wheeled me up to the room.

The next morning I woke up in the sunken bathtub of my suite. I made it through practice by the skin of the bile in my empty stomach, and all I could think about doing after practice was getting into my bed for a major nap.

Then I realized that my credit card was still with the waitress at the strip club.

I called Amex to cancel my card and the whole ugly truth came clear. The waitress obviously drugged my drink because she knew I was the cardholder, and when I got carried out she hit my card with $6,800 in bogus charges. What can I say or do to prove I'm right, especially after everyone in the place saw me behaving as if I'd been drinking for days and then get hauled out on my shield? Nothing but learn a lesson. Strip club waitress 1, Sean Avery 0.

The hockey world has an expression for what came next: playing guilty. The idea is, when you're hungover and everyone knows you're hungover, or when you've done something stupid and everyone knows it, you play better. Playing shitty when everyone knows you're guilty would be too much to bear. So you find some otherwise unavailable store of energy. Everyone has it. And just about everyone in the NHL has played guilty, some of us many, many times. That night, it was fucking "game on."

On that steamy September evening, the NHL went the full Vegas route in the MGM Grand Arena, featuring a hot tub filled with strippers ostensibly promoting beer and giving lucky male fans back washes during the game (I'm not kidding). Meanwhile, I gave the NHL a taste of the character I was becoming: Sean Avery, master of mayhem.

I drive future Hall of Famer Peter Forsberg so nuts during this exhibition game that he finally drops his gloves and comes at me like the bull he is. Everyone talks about how classless Sean Avery is, how below the belt I go with my trash talk, but that gives me far too much credit. I used the oldest trick in the book to enrage Peter the Great, simply pointing out to him, on an endless loop, how slow he looked because of his bad ankle which was a result of . . . wait for it . . . old age.

The deadliest thing an older sports superstar can ever hear are those two words, because your career is defined by how you can make your body do things other mortals cannot, and now Time has called time, as it were. No way around it.

Now, I obviously called him a whiny bitch and all the other classics, but what got him going was the truth. That's the key to chirping at someone. It doesn't hurt if it's not true. My yapping took this game-changing player completely off his game. And we ended up in a line brawl. The fans from LA and Colorado went crazy in a way I'd never seen at a pre-season game. MGM Arena was rocking. It was like the playoffs. And for those people in Vegas who'd wandered into their first hockey game, all I can say is you must have been hooked for life. Meanwhile, I scored an assist, took forty-two minutes in penalties, and we won, 3–1. Forsberg got twenty-one minutes in penalties, and not a single point. I'd beaten one of the best players in the world.

Anyway, good luck to the visiting teams coming to play the Las Vegas Golden Knights. After a night in Sin City, they'll be skating uphill before the puck drops. I don't gamble but I understand why other guys do.

Also, I've never been back to a strip club.

The first game of my first full regular season with my new team is in . . . Detroit. Against the Red Wings. I mean, in case I didn't miss the guys or the city enough, the NHL hockey gods obliged by starting me off with my new team back where it all began. I was excited about playing in Detroit, and about seeing the guys, and even about going back to Roma Café for my pre-game meal.

How can I not be nervous? Detroit is the team that gave me my shot in the NHL, and I still have a lot of lifelong friends there. Detroit supported me as I learned the ropes as a rookie, but what Ken Holland said after he traded me still stuck in my head because I was also learning about loyalty in this business. Holland said he'd traded me because of my "lack of respect for the game and for the people of the game."

If I didn't respect the game, why have I played it and practiced since I was five years old? Why have I dedicated painful summer hours to train harder than ninety-five percent of players in his organization and put my long-term health on the line if I didn't respect the game?

Fuck you, Ken Holland.

He said I don't respect people in the game. Is he referring to me trash-talking superstars in the league while I played for his Red Wings? If so, why didn't he pull the jersey off my back and send my ass down to the minors instead of letting me play thirty-six games the year his team won a Cup?

Fuck you, Ken Holland.

I played a strong game against Detroit and finished with an assist, but I was on the ice with twenty seconds left in a 2–2 tie when Steve Yzerman beat Éric Bélanger up the ice and took a pass from Ray Whitney that got by a weak-defending Ian Laperrière. The great Stevie Y took the pass on his forehand and before you could blink he took a low, hard slap shot that beat the reliable (cough, cough) Roman Čechmánek for the game-winning goal.

I shower after the game and think to myself that if I'd taken a better angle on the forecheck I could have stopped the outlet pass and maybe I would have earned a shift in overtime, and who knows what can happen then? But the reality is that we have eighty-one more games to play, and so you move on to get ready for the next one. And you hope that you have a group of guys who pay attention to all the little things in the game because it's those little things that make the difference over an eight-month season. Everything in life is about taking care of the little things. Or so I think. But I won't be playing our next game in Pittsburgh because of a Very Big Thing. And if wishes could make it undone, then it would be undone a million times. But they can't.

On October 5, 2003, before the first game of the season, I'd received a call from my best friend, Adam Campbell, who was my teammate when we were sixteen-year-old rookies in the Ontario Hockey League, which is the highest level of hockey any sixteen- to nineteen-year-old can play. Adam asked me if I was sitting down, which is something I'd never been asked before.

Adam told me that Dan Snyder, my former roommate and captain, was dead. Dan was the passenger in his Atlanta Thrashers teammate Dany Heatley's Ferrari, which Heatley had wrapped around a tree while speeding in Atlanta a few days earlier. Dan had suffered massive head injuries in the crash, and the medics put him a coma to try to help his brain heal. His vital signs had been good, and there was hope that Dan would wake up and live a long life, but that didn't happen. And now he was dead, at age twenty-five.

The first time that Dan threw me his keys to start the car before we drove to school one winter morning in Owen Sound, Ontario, population 22,500, I walked out to the car in my team tracksuit and Sorels, jumped in, and turned the key. The car lurched forward and drove through the garage door. I could see Dan in the rearview mirror. He was standing there, shirtless, with his hands on his hips and smoke coming out of his ears.

I'd never driven a manual transmission car before, and certainly didn't know that Dan had left the stick shift in first gear. Dan chalked it up to something a captain needs to accept and he didn't lay a beating on me that morning. He was a good guy.

The funeral is in Dan's hometown of Elmira, Ontario, about an hour's drive west of Toronto. Five hundred minor hockey league players of all ages lined Snyder Avenue—Dan's family has a long history in this town—and they tap their sticks on the pavement in a hockey salute as Dan's family and his Atlanta Thrashers teammates walk into the Mennonite church.

This is the first time that I've been touched by death up close, but I don't cry at Dan's funeral, and I wonder why. Would Dan have cried if he was at my funeral? I don't think so, but how can I really know?

I was more upset at seeing his mom and dad and sister and brother try to get through this day. Because it's so painful to me, and I can't imagine how they can bear it.

I guess maybe they did the way we always do, by remembering the great things about the person who has died. And Dan's heart—his desire—was the greatest thing. I know he would have been in the NHL for a long time, because he made it there against all odds. He was drafted to the OHL in the last round as an overage twenty-year-old and came into the league at five-nine-and-a-half and 170 pounds soaking wet. He was again picked in the last round of the NHL draft, and a few years later this skinny kid was an NHL player, because he was always the hardest working guy on the ice. It's not just the kind of bullshit teachers and parents tell you. You really can make it. Nobody liked to burn the candle at both ends more than Dan Snyder, but he always showed up to play hard.

Dany Heatley is at the funeral as well, with his leg in a cast. He looks like death, and he's going to be charged with vehicular homicide, though we all know that the last thing he wanted was to hurt his friend. And then something amazing happens, something that makes every little problem I think I have just seem so small and worthless.

After the memorial service, Dan's mom and dad, Graham and LuAnn, read a statement to a news conference in the arena where Dan had first played hockey. And this is what they said:

"We want you to know that we do not lay blame on Dany Heatley for the accident that took our son from us. Dany is a good person and no one feels more sorry for what happened than he does. Forgiveness is also a part of being human and we know there is nothing to gain from harboring resentment or anger towards others. We are here to support him through this difficult time and know that he, too, is hurting so much."

The house that Brad Norton and I have rented is one block away from the Pacific Ocean and belongs to Steve Shields, a goalie for the Chicago Blackhawks. We pay $6,000 a month which we split down the middle, and it's a very reasonable amount to pay to be able to live a block from the beach.

We play rock-paper-scissors to see who gets the master bedroom, which sits on the top floor and has its own deck overlooking the ocean. Norty wins. He didn't cheat.

This house becomes a regular spot for many after-parties that spring up after some beers at Harry O's, the local hockey bar in Manhattan Beach which a retired hockey player named Billy Harris owned at one point, and which I do not frequent. Guys from the team would drop in to our place, along with the occasional floater, maybe a few hockey groupies, plus some Hollywood actresses or local surfer girls.

I wonder sometimes whether living out here in something resembling paradise is making me soft. One thing for sure—it makes the ice soft at the Staples Center. But the Kings' assistant equipment manager has it figured out. For arenas that were hot, like LA or Anaheim, Rico would give me a duller blade to skate on, because the ice would be softer and you don't want it to dig in. For hard ice, he'd make them sharper, to give me maximum power. The idea behind skate sharpening is basically balancing control and speed. The sharpener creates a valley—or a hollow—in your skate blade. The deeper the hollow, the sharper the edges of your blades for turning fast and stopping hard, and the shallower that valley is, the more the blades touch the ice, so that you get more glide. Too much of either is bad.

Every NHL player likes his skates sharpened a different way. Jaromír Jágr used to have his skates sharpened four times during a game when I played with him in New York, and some guys would have their wheels (which is what we called our skates) sharpened only on game days, because they wanted to keep their blades for as long as they could without having to break in a new pair. Some guys would just replace their blades and keep the boot, though I liked to get new skates because it made me feel like I was literally getting a power reboot. As a skate breaks down it gets softer, which means that it absorbs the power of the stride rather than transferring it to the ice.

One reality that is perhaps so obvious that people don't really talk about it is the fact that hockey players do everything from the vantage point of a sharpened piece of steel about an eighth of an inch wide and a foot long. When you get a genius sharpener like Rico, you really appreciate it. I guarantee that no professional player from another sport could ever become an NHL player and I guarantee that a hockey player could, with enough practice, become a professional in another sport.

I use music before a game to get me focused and pumped up, and more than a few fellow hockey players thought I was weird for the music I chose, bands like Radiohead or Sigur Rós. That's a pretty stark contrast to the usual thumping and wailing that you hear in the dressing room before a hockey game, songs like AC/DC's "Thunderstruck," which have played in hockey dressing rooms since I was twelve years old.

NHL hockey teams play music in the dressing room from 5 P.M. until you go out for warm-up about forty-five minutes before game time. They have a set playlist that usually stays the same for a few months too long, and after a while we're sick of certain songs. When I say "we," there's a hierarchy. The goalie is at the top of the pole—if he doesn't like a song, it gets pulled from the list. You hope like hell that your goalie not only likes music but has taste, because if he doesn't you'll be listening to the sound of black holes collapsing or chipmunks mating for the entire season.

After the goalie come the star players, then the more veteran players, and then the rest of us. Of course, we're free to create playlists, but the team gets to decide, in the order I've described. My playlist never made the cut.

Warm-ups in Los Angeles are legendary because it's Hollywood, baby, and you never know who's watching. So you enjoy those twenty minutes of cruising around with the breeze in your hair. (Your helmet is on the bench so you can show off your freshly cut hair with just enough product in it to keep a nice hold, but not so much of the stuff that it will run into your eyes the moment you start sweating.) In the middle of a game, you're not thinking about what you look like, but during warm-ups? For sure.

For some reason, every team warms up the same way. Cross-ice saucer passes and shots on net. But you're not picking corners on your goalie. You want to put the puck in the goalie's pillows (his pads). I've seen Dominik Hašek skate off the ice during warm-up in Detroit because guys tried to score on him. Saw it with Henrik Lundqvist in New York as well.

People also think that we have some elaborate superstitious ritual when we leave the ice after warm-up. We don't. There's just always one guy who likes the attention and who chooses to be the last man beside the goalie to head off to the locker room. In Detroit, Darren McCarty liked to whack Hašek's pads as the last guy. In LA, it was Ian Laperrière.

I wasn't really the pad-tapping type. My warm-up was more likely to include a bit of eye contact with the hot blonde eleven rows up. It's like seeing her in a coffee shop, except that you're on the ice surrounded by 20,000 people who have paid to see you. I know I'm a monster for saying this, but here's the thing: these women may not be yelling down to the ice, "Hey big boy, want to fuck after the game?," but her look can say it, and if you send that look back, well, you're in for some sexy time in about three hours. It's a pretty cool feeling even if I never went for it, but a lot of guys did.

The other thing that's dead certain three hours or so after warm-up is a media scrum in the locker room. Win or lose. Think about any other job in the world where after work a bunch of total strangers come into your office to interview you about that day's work—about the things you did right, but mostly about the things you did wrong. They also ask you to gaze into the future and predict what work will be like tomorrow, or at the end of the year. Will you win or lose?

Oh yes, there's one more thing: you and your co-workers have taken all your work clothes off and so you do these interviews naked. Crazy, right?

That pretty much describes an NHL locker room when the beat reporters descend to get quotes for their reports and roundups. Grown men—some of them happy to display their anatomical gifts—being interviewed by attractive women. With the Kings, our locker room flasher was Éric Bélanger. French-Canadian guys were very pretty, and had a European style sense that was different from the rest of the country. Belly thought he was the slickest of them all, and he loved his body, so he loved to show it off. Most of the time during post-game interviews his towel was so low you could see his pubic hair. When there was a female reporter in the room—in LA there were women who worked for Fox Sports—then towels "accidentally" fell to the floor and Belly's would certainly be the first.

This is something nobody speaks about, but there should be some sort of labor law that preserves the dignity of both parties. All you have to do is imagine this in your own workplace and you get my point.

Speaking of workplace etiquette, the LA Lakers practice at the same facility as the Kings in El Segundo, and I see Kobe Bryant on a regular basis walking into the building from one of the parking spaces designated for the athletes. When I walk by Kobe I get the feeling that he looks at us hockey players like we're the help, not like fellow professional athletes who share the same oval inside the Staples Center. There's no greeting or even a nod of professional courtesy. I asked him to sign a basketball for me once, and he didn't even meet my eyes when he said "No." It could be that he's just an asshole, which some say that he is. In the hierarchy of professional sports, the tall guys who put the ball through the hoop—and who play a game whose last minute can be longer than an NHL period—often are.

Perhaps you're thinking "Hold on, *Sean Avery* is calling someone out for being *rude?*" Fair enough. Sometimes it was the job to be rude. But that's not who I am personally. Still, sometimes, the two intersect when I meet up with another player who I hate. It's dangerous, because you want to keep control of your emotions in order to have maximum effect when you do what I do, but Scott Hartnell is a guy I can't stand.

He came into the NHL around the same time as I did. He's from western Canada, he played for Canada in the 2006 World Championships (they came fourth), and he's considered a true "Hockey Man" even though his style is chippy and ornery. It's weird. A lot of the same people who think I don't fit in with the league love Scott Hartnell, but he's not that different from me. So we were probably destined to hate each other. That hate began November 19, 2003.

I score on my third shift of the game. It's my second goal of the season and it puts us ahead of Nashville 1–0.

First goals of the game are always big goals, and when you score early in a game it changes everything. All of a sudden your legs don't have that heavy feeling. You're light on your feet and gliding from goal line to goal line. You skate with your head up as soon as the puck hits your stick because everything feels easier.

On my fifth shift I move fast toward Hartnell as he moves toward a puck going hard around the boards. He has to skip a beat to control the puck, and to a guy like me that's the green light for a big hit. A guy thinking about the puck at his feet isn't thinking about the guy moving in to crush him. Just for a split second, but a split second is usually all it takes to line a guy up. But Hartnell knows what he's doing. He knows he's got a target on his back. He hits everything that moves, so he knows no one is going to pass up an opportunity to take a run at him. He can feel me moving in, and turns slightly at the last moment.

I can't adjust. My shoulder-to-shoulder check is now heading straight into his numbers. Like all great agitators he crumbles like a game of Jenga. Everyone in the building thinks I've killed him.

Players like Hartnell and me learn how to sacrifice our body for the penalty. We know how to position ourselves so that somebody coming full steam at us will look like they've destroyed us, but because of the way we place our feet and square our bodies, we hardly even feel it. It's like taking a fall when you're a stuntman. Do it right and you only look hurt.

After I've sent Hartnell into oblivion (not), the whistle blows and there's a lot of chirping. The Predators are yelling that they're going to go after our star, Ziggy Pálffy, which is hardly a fair trade and which they don't do. Pálffy ends up with twenty-one minutes ice time and an assist. Nevertheless, it's the end of my game. I've played fewer than five minutes, and I've been docked with a five-minute major penalty for boarding and two ten-minute misconducts for the language I used to point out the referee's utter stupidity in falling for Hartnell's trick.

In any case, Scott Hartnell recovered enough from my attempted murder to play more than eighteen minutes that night, and while we beat Nashville 3–0, that fact rubbed salt into my self-inflicted wound. I vow to pay Hartnell back for this.

I had to wait a couple of seasons to get my next shot at him, but I was patient.

Hartnell was going through a divorce at the time and that gave me my chance for revenge the first time I lined up beside him. I asked him what it was like to be a star player making millions of dollars a year. He looked at me confused, as if I'd popped a trick question, but he answered it like a true Hockey Man. "It feels pretty good," he said, and then I delivered my punch line. I asked what it felt like to be the only star NHL player making millions a year to actually get dumped by his wife while in his prime.

That is how trash talk works, and why I was so good at it. You pick your moments and your material, something that will go straight to the heart of the matter. Just swearing at a guy does nothing, but finding his Achilles' heel is as good as scoring a goal.

Now that I am a full-fledged NHLer, I start developing routines. I'm eating the same pre-game meal every game day—garden salad with Parmesan cheese and French dressing, half a dish of spaghetti Bolognese, and two grilled chicken breasts. I'm napping from 2 to 4 P.M. daily, which is a job requirement, but sometimes it's hard to fall asleep in the middle of the afternoon when it's eighty degrees and flawless outside.

I'm having the same problem at night, so I start taking a single Ambien after games to help me sleep. Yes, I've read about the side effects—drowsiness, dizziness, weakness, lightheadedness, "drugged" feeling, tiredness, loss of coordination, stuffy nose, dry mouth, sore throat, nausea, constipation, diarrhea, stomach upset, headache, and muscle pain. But after a game when you're wired from winning, or replaying all the "coulda shouldas" if you lost, you need to sleep if you're going to be of any use to anyone the next day.

I'm also doing the same exact routine during pre-game warm-up. I take the same number of laps in a certain direction, I take my shots in the same order, and I pick the exact same corners in shooting drills. Why? It's not superstition with me, though it is for many guys who believe that there's some cosmic hockey wizard making sure we stick to hockey habits. I guess I do it because it's one less thing that I have to think about.

The daily routine becomes the rock of a long career—I mean, it's the one thing that you can control, and it's one of the reasons athletes have such a hard time after retiring from the game. You're going from a glamorous, high-octane life with dozens of demands made on you every day to a life of "nothing happening," just like that. It's one hell of a shock to most athletes. I'm thinking about my transition even now, and I promise myself that the "nothing happening" won't happen to me. But still, I worry that it might not be my promise to keep.

On the night before New Year's Eve, the New York Rangers are in town to play us at the Staples Center. I talk shit to Eric Lindros all night. Every time he skates by the bench I'm yelling, "Pick up the pace, Bonnie, you fat fuck." Bonnie is Eric Lindros's mother and she was notorious for being involved in his career. I tell him repeatedly that he's never going to win and that will be his legacy. It bothers him. He must be thinking, "Who the fuck is this kid saying this shit to me?" His teammate Matthew Barnaby wants to kill me. Barnaby is the bad boy of the NHL at this point, and he's intimidating, and I'm a little bit starstruck.

Barnaby was insane. He's the only guy I've ever seen who talked more than me on the ice, but what he said was gibberish. It was like a crying baby on the airplane, except this baby was screaming out "Cocksucker!

Faggot! Motherfucker!" non-stop. More dangerously, Barnaby was one of those rare guys who you couldn't hurt. You could hit him with a sledge-hammer on the head and he wouldn't stop smiling. He liked to get hit, and he liked to fight, and he liked those high-pressure, game-changing moments, so it was a very risky thing to get into a fight with Barnaby. I knew what he was capable of.

But my game wasn't so different, and I guess our coaches wanted to keep us apart. We didn't get on the ice against each other more than a few times, and, as it was a close scoring game, he didn't come after me in case I sucked him into taking a penalty. I could send a team into complete chaos before the morning skate was over. I believe that I'm probably the most talked-about third-line player in NHL history when it came to coaches giving their pre-game speeches and warning their guys to be careful around me. Getting me inside their heads before they even saw me. I'm not bragging about this; I'm just telling you how it went down.

Part of the reason I got away with taking so many penalties was that I drew so many penalties, and better still, I had the ability to do it when our team needed a power play. The downside of this aspect of my game was that I'd also be given penalties for things that eighty percent of players would never get punished for, simply because the refs had to keep the game somewhat close and wouldn't call it. Unless it was against me. On some nights I should have drawn ten penalties against my opponent, which is not that many when you consider sixteen of the twenty-three guys on the other team wanted to kill me.

The one guy in all my time in the NHL who really pissed me off was Darcy Hordichuk. I don't know what he was on, but he was so out of his mind that he was just a dumb agitator. He would repeatedly call me a "faggot" and "chickenshit" and say that he was going to eat me and eat my children and spit them out. I was like "Dude, I don't even have children. Shut up. You're an idiot."

He also knew that he was tougher than me. He was a heavyweight in the NHL. He would have killed me in a fight and I knew that, so he was just stating the obvious. Yawn.

When I came to play in my hometown of Toronto I made sure to let the media know that Toronto was the last place on earth that I wanted to play. Not because of the media scrutiny, but because I'm starting to get an identity as a character in Canada, and if I played in Canada there would be no escape from this character. In LA, I can explore other things in life—I can even go to a cocktail party and no one will talk to me about hockey. In Toronto, it would be 24-7 hockey, and I don't want it.

Then there was also the Toronto problem of Don Cherry, host of "Coach's Corner," who hated me. I saw him in the corridor at the Air Canada Centre and I asked him if he realized that all the players thought he knew nothing about the game. He muttered something under his breath and one of his handlers took him away. If I'd played in Toronto I would have been his whipping boy. I was no one's whipping boy. I now had a real edge in the NHL and it made the game fun for me because I liked playing the bad guy. I liked the way it felt when I could see my opponents' eyes filled with anger, an anger that hurt how effectively they played and gave an advantage to my team.

But make no mistake, I was playing a character. I'd put the bad guy mask on before I hit the rink and I'd take it off when I got home. It was a role I played in an arena, just like an actor would play it on stage. I enjoyed it, but I also enjoyed being able to turn it off. You can' t live with that kind of intensity twenty-four hours a day.

That said, the on-ice guy had to come from somewhere, and of course, my long struggle to make the NHL despite being told I never would was a deep injustice I felt off the ice, and it spurred me on to prove the doubters wrong. The on-ice Sean would make an appearance in the real world from time to time. It was not always a good thing.

For example, I was having a dinner party with ten friends in my house in Los Angeles. I was helping cook dinner, listening to Joni Mitchell, relaxing. A new neighbor called the cops because apparently my pre-dinner conviviality was more than he or she felt appropriate. The cops show up and immediately start in with attitude—the kind you'd get from an opponent on ice trying to intimidate you. So I gave it back, but in a controlled way. I asked them, How loud was too loud? Did they have a sound meter reading that I had violated? I can be very literal, and of course, the cops got angrier because they couldn't answer my questions. I told them I was not turning the music down because it was not too loud, and my neighbor didn't get to dictate total silence to the neighborhood.

The cops went away, the neighbor called again, and the cops came back, looking for a win. They charged into the house and tried to turn the music down themselves, and I wouldn't let them in the same way I wouldn't let an opponent disrespect a teammate. I trash-talked them, I blocked them, and they responded the way cops do. They hauled me off to jail for slamming the door on them. I got out on $20K bail, they dropped the bogus charges, and that was that.

So this character of Sean Avery was a double-edged thing, but I really enjoyed playing him.

The last month of the 2003–04 NHL season is easily the worst month of my life. To put it as starkly as I can:

STL 5–LA 3 . . .
SJS 5–LA 3 . . .
DET 5–LA 2 . . .
EDM 2–LA 1 . . .

VAN 1–LA 0 . . .

EDM 3–LA 1 . . .

CGY 3–LA 2 . . .

COL 2–LA 1 . . .

SJS 3–LA 0 . . .

CGY 3–LA 2 . . .

SJS 4–LA 3 . . .

I'm playing on a team that's lost eleven games in a row. Our last eleven games of the season.

Our reason for this embarrassing and depressing slide into the ditch is that our team has given up on our coach, and we're mailing it in to get him fired. Which doesn't mean guys are purposely playing bad, it means they've lost their motivation. When a coach "loses the room" it means that guys will not go the extra mile to win it all. They'll only do as much as they need to do. Not only did most guys dislike our coach, but they didn't respect him, and when a team doesn't respect their coach it's a lost cause. He told us that if we didn't play better he was going to get fired, which showed how out of touch he was. He wasn't blaming us—he was trying to motivate us. What hockey players need is Mel Gibson in *Braveheart*, not the exasperated substitute teacher asking the class to settle down.

I think we can all relate to having a terrible boss, one whose total incompetence frustrates all the good things that you want to do for your organization and for yourself. I can tell you it's just the same even when you're a professional athlete. From the outside it looks like you're enjoying a fabulous life, but from the inside, it was miserable.

And yet . . .

I put my head down and got on with playing my game. I was playing fifteen minutes a night during this stretch and I was playing hard. I wanted to send notice to my peers and coaches and general managers around the leagues, to fans and babes and every shithead who told me I was too small to play in the NHL when I was just a little kid, that the LA Kings were not losing because of me.

11

EVERYTHING IN ITS RIGHT PLACE

Two days after we put a bullet in the head of that terrible season, I drove to our practice rink in El Segundo to pack up my bags. This is the day when you grab sticks, tape, new skates, workout clothes, and anything else you need for your summer training wherever you plan to spend the off-season.

This year the guys roll into the room with mostly fake somber faces, bluffing their way through the day as if they really feel badly. But I know they're glad to get away from this misery. They close the trunks of their sports cars and peel out of the parking lot for the open road, free for the next four months.

I drive off in pursuit of some culture. I head to Indio, California, to the Coachella Valley music festival run by AEG Live, the Los Angeles Kings' owner Phil Anschutz's entertainment company. I throw my bags into my Hummer. My wingman is Lawrence Longo. It's a two-hour drive east, toward freedom.

As we blow out of LA on the I-5 and light up our first joint of the summer, I look in the rearview mirror and into my own eyes. I have no guilt. I played my ass off this year, and that's all you can ask of a professional athlete. Now I'm going to play in a different arena.

Coachella is an excuse for every California girl who loves music or a big party or both to wear short shorts and bras and layers of jewelry, and to come forth and make music. I was single at this point, and although I liked to have a good time with the ladies I was always paranoid about getting a girl pregnant. So I wasn't an uncontrolled sex machine at Coachella, though it was a great place to watch the lovely ladies pass by to the soundtrack of some great bands.

In LA, I had to learn to parse the ways of different women. There was the Actress, who is a chameleon and can be maddening; the LA Party Girl, always looking for fun here, with you, or over there, with the better offer; and the LA Model, who is usually a really hot girl not tall enough to be a New York model. I'd been hanging with an actress-model-and-mainly-party-girl named Nicole, and I met up with her and her friends when we landed at Coachella. She looks like the original California flower girl, and she's smart and interesting and confident. She doesn't expect anything from me, and that takes the pressure off. I have my all-access pass, I'm with an absolutely stunning girl and my best friend, my energy is at a high, and a photographer friend back in LA has given me something to try specifically for this festival. Inside a small folded piece of paper is pure MDMA. Otherwise known as ecstasy.

The drug makes all my worries disappear. I'm not bashing myself for not working out hard enough, or running over scenarios where I'll soon be sent to play minor-minor-minor pro in Dogfart, Flyover. I feel at total peace with myself and the world and wish it would last forever.

That night was about experiencing something most of my friends have been doing since high school—getting high at a concert. I'm playing catch-up in many areas of life. That night in the desert I experienced MDMA.

I know everyone's probably going to hang me for my "experimentation" with drugs because it contradicts the idea, welded into our cultural DNA, that every athlete must be a role model. But what is a role model? If it means someone who is a good citizen, who believes in treating people decently, who works hard and honestly, well, that can be anyone. If it means someone who makes a lot of money because they play a game that kids play anyway, and they don't get in trouble for doing stuff adults do, well then, no, that's not something I'd want any kid to aspire to.

That said, the passion and discipline you need to become a professional athlete is at the heart of being a good role model, so if that's what a kid takes away from it, great. But athletes live on the edge, and we crave intensity, and that tends to put you in some places you don't want a kid to go. I'm not advocating recreational drug use. At least not until you've worked your ass off and accomplished your dreams. Then go for it if you want.

I never really worried about getting in trouble with the NHL because the league's drug testing looks only for anabolic steroid use. NHL players can do coke, pot, acid, crack, or meth and not get suspended. I know of roughly fifty NHL guys who used recreational drugs at some point during the 2003–04 season as well as in the off-season.

Now, I didn't party with all fifty at once, but I saw it in social situations and it adds up. I mean, we'd see players out on the town after road games. You play in a place like Chicago, and you might see some of the Hawks in the clubs afterward, and you might see certain well-known players indulging in substances both legal and not. If someone told me that no NHL player ever did a bump in the bathroom on the team airplane, I'd tell them they didn't know what they were talking about. Same thing if someone said we didn't fire up a joint on the drive from the arena to the airport after a home game. Happens all the time.

It's not a criticism. By Game 60 of an NHL season even rookies feel like veterans. You feel the intensity each time you skate out on the ice sixty times over a three-month period, but there comes a game, say a dreary Sunday afternoon tilt in Nashville, when you just can't get your head into it.

Someone will say it in the room: "How the fuck are we going to get up for this one?" Take more drugs is one answer, but I've also heard players—and myself—say, "Let's play for the people who pay our salaries." In the playoffs, guys say "Let's play for the crest on the sweater," and no one ever mocks that idea. But yeah, drugs work too.

The other astonishing thing about drugs and the NHL is just how easy it would have been to take them across the border. When you fly into Canada, the customs guys come on the plane and walk down the aisle, looking at our passports, and more often than not, asking a player to sign a couple of souvenirs they've brought along for the occasion. They never looked in our bags. I could have been an international cocaine smuggler the entire time I was playing, and made a lot of money, and no one would ever know. It might even be happening now, in our age of so-called ultra border security.

The NHL has the most lenient drug testing of the four major league sports, and also has the lowest number of players arrested for crimes. Is that because NHL general managers hold players more accountable than in other sports? Or is it because most NHL players come from small towns in Canada or the U.S.A. or Finland or Sweden or Russia, and not from the crime- and drug-infested inner cities of North America? I don't know. But it's a question to ask when you're trying to define just what you want a role model to be. If you don't have one in the house you grow up in, then you have long odds to be one in life.

After what was a truly stimulating weekend in all senses of the word, we headed back to LA from Coachella. My friend Bobby Carlton tells us to swing by his friend Rachel's home, which is perched on a hill above Sunset Boulevard in West Hollywood. I had begun the day with a four-mile run in the desert before Lawrence had woken up, so I was feeling presentable after the hard and absolutely brilliant two days we had just put our bodies and minds through.

The house was filled with teak and had a major Moroccan vibe going on. Bobby was sitting out back near the pool with this beautiful blond woman. Now, we're in SoCal and beautiful blond women are wherever you look, but this woman rose above them all, and I immediately recognized her. I was glad that I hadn't made the trek back to LA unwashed and hungover.

Rachel Hunter was thirty-four years old and had lived a lifetime compared to me. She'd been married to Rod Stewart at the height of his fame (or one of the peaks, as the dude has been on top for a long time), and she was a supermodel during the 1990s. Rachel had seen the entire world ten times over.

The sparkle in her amazing emerald eyes told me she wasn't just being polite but was genuinely interested in me. I think she was attracted to the fact that I was an outsider in Hollywood. She'd been living here for ten years under a very bright light, and she was getting tired of the LA bullshit.

We hung out for a few hours that Sunday afternoon, and on the drive home I asked Bobby for her phone number. That night I sent her a text message, asking if she wanted to cook me dinner one night that week.

There's some calculation on my part behind the ask. I'm sure Rachel gets asked out to paparazzi-heavy hot spots like Ago or Koi all the time, so her dates can open *Star* magazine and see pictures of themselves with a celebrity. So I purposely made a point of asking to see her in the privacy of her home. I don't want to be the guy who needs to have everyone know I took "Stacy's Mom" out on a date. (If you don't know the song, check out the music video and you'll see Rachel in action, and I dare you not to fall in love with her, too. Let's just say that she was cast to be about as hot as a mom can be.)

I also think famous women probably like a man being a little bossy with them, especially when the motives are good and they're tired of everyone kissing their ass all the time. We decided on Wednesday night.

Rachel had been sober for a few years, so I stop and grab some Arizona Ice Tea. I'm more excited than nervous because this is much more real than anyone I've met so far in terms of potential romance.

Dinner goes great. Rachel makes roast chicken with peas and mashed potatoes, which shows both her talent as a cook and her sense of humor—such simple fare couldn't offend the palates of two colonials from Canada and New Zealand. We spend most of the night talking about what we do and where we come from. Rachel is the mother of two children (Rod Stewart is their dad) and she had them young. Her son, Liam, is ten years old and actually plays hockey for the Junior LA Kings, while her daughter, Renee, is twelve.

We talk until I'm fighting to keep my eyes open and I still have to drive from West Hollywood to Manhattan Beach, which even at 2 A.M. will take me twenty-five minutes. I think about the evening I've just had with this lovely woman on the drive home, and I get way ahead of myself by making assumptions that the two of us will still enjoy each other's company after the second or third date. Is the age difference too much? What if it's true love and she doesn't want any more kids? What if the famous ex-husband—make that extremely famous ex-husband who hasn't officially divorced her yet—comes back into the mix? I guess the questions mean I like her. All I can do is ask her for a second date. She says yes. It's the beginning of my first adult relationship with a woman.

It got serious pretty quickly—in fact, we talked marriage. It was not heavy-duty serious talk, but we did explore what our marriage would look like, and if it was realistic based on our age gap. Looking back on it, our age gap was nothing.

So now here I am, dating the woman of my dreams. Rachel had gone to the rainforest to save gorillas, she'd been married to a guy considered one of the sexiest rock stars ever, she'd lived in castles, she'd met the Queen.

I was never going to impress her with flashy things. She was more interested in the relationship that I had with her son. I'd never been a dad, but my friendship with her son turned her on more than me showing up in a Ferrari to whisk her to my private plane (I don't have a Ferrari or a private plane).

I was still painfully aware of all the things I'd missed by devoting myself to hockey. I was getting pretty good at pretending to fit in (I often had no idea what was happening around me), but I still felt nervous and insecure off the ice. But that was overridden by my desire to learn. And I wanted to learn about art.

My first real introduction to the art world was during a day spent cruising the art galleries of Beverly Hills with Bobby Carlton. To me, art galleries were as intimidating in real life as they are in the movies. They seem like secret societies, whose members will laugh you out of the room if you don't say the right thing.

I grew up in a house with lots of love, but not with many books and no art. I listened as people at parties in LA talked about artists, and I read about them in magazines. I was aware that not only could art be beautiful, it could also be a business. A piece of art that caught my imagination could also one day be worth much more than I'd paid for it. So art spoke to me on two levels.

At this point, I didn't own anything you could put in a frame and hang on the wall partly because I did not own any walls. The first gallery that we visit has many paintings—Picasso, Ruscha, Twombly, Warhol, and de Kooning. It also has work by photographers, one named Helmut Newton and the other a very attractive woman named Taryn Simon.

I asked Bobby if photographs are considered art, because the one thing I promised myself was that even though I knew nothing, the only way to learn was to ask questions. Learning is about taking in new information and connecting it to your mainframe of knowledge. Whenever someone would say something negative about my ignorance on some topic, I'd always point out to them that from the time I was four years old I'd been practicing to become one of the best hockey players in the world, and in that journey I learned many things that they hadn't. That would always put them on their heels a bit. But yes, Bobby tells me, photography can be art.

Of course, there is also a type of photography that is definitely not art, and it's practiced by that gang known as paparazzi. The first time I ever had paparazzi take a photo of me was with Rachel. We were now dating and we were getting lunch in Beverly Park, which is an even richer area than Beverly Hills, and just above it as you head up the hill to Mulholland Drive. We were halfway through lunch when Rachel started to stare off into the distance as if she had just seen an old enemy and was willing them to disappear. I asked her if she was OK and jokingly asked whether "Rod the Bod" was coming to sort me out. At this point I hadn't met "Maggie May"'s creator, but certainly had some insecurities about dating his ex, even though Rod was thirty-five years older than me.

Rachel chuckled and then, under her breath, whispered "Paps." "What are Paps?" I asked her, thinking it sounded like some kind of virus. And so they were, as I came to learn about the paparazzi, who think it's completely normal to photograph you while you're eating your lunch and not doing anything celebrity-ish at all. That's "normal" life for a celebrity, but it's never normal for the person with them, and that makes it more uncomfortable for everyone.

In truth, I had nothing to worry about from Rod Stewart, as Rachel had a great relationship with him. I never heard her once complain about him. She loved him. I'd been a huge fan of his, especially when he was with Faces, so I was nervous when we first met at his mansion in Beverly Park. I was nervous because he was Rachel's ex, and because he was Liam's dad, and because I was starstruck.

He lives in a private gated community on top of the hill that is the most exclusive neighborhood in the U.S. Eddie Murphy, Denzel Washington, and Sylvester Stallone all live there. Major money. When I went to Kid Rock's house in Detroit you blew an air horn at the end of the driveway and Kid Rock would roll out to let you in. When I went to Rod Stewart's house you had to go through two security checkpoints to get into the inner sanctum, so I was already a little intimidated. And then I saw his house.

It was a true rock star palace. After you go through a gate announcing "God Bless Celtic"—Rod is a huge fan of the Glasgow soccer team—there's a big fountain with statues blowing water into the air, a fleet of Ferraris in the driveway, and 28,000 square feet of a sprawling house, with vines growing up the side and Pre-Raphaelite paintings decorating the stairway wall in the entrance hallway. There was a 200-year-old French crystal chandelier hanging in the living room, a huge swimming pool, a tennis court, a five-aside soccer pitch, and serving staff in uniforms. Now I was really intimidated.

Rod, however, was very down-to-earth. He was in his early sixties, but looked a lot younger, and dressed in English gentleman casual—the country squire on the weekend. He put me at ease by talking to me about hockey. Specifically, his son, Liam's, hockey career. Then he asked me to explain the offside rule. It's always the one that confuses people who are new to the game. Rod had been a pretty good soccer player in his youth, so I just told him it was kind of like offside in soccer. You can't cross the blue line ahead of the puck, in the same way that you can't go past the defenders ahead of the ball in soccer. He got it.

I have to move house in the off-season, and I find a great two-bedroom apartment on the top floor of a home a few hundred feet from the sands of

Manhattan Beach. To help with the rent, my buddy Jeremy Taggart is taking the second bedroom because he's making the next Our Lady Peace record with famed producer Bob Rock in his studio in Malibu, which should take them the better part of the coming year.

Now that I'm seeing Rachel I will not be going back to Ontario to live with my parents, which is the perfect illustration of what I meant about California offering me opportunities to broaden my horizons: inside of a year, I've gone from bunking in my family home to living with Rod Stewart's ex. Crazy, but I'll take it.

The LA summer address also means that I won't get to work out with Kris Draper, as I've done for the past six years. This makes me nervous, but I set up a system to have my old trainer John Renzetti email the week's workouts every Sunday evening. I told John that when I made the NHL I would give him $20,000 and I did, but during the summers both Drapes and I pay him $12,500 each for his services, which is a nice cash bump for a teacher.

I have full access to the Kings' training facility and no possibility of a contract dispute this summer. This past season I made $440,000, and for the LA Kings to retain my rights they only need to pay me a ten percent raise, so in my next season I will make $532,000 (or a little less than half that when you shave off all the fees and taxes I mentioned earlier).

Even though I'm making great money by the standards of the world, it's on the low end in the NHL, something that you're reminded of all the time when you hang with massively paid superstars like Brendan Shanahan. And when he was at about the same stage in his career as I am in mine, he was pulling down nearly $1.4 million. He bought a lake house to live in during the summer months where he could relax and entertain family. Shanny's cottage was on Ball Lake in the summer holiday mecca that is the Muskoka Lakes region of Ontario, and he invited me and my girlfriend to come for a visit. So I booked two airline tickets to Toronto for myself and Rachel.

Shanny is the closest thing to an older brother/mentor I have other than my father. He projects a slick and professional face to the world, with a hint of amusement creasing his eyes, but when he's not in public, Shanny has a dark and cynical view of humanity. I do not, except when it comes to NHL execs, but Shanny's willingness to question things matches my own genetic resistance to conforming, and so I learn from him not to take what I see at face value.

When we land in Toronto we take a taxi to a small airstrip to catch a seaplane that will fly us north, so we can avoid the four-hour car crawl to Muskoka on a Friday afternoon. The seaplane lands 300 feet out from Shanny's dock and glides in nice and smooth to Clark Kent awaiting us with his famous fists on his hips.

He doesn't look like he belongs in Muskoka, which is Toronto's summer playground, a mix of discreet old money and noisy new money with Porsche SUVs and Jet Skis and lots of booze and BBQ. Shanny, in his crab-print shorts, is more of a Martha's Vineyard kind of guy, with champagne cocktails in hand and a Great Gatsby vibe that makes it all so much more of a spectacle.

He's trying to maintain his customary cool when Rachel steps out of the plane and onto the dock. He has this big smile on his face and gives me a subtle nod of approval. Rachel wastes no time in cementing his first impression by heading straight for the host to give him a big, warm New Zealand hug. Shanny rests his head on her shoulder and sticks his tongue out, teasing me. It took a lot to impress Shanny, because of his natural skepticism, but I could see that Mr. Miyagi was proud of the Karate Kid.

Shanny was up at the cabin on his own, and he took us out on his boat, which was a thirty-foot power cruiser. I was surprised he could even drive the thing, as he wasn't an "outdoorsman" by any stretch. But he managed to keep us from sinking, and while we were drifting along on Ball Lake, Shanny talked to me about business. He said we were going to lose the negotiations with the NHL. It was the first time I heard a player say this, and it shocked me—even coming from Shanny, who usually expected the worst. I'd been drinking the NHLPA Kool-Aid and I knew little about how the real world works, so I just told him he was crazy. He laughed at me, but I was convinced I was right.

We stayed with him for a day, then we made our way back over to the Yzerman compound to stay for our final night. This was really so that Rachel could meet Stevie Y's wife, Lisa, who was around the same age and had similar tastes. Lisa was a down-to-earth lady from Ottawa, and a reflection of Steve: calm, cool, collected, and beautiful. Rachel fell in love with Muskoka, and actually has a girlfriend who lives in the area during the summers, one she knew from her rock 'n' roll days. This is Kelly Van Halen, the ex-wife of Alex Van Halen. I have a feeling we will be back in Muskoka. But like many things I felt sure about that summer, I was wrong.

12

LOCKED OUT OF MY LIFE

In the summer of 2004, the NHL and the NHL Players Association (NHLPA) are in negotiations for a new collective bargaining agreement (CBA). We've known this was coming since the last CBA was signed, and at the start of the past season the NHLPA recommended that each player put a portion of their 2003–04 paychecks aside just in case a lockout or strike actually happened during the 2004–05 season. We think that's overly cautious, but I do it anyway.

The NHL wants to impose a hard salary cap because they say that increasingly lavish salaries will destroy the smaller-market teams. A hard cap means each NHL team will have an upper limit on what they can spend on players' salaries. Unlike baseball, where you can overspend and pay a penalty, the NHL wants to make the cap a hard number that no one can exceed.

By July the NHL is aggressively pushing for it and I'm with the NHLPA in pushing back: I say no way will the players ever accept a hard cap system because that means the top players will still get paid the big dollars while the rest of us will have to split the smaller pie that's left over.

Bob Goodenow leads the NHLPA. He was captain of the hockey team at Harvard University, where he earned a degree in economics and government. He later received a law degree from the University of Detroit, and as a labor lawyer there, became an agent for several players, including my buddy Brett Hull, who was then with St. Louis. Goodenow got everyone's attention when he increased Hully's salary from $125,000 a year to $7.3 million over three years.

In 1992 he led the NHLPA in a ten-day strike, the first time this had ever happened in NHL hockey, and he won the players some concessions. The NHL struck back by hiring Gary Bettman as its first commissioner (before then the title was president). Bettman is also a lawyer, and he'd come from the NBA, where he was the guy who invented the salary cap, the first in modern-day sports.

You could see where this showdown was heading from that moment on.

It's the worst-kept secret in hockey that Goodenow and Bettman despise each other. Bob would tell us in NHLPA meetings how much he disliked Bettman, and how this was a war we were in. Neither guy is the type you'd want to sit next to on a long plane ride, but I know that Goodenow's desire to crush Bettman—who serves the guys who sign our checks—is going to hurt us in the long run because if this is war, the owners have a bigger war chest.

Every team has an NHLPA union rep, whose usual task is to hand out the swag at Christmas. I'm an assistant rep on the Kings, and now the NHLPA is asking us to take time during the summer to educate the players on a decision that will cost us, personally, millions of dollars, and the NHLPA hundreds of millions of dollars.

Some NHLPA reps, including myself, do not have high school educations, and while education in no way guarantees that you're smart, the fact that we aren't as well-educated as the guys leading us, and the guys opposing us, stokes our insecurities. I can think, and I'm not afraid to ask questions when I don't know something, but these lawyers can unleash floods of tricky legalese at us, and it's sometimes as if you're being spoken to in Martian. At a certain point, we have to trust the union. And that turns out to be a problem.

At first we'd get emails from the NHLPA informing us of what was going on or not going on in the negotiations, but after some of those emails were leaked to the media, they changed the system. All information would now come from the "players only" website, which was password protected. But that information got leaked as well, so now we'd have conference calls that involved two reps from each team, so sixty guys, along with Bob Goodenow and his staff, and good luck to anyone who wanted to eavesdrop on those things.

These calls quickly turned into circuses, with certain guys rambling on and on about how they felt, and absolutely no one managing the show. Sometimes we could hear crying babies in the background, or the sound of a busy hockey player playing Halo. Athletes do not have the ability to sit on an hour-long conference call in June and July and August. We're built to keep moving, and while we have the discipline and desire to push our bodies to the breaking point for five or six days straight, we don't have the discipline to sit on the phone for an hour to talk about revenue sharing. This is why we had no chance in the CBA negotiation.

I got my NHLPA education from Chris Chelios, who had a very realistic view of what was going to happen. He thought Goodenow was going down the wrong path, and while he didn't say anything publicly, he made it known in our conference call meetings, or when Bob would come and meet with teams individually. Bob would listen, and then stick to his own plan.

Goodenow had too much authority in the negotiations, and if any player went rogue, he had ways to drag the guy back in. He was a lawyer, and very persuasive. He dazzled us with great PowerPoint presentations, and if he couldn't persuade a guy, he'd call him personally or he'd suddenly be in Detroit for some meetings and want to take Cheli out for lunch.

Out of the thirty to forty calls I was on during those negotiations, I remember only a handful of times when a player making more than $8 million a season was on the line. NHL superstars didn't get very involved during the 2004–05 CBA negotiations, unless they were doing it behind closed doors. And for some, that also meant going behind the players' backs and helping the league. This came out later on down the road.

As negotiations go on and seemingly nowhere, I start to spend more time at Rachel's Hollywood Hills home and less time at the beach house that I've rented with Jeremy. We're not seeing much of each other, because he heads to the studio around 4 P.M. each day and they record into the night, and I'm lying in bed with Rachel, wide awake and wondering: what the hell am I going to do if we don't start the season on time?

Things are not looking good. Thursday, September 16, 2004, should have had me putting on my hockey equipment for the first day of training camp. Instead I was sitting on the patio of Café Med in Sunset Plaza with the wind knocked out of me. The day before, the CBA had expired, and we were officially "locked out" of work by the NHL.

Despite this chest-thumping, I cannot believe this lockout is going to go on longer than two weeks. There's too much money at stake. That said, and even though I was on all the calls that the NHLPA had with its players, I was still twenty-four years old and had no idea what was really happening. It could last ten years for all I knew.

I had no calls from my agent, Pat Morris, throughout the negotiation, and certainly not on that dark day, though I longed for one, where I would hear him tell me that he'd found a team in Europe that wanted me. I would have said, "Thanks for that, Pat. When do I leave?" I guess Pat had more important things to do.

I've decided to set myself a two-week deadline to see how this lockout plays out before I do something else, like look for a team in Europe. In the meantime, the NHLPA has authorized a $5,000 per month stipend to all players who played on an NHL roster the previous year. To players making more than a million dollars a season, it wasn't going to turn them into raving union supporters, manning the barricades and calling for Bettman's head, but for me it's a big help. I made $440,000 the year before. After paying taxes and agent fees and living in one city during the season and another during the summer, even a shrewd saver could only hang on to $50,000–$75,000 at most. So after only playing a couple of years in the league, it's not like I am rolling in dough.

One negative aspect about living in LA and not in Canada during the off-season is that the cost of living is more expensive in SoCal, so the money goes faster. The upside is that Rachel is there and I'm in love with her.

My self-imposed two-week deadline comes and goes and we have no agreement. This is the first time in sixteen years that I'm not playing hockey in October. I should be getting paid $20,000 every two weeks after tax, but instead I'm heading to the Beverly Hills sports club every morning to train—pushing myself so I'm ready. Part of the lockout's collateral damage was that we were also locked out of the Kings' training facilities.

A lockout is like a bad acid trip: one minute you're loving it, with your feet in the sand while you're sipping a cold blended fruit drink and your favorite song plays, and the next minute you're struggling to find the words when someone at a party asks, "So what do you do?"

"I think I'm a hockey player" is your answer, which is hardly bursting with confidence, so you add, "I mean, I have an NHL contract, but I'm not really sure when or if I will ever go back to work . . ."

As the days go by you start to have more bad trips than good trips. I think that maybe if I'd been thirty-four years old it would have been easier because I'd have had a dozen NHL seasons behind me and perspective: I would have accomplished something. But having my career pulled out from under me at age twenty-four, just as I get a taste of how great it is, makes me realize that this is the hardest thing I have ever gone through in my life. I mean, hockey is my life and I have no hockey.

Looking back now, I can say with absolute certainty that the only way the NHLPA would have ever been able to beat the owners would be to always have an extension done fourteen months before the deal expires, and of course, if the CBA was that easy to extend, we'd have never lost a season. What I'm saying is that the players will never be able to win even if they're still playing pro hockey a million years from now (which I doubt they will be, given the way the world is going).

When I look back on the lockout and the union telling its members to get ready to fight and promising us "We will not back down!" I can't help but shake my head and say, "Sorry guys, but you will never win. The union will always break before the owners do and you will always get a worse deal the longer you wait. That's why you need to always get a deal done." But I don't know that as 2004 slides into December, and the talk in the media is that we're going to become the first professional sport to lose a season. That can't happen. Can it?

Rachel is keeping me sane, or as sane as I can be, but one day bleeds into the next. A few days after New Year's, I have a breakdown. I mean, I wasn't sobbing naked in the street (nor am I making fun of those who break that way), but I realized that I couldn't define my life without hockey and I needed to connect to it or I'd become unmoored and then anything could happen. So I called Pat Morris. This is the first time we've spoken since the lockout, and I tell him that I'm ready to go play somewhere, anywhere. I tell him that if he's speaking to any teams overseas looking to sign some players, then I'd love him to drop my name into the conversation. What I really meant was please, throw me a lifeline, quick. If the league was trying to bring us to our knees, it was doing a pretty good job of it. Pat said he'd keep me in mind. I was even grateful for that pretty staggering shrug.

In early February 2005, the NHLPA summoned all its players to Toronto to vote on a proposal that the union was preparing to send in to the NHL as our "final offer." Some European players actually flew over for this summit—for the "free" trip (we'd pay for it in the end) and a chance to get away from home for a few days. There were other players who needed to be among friends to share their woes and try to release the anxiety and anger and identity issues that we were all feeling, as we were now staring down the prospect of losing an entire season.

Roughly 200 players rolled into Toronto on the first Friday in February, and we checked in to the Westin Harbour Castle, which is a nice, if generic, corporate hotel, with massive conference rooms. We were told to dump our bags with speed and get to a meeting in one of those conference caverns.

That was a difficult room for me to walk into because there were at least thirty guys in there who would not piss on me if I was on fire, and four or five who would curb-stomp me if they had the chance. The only person who was hated more was the little man with the nervous twitch from Madison Avenue, Mr. Gary Bettman.

But we were all on the same team now: locked out NHL players. Even so, I waited until almost everyone was seated, and because Chris Chelios was such a good friend, he saved me a seat beside him at the end of the last row. I think Cheli was the second-most hated guy in the room, or perhaps he was No. 1, because he was challenging guys like the NHLPA's president, Trevor Linden, and calling foul play when decisions were being made that didn't follow the constitution. Cheli thought the NHLPA leadership was too cozy with the NHL, and maybe he was right.

The NHLPA wanted to get us all into the same room and get it all done and dusted quickly for a few reasons. The official version is that they needed to present to us ASAP in case they needed to redline the fine print in hopes of hitting the deadline the NHL had set. But I'm guessing that they also rushed us because they knew the guys had all traveled that day, which would make it hard for them to sit in a conference room for a few hours. Plus most guys hadn't seen their peers for months and now we were all together in Toronto. The boys couldn't sit still, thinking about how hard they were going to hit the town that night.

The union had set up a world-class feast for us—lasagna and steak and fish and every salad and vegetable dish you could think of—and after guys had put themselves in a food coma, the meeting started. By the way, the corporate world does not serve up spreads like this before big meetings because they know it sinks concentration levels to what they'd be just before you fell asleep, once that food settles in your gut.

But finally, we had 200 NHL players sitting in a big room, each guy with his own binder of papers detailing the potential deals. We're finally going to get down to business and sort out our livelihood.

And then it happens . . .

Those big banquet-room doors swing open and the Westin Harbour Castle's most attractive female wait staff are rolling in big gray hampers that are usually used to transport laundry but are now filled with the only ice the guys in this room have seen in eight months, and tucked into the ice is the coldest Canadian beer in the country at that moment.

The beer works its magic, and pretty soon voices get louder and opinions get harder. And it's not long until attention focuses on Tie Domi and Krzysztof Oliwa. Domi, the Toronto tough guy, wants to accept the deal, and he has a lot of friends in the business world, so some guys think he knows what he's talking about. Oliwa, the six-five enforcer now with Calgary, is an NHLPA hard-liner who does not want to settle, and as they argue they're getting closer and closer to each other and louder and louder, and then they're basically squaring off at the front of the room and having to be restrained by guys before they start punching each other. Then those big doors opened again for another beer delivery. I stopped counting how many beers Keith Tkachuk had had after I watched him polish off eight

QUEST FOR THE CUP → 18-PAGE SPECIAL

FORSBERG: THE WARRIOR RETURNS BRIERE: SO LOVED, SO HATED ROBIDAS: THE UNDERRATED STAR

The Hockey News

⏱ thn.com

THE
FREE
AGENT
ISSUE
:::::::::: the impact
on your team

SECRET
OF THE
HABS
SUCCESS

WHY
PARITY
STINKS

PLAYOFF
OFFICIATING
GET OVER IT!

Sean
Avery
THE
NHL'S
EVIL GENIUS

I know a compliment when I see one. If I can get on the cover of a magazine just by playing my game, I must be doing something right. But *evil*? That's not me. *Genius*? I'll let others judge. (COVER COURTESY *THE HOCKEY NEWS*, USED WITH PERMISSION)

Me and Mom. See? How could that kid be all bad?

That's my dad on the right. He's the guy not getting punched in the face. One thing we talked about a lot when I was a kid was that violence never solves problems.

My brother, Scott, hanging with the Stanley Cup inside Warren 77.

Me and Mom today. I don't need everyone in the world to like me.
But I'm like anyone else—I want to make my parents proud.

Making it to the NHL feels pretty great. Winning the Stanley Cup in your first season
feels pretty good too. I highly recommend it. (CREDIT SHELLY CASTELLANO PHOTOGRAPHY)

At Derek Boogaard's funeral with my Rangers teammates. You can see from our faces that some things in life are more important than winning hockey games. (AP PHOTO/THE CANADIAN PRESS, MARK TAYLOR)

The fans in Philadelphia will always have a special place in my heart. As you can see, Fly fans loved me—as long as they were safely behind the glass. (BRUCE BENNETT/GETTY IMAGES)

For some reason, Marty Brodeur didn't like it when I set up in his crease. Sometimes I got the impression he was angry. (AP PHOTO/BILL KOSTROUN)

It's funny. Scott Hartnell plays the game the way I did. He can score, he can hit, and he loves to get under guys' skin. Sounds a bit like me. But for some reason, he's thought of as a gritty character guy, while I was considered, well, an evil genius. Seems kind of unfair. I did enjoy punching him in the face, though. (AP PHOTO/JULIE JACOBSON)

There are a few places on the ice where truly gifted hockey players don't have to go if they don't want to. The front of the net is the least pleasant of those places. I spent a lot of time in front of the net. If you think it's easy, you should try staying on your feet while a 225-pound defenseman pounds you, and your own team bombs 100-mph slapshots your way. (AP PHOTO/KATHY KMONICEK)

This shot should tell you why guys like me are effective in the NHL. Todd Marchant is looking at me, probably contemplating revenge of some kind. I'm looking at the puck. Who do you think is about to make a play?

Brendan Shanahan showed me more about the league and about life than anyone else I played with. Here we are at New York Fashion Week. He may be the only guy I played with who has ever been. (AP PHOTO/RICHARD DREW)

Me and Elisha. I'm generally proud of my taunts and insults, but there is one I would definitely take back if I could.

That's me hanging out with Bill Murray.

And here I am with friends in Jamaica. That's my buddy Lawrence Longo, four over from me to the right. The incredibly beautiful woman beside me is proof that I'm a lucky guy, and also proof that you make at least some of your own luck. If I hadn't played hockey, and hadn't played in New York, and hadn't opened a restaurant, I would never have been lucky enough to meet her.

A lot of guys will say that just being in the NHL is a dream come true. And it is. I dreamed about it my whole life. But the thing is, it's also a gateway to a whole world of other opportunities. Here I am with Trey Anastasio from Phish in the hallway of Madison Square Garden.

On the opposite page, that's Hilary and me on our wedding day. Most guys think their wives are the most beautiful women in the world. I feel pretty lucky that mine actually is the most beautiful woman in the world. And underneath that photo, you'll see a young, curly-haired version of me partying with the Stanley Cup and my "big brothers" on the Red Wings. That's Brett Hull on the left, and Chris Chelios in the back. The guy with his arm around me is Kris Draper, who helped me land with the Red Wings and also got me my first modeling gig. And the guy with his right hand on the Cup? That's Kid Rock.

(CREDIT HANNAH THOMSON)

Some other places I might never have ended up if I hadn't busted my ass to make it to the NHL. On the opposite side, that's me living the glamorous life of a pro athlete on the road. Below is me leading the considerably more glamourous life of a *Vogue* intern. I guarantee I wouldn't have been there if I hadn't also been a New York Ranger. And above is me about to take a "Muskoka shower." Muskoka, about two hours north of Toronto, has the highest concentration of off-season NHLers known to man.

If you work hard, you're allowed to play hard. That's what I do, anyway.
Here I am at Bonnaroo. (DANNY CLINCH PHOTOGRAPHY)

cold ones in thirty minutes. And he was by no means alone in setting beer-drinking records that night.

It was apparent that this meeting was a very well-executed event designed to get us drunk and bloated and to result in absolutely nothing productive getting done. And so nothing was.

More meetings were scheduled for most of Saturday, but I decided not to go. I wasn't going to learn anything new, and yesterday's beer fest/ shouting match wasn't something I wanted to do again. So I took a cab out to Pickering to spend the day with my parents. We talked about the state of the NHL, and my genuine fear for the future. I mean, these were the people who heard me when I first said I wanted to play in the NHL when I was a little kid, who drove me to every practice on every grim winter morning, who took me on travel team trips, who supported my belief that I could make it, and who wiped away my tears when others said I didn't have a hope in hell of making it. Now, though, my mom and dad didn't really know what to say. We had arrived at the point where the unthinkable was on the verge of happening, which taught me—and small consolation, this—that if you can think it, it *can* happen.

My parents always believed that I had a plan and things would work out, but they were clearly worried about me, so they came back into Toronto and we had dinner at the Keg. I went to the restroom to take a leak and two guys walked in, and while waiting for my stall to open one of the guys started talking about how much of an asshole I was as a player. It would be a better story if I said I swung around and decked them both for insulting the company my parents kept, but I didn't. I just walked away. They didn't even see me.

On February 16, 2005, the NHL became the first professional sports league in history to cancel an entire season.

Pat Morris finally called me and said he had an offer for me. In Finland. Lahti, Finland.

Lahti is a city of about 100,000 on the same line of latitude as Whitehorse, Yukon. Sixty degrees far north. And the Lahti Pelicans are at the very southern end of the standings in the Liiga, the Finnish premier professional hockey league. What's not to like? I signed for the remainder of the season with the Pelicans, and got on a flight to Helsinki, which was followed by an hour-long car trip north to Lahti, which is a pretty town on a bay.

Hotels in Finland are a cut below what we're used to in the NHL. The rooms have twin beds with mattresses as thin as a pillow. The electricity runs on a different voltage from North America, and the TV features a whopping eight channels. All in Finnish.

The breakfast buffet at the hotel offers boiled eggs, pickled herring, caviar in a squeeze tin, and a ton of bread, and by my fourth day in the country I actually liked it. Before each practice we would put team tracksuits on and go for a mile run in this winter wonderland. The temperature outside was sixteen degrees and everything is white. The city's perfectly manicured sidewalks have snow neatly piled four to six feet along their borders, and the Lahti Sports Center has these giant ski ramps eight stories high. Ski jumping is a major sport in Finland. I don't know anyone here, and all the men and women look the same—blond and bundled up against the cold that's worse than Canada's. I'm as far from LA as I can be.

On my first weekend with the Pelicans—teal jerseys, lighter than those of San Jose, with black and white trim and a pink pelican head logo—we have two home games at Isku Areena, which seats 5,500 fans. I don't know anyone on the team and I'm the only NHL import, but everyone's cool with that—I mean, no one wants to give me grief for taking some Finnish player's spot. They're happy to have me, and I'm very happy to score a goal during our first game that Friday. Despite my happiness at being back on the ice, I definitely feel like it's been months since I've played hockey at a high level, which, of course, it has been.

My lungs are screaming after my first shift. No matter how many quarter-miles I've run to stay in shape, you cannot replicate the burn you get from playing your first game in months. For me, it's the best pain in the world.

Actually, it's the second-best. After a shot of Toradol.

After my lungs yell at me, my legs are next. I don't have the quick first step on this Finnish ice that I know I have in the NHL. It's not noticeable to the fans, but as a player you know. Milliseconds of delay feel like days, and the demons start to collect inside your brain, spreading their gossip of worry.

Has he lost his step?

Will he ever get it back?

Maybe this lockout is the end of him . . .

The good thing is that while you're on the young side of your career you can literally count how many days, games, and practices it will take before the switch goes off and your legs are back. And thank God you are back. But you also know that the moment that step doesn't come back is the moment you need to start thinking about what the next sixty years hold for you.

In my second game for the Lahti Pelicans I score two goals and get kicked out of the game for fighting Jarkko Ruutu, a guy who plays a similar game to me but at a much, much lower level. I have the puck as I'm skating out of our zone on the left, and make a cross-ice pass to our winger. Ruutu tries to hit me late, so I put my hands and stick up to defend myself and wind up cross-checking him in the side of the head. Then I drop my gloves before he has time to turtle and go after him. My teammates love it and so does the crowd, because no one ever fights here. It seems from the fans' cheering of my win over him that even the Finns don't like Ruutu.

He was a guy that NHL players talked about with disgust, which is different from the way they talk about me. They talk about me with hate.

As I'm taking off my equipment after the game in a room full of strangers here in dark, cold Finland, I feel alone. And I feel sad.

I should be celebrating in the dressing room of Staples Center after my Gordie Howe Hat Trick just helped the Kings win 4–3 in overtime, and I need to hurry up because my hot movie star girlfriend is hungry and wants to jump shotgun into my Porsche 911 Turbo for the fast ride through the streets of LA with the top down as I smoke a cigarette with an ice bag wrapped around my knee which doesn't get in the way of the glorious blow job I'm getting because my girlfriend enjoyed the great game I played.

Instead I end up in a sauna in the basement of a bar in Lahti, listening to a bunch of people talk in a language I don't understand, soundtracked by music that was in the Top 40 three years ago in America. This is another reason the owners will always beat the players in a CBA negotiation, because once you've had a taste of the NHL, it's the best taste in the world.

I woke up on that Sunday morning and I just knew. I had the hotel shuttle bus drop me off at the arena, where I told the caretaker I'd left my cell phone in the locker room. I quickly packed up my equipment and hurried out to the waiting hotel shuttle and told the driver to drop me off at the bus station. I bought a ticket to the Helsinki airport and didn't feel any relief until I landed in Norway to switch planes for my flight to New York. I didn't call Pat Morris for a week, but I had a pretty good idea that the Finns would have told him I'd left. When we did finally catch up, he said, "The over-under in the office on your staying in Finland was a week." Then he laughed. I guess he won the bet.

When I landed in New York I discovered that it was Fashion Week. Well, I actually knew that it was. I was paying a lot more attention to style. People have to look good in LA, and so you kind of inhale it. But I also like to look good, and had started reading *GQ* and *Vogue* and finding their fashion pictorials as fascinating as any book. I loved the buzz of Fashion Week in New York, and enjoyed checking out the shows, which last about fifteen minutes but have months of prep, very similar to pro sport. I loved the champagne parties, and the interesting, accomplished people from fashion and business and culture, and that same overwhelming sense of possibility I first felt when I came here to model tuxedos on *Good Morning America*. This time, though, I felt like I belonged more to the city. I have made progress in defining myself off the ice, and feel that I can move at New York speed. The city, for a week, makes me not forget my problems, but file them away.

But I don't live in New York. I live in Los Angeles, and so the party ends and I fly home to confront reality. Things with Rachel are not great. She's her wonderfully understanding self but I feel like a failure. I feel like I'm not giving very much back to her. I know it's from the effects of this lockout. I'm twenty-four years old and I don't have a job and I'm living with my girlfriend and this ramps up my insecurities about working again, and being good enough for Rachel. I mean, I'm dating a famous divorced woman with two kids who is so good at keeping everything on an even keel. Everything except for me.

I've just finished running the stairs at Drake Stadium on the UCLA campus in Westwood when my phone rings. I'm wiping sweat from my hands so that I can swipe the iPhone to answer this call from the Godfather. Even though what he's telling me is almost unbelievable, I know Chris Chelios doesn't waste time playing practical jokes so I perk up and listen very carefully. The owner of the Motor City Mechanics was willing to sign Cheli, Derian Hatcher, Brian Smolinski, Kris Draper, and the former No. 42 of the Detroit Red Wings—that would be me—to play in the United Hockey League.

Cheli had already negotiated our deals: I was to get a $20,000 signing bonus and we would get $2,500 for each win and $800 for each loss. And on top of this unexpected bounty, we didn't need to play away games. Cheli is such a shark that he realized we couldn't get a piece of the gate at away games, so he negotiated us not having to play them.

Two things were certain: I needed the money and I really needed to play some games to clear my head and keep myself sharp so when next September came around and this labor madness was sorted I could hit the rink at as close to NHL full speed as possible. Even though I'd bailed on my Finnish hockey adventure, I really need to play hockey. Cheli saved the day.

Cheli told me that I would stay in his guestroom, which made sense considering we would probably be hanging with each other day and night—make that late night—as we did not so long ago. To be honest, I was relieved as I said goodbye to Rachel and the kids, because I was sure they would enjoy the break from my daily frustrations. We didn't know when we'd next see each other but I was hoping that my renewed lease on life—and a little distance—might help get things back to a more balanced place with Rachel.

Cheli lives in a big house in Bloomfield Hills with his four kids and his wife, Tracee, whom he married young. She's just great—very down-to-earth and tolerant, which she'd have to be with a brood like that. Each of the four kids was polite and respectful, but they had their father's competitive edge, and the house was a lively place to be. I had a room on the ground floor, next to the kitchen, so I heard all of it.

It feels great to be with Cheli every day, and it reminds me of the old days (two years ago . . .) when we were driving to the rink together for practice or going for lunch at Cheli's Chili Bar. We do workouts in the sauna in Cheli's basement and somehow, despite all this, we still find ourselves out on the town a few nights a week.

The Mechanics only started to play in the UHL in the fall of 2004, so they haven't even completed a full season yet, and when I roll into Detroit they have eighteen wins and thirty-nine losses (a few of the latter in shootouts). When I turn it on I can pretty much dominate the game, and while it doesn't feel great to say I'm dominating the low-level minor pro league that is the UHL, it does feel great to be playing. Just being able to skate with the puck and make moves with speed around players is a great shot to my confidence.

I'm also playing a pretty nasty game because I have a ton of simmering anger about the lockout that I need to blow off. And I need to play this way so guys think twice before they take a run at me. In the NHL you have many more options as an agitator, with words being one of your foremost tools. But here in the UHL it's the deed that makes the point. My stick is a sword and when any guy comes near me they need to know that if they're going to make a move on me then they may lose an eye or a few teeth. I'm not fucking around in this league as I have way too much to lose.

We're playing the Flint Generals and they have a guy who's a real shit disturber named Kevin Kerr. He was drafted in the third round of the 1986 NHL Entry Draft by the Buffalo Sabres but, like many guys good enough to make it to the NHL, never did. Kerr is pissed off that guys are losing their UHL jobs because these hotshot NHLers are slumming it in the UHL while their billionaire owners argue money with their million-aire player reps. I don't disagree with him, but it reminds us all that this game is a business, and the Motor City Mechanics are taking advantage of a market opportunity.

I can't remember what exactly our coach, Steve Shannon, said during intermission, but apparently he put a $200 bounty on Kerr's head. Somehow this bad decision ended up leaving the dressing room and wafting into public knowledge, and the UHL president Richard Brosal suspended Shannon for the remainder of the season. Kerr was a little bit shaken by a clean check in the game but no one tried to take his head off. I mean, who'd want to be on the other side of injuring a guy for a $200 prize?

The thing is, coaches say "Take his fuckin' head off" about opposing guys all the time (without putting a bounty on it). Do they mean it? Sure. They just don't want you, or them, to get caught. Steve Shannon got caught because he made it a hockey crime with the cash bump for the hit.

I did feel guilty about not playing road games with my fellow Mechanics, and decided to play my first away game in Flint, which was not the easiest place to play. I'm hated in every NHL away arena I play in, but in the NHL we have some protection in place, a buffer zone between the players and the fans. In the UHL that protection does not exist, and the fans are waiting when our bus pulls up. I hear the usual bullshit as I walk in: "Faggot-Pussy-Bitch-Faggot." I've been known to get in the faces of these individuals and enjoy watching them shit their pants as I approach them with a pep in my step. They always back off.

I think I may have made Cheli feel guilty about staying home while the team is away, too, because he agrees to play our next road game in Kalamazoo. Since we don't have a replacement coach yet, Cheli is bringing Bob Ritchie to coach the team. So incredibly, Kid Rock ends up standing behind the Mechanics' bench with a beer in a brown paper bag, calling out line changes. He's having the time of his life and the players on our bench, and even the guys on the Kalamazoo Wings, are absolutely loving it. This is the closest thing to *Slapshot* I've ever seen.

Even so, I'm feeling guilty about the amount of money we're making under the table, and I'm not going to mail in my game. But a couple of games later in Detroit, what I feared could happen, happens. Looking down at my right index finger as I skated to the penalty box after laying a beating on some poor guy in a small scrum during the game, I could see the bone of my knuckle. The skin on both sides had peeled over like a blooming onion. My punch had landed flush on the guy's two front teeth and now my finger was in bad shape, worse than any other injury I'd taken to my hands in previous fights.

I skated directly to the dressing room and the doctor came down from the stands to check me out. He quickly decided that I needed to go to the hospital to have X-rays and then hopefully a good plastic surgeon would be around to stitch me up if I didn't actually need to have surgery.

I started to sweat more in the car ride to the hospital than I was sweating during the game because this was serious. A hockey player's hands are very important for obvious reasons, but the complicating factor here was that any injury that a player sustains while playing in a league other than the NHL during the lockout would cancel that player's guaranteed NHL salary for next season.

Whenever that next season was going to happen.

The X-rays came back looking good, and a doctor who worked for the Red Wings happened to be on call that afternoon in Detroit, so you could say that I was very lucky. Doctors who work for hockey teams are some of the best, and are usually as good with sutures as any plastic surgeon because they get a lot of practice. It took twenty-six stitches to sew my right index finger back together, and then the doctor applied a finger splint with a pretty substantial bandage wrapped around it. I was to go back to the doctor in a couple of days to see if I could have the stitches removed.

(Usually stitches should be removed three or four days after they sew you up, otherwise the skin will start to heal overtop the sutures. It's very painful when you remove them too late because you basically need to cut the skin again so you can dig them out. You always want to take stitches out the day before you think they're ready, when the skin is still pink and tender with a little bit of blood still oozing from the cut. Not pretty, but true.)

The deal we had with the Mechanics was that we would get paid per game, and Cheli didn't think it was reasonable for me to expect to collect if I didn't play. We were now winning most of our games, and this was going to be a $7,500 weekend if we won all three games. So I decided to play.

I was planning to keep my game to the perimeter and avoid scrums and chippy stuff, and I had to wrap my hand with a little more padding to make sure it was protected. The Mechanics' equipment guy (I love equipment guys, they're the best, everywhere) also figured out a way to make the finger on my glove a bit roomier so that I could fit the extra padding around my mangled finger. I played in all three games, and we won two, lost one. The $5,800 makes my finger feel much better.

My heart, though, is hurting. Rachel hasn't come to Detroit while I've been playing here. Even though we haven't been a couple all that long—less than a year—I can feel that the end is near. Part of me wants our relationship to end, but part of me wants it to last forever. This has been a tough time for me to be in a relationship, and it's not going to get any easier. I decide to do the decent thing and tell her she should carry on with her life without me as her partner. The lockout is still on, but I know that it won't last forever, and I need to focus on training and getting ready for the 2005–06 NHL season, if there is one. Rachel isn't surprised by my offer, and she isn't angry about it either. She feels the same way. She is very wise, and very nurturing, and very clear-eyed about where we are both going as people. I was the first person she'd been with since Rod, and she didn't take that lightly, nor did I. We remained friends. Later I would wind up living one street away from Rachel and the kids, and I would go to see them regularly.

I keep playing in Detroit, and I keep watching Cheli and how he works—not on the ice, but off it. He's really dedicated himself to the lockout negotiations, but his superhuman energy has not been engaged in negotiating with the league. Instead he has focused on trying to control all the back-door negotiations going on in our own union. Guys are holding separate "unofficial" talks with the NHL and the owners, and it's weakening our cause.

I was beside Cheli while he was in the thick of things, and he told me everything. He uncovered a lot of information as he tried to police a group that had gone rogue—guys who were having secret talks that didn't align with the membership. He hired lawyers at his own expense, he tried to subpoena NHLPA email records, and he flew all over the country to talk to guys. The beautiful thing about it was that this superstar was doing it all for the average player, and aside from the lawyers he hired, there was no one helping him. It was like a street fight, with Cheli on one side and the rogues on the other.

Trevor Linden was at the forefront of the rogues, and Trent Klatt, my teammate in LA, was somewhere in the middle, though he sided with Cheli in the end.

I implicitly trust Shanny, but it might have been that other guys in the room didn't feel the same way. Was he smarter than all of us and just trying to bridge the gap between reality and hope by working both sides of the room—the NHL and the NHLPA? Maybe. I don't know. But at the time Cheli perceived this group of players as being too friendly with the NHL and therefore damaging our bargaining unity. Whatever Shanny did hurt his friendship with Chelios beyond repair. They played hard whenever they were on the ice together, but off the ice they were estranged.

June 2005 comes and goes, and it's the first time since 1919 that there has been no Stanley Cup Final. The league and the union still have not agreed on a deal, but I know that the players will cave if it comes down to us going back to work in September or not. The media has been full of "the sky is falling" reports that fans will be lost and that it will take years to restore our "brand," but I don't believe that. The lockout has made people realize that they follow the NHL because they love it. You always want the fans to love the game as much as you do.

But what people don't realize is the toll the lockout takes on the players. Marriages and relationships start to crumble under the stress. A player's whole domestic life has been built on the rhythm of him being away—at practice, at games, at home and on the road—and now the radical change in that rhythm has forced all kinds of adjustments that are a struggle for many. I don't know anyone who got divorced right after the lockout, but I know that when we had these NHLPA meetings guys were clearly expressing their frustration: "My wife doesn't know what to do with me. My wife is going to kill me. I don't know what to do with me." That kind of thing, from all over the league, and it became sort of a running joke, whenever it could be inserted in a conversation: "If this lockout doesn't end soon, I'm going to wind up divorced."

I know of a few players who had to go to a company in Florida which was loaning guys cash and using their guaranteed contracts as collateral—not guys making the NHL minimum, either, but guys who were making millions and living the high life. Talk about risky, because who knows what will happen to those contracts once we settle?

The only thing that I think players would fight for until the end of time is to keep guaranteed contracts. Your career can be over in a flash because of the kind of work you've been hired to do. It's immoral and certainly should be illegal to cut a guy loose from his contract because he was too injured to continue, or because a labor dispute changed the game.

But from where I sit in June of 2005, I know more than ever that players will never beat the owners in a work stoppage. It would be the worst bet to take in the history of gambling.

13

A NEW LIFE IN PARADISE

There's no time like being out of work and filled with doubts to end a relationship and move, but now that Rachel and I had parted company, I had to move out of her house. I didn't have much stuff—I can fit my life into a bag. Rachel was away in New Zealand with the kids for a work-vacation, so the place was empty. It hit me hard, because I loved her, and I didn't know if I was making the right decision. We didn't break up because we had lost that love, we broke up because of circumstance. I needed to bear down and get even more focused for the future. I had just lost a year of my career, and the average length of a pro hockey career is five or six seasons. So possibly a fifth of my career. If you work for forty years in a profession, it's like saying goodbye to eight of them. I wasn't feeling sorry for myself at all, but I had a pretty damn strong sense of urgency to get back to the thing that gave me meaning: my game.

I rented a room in the Sunset Marquis in Hollywood, which is a rock 'n' roll hotel with a very different LA style from the Chateau Marmont. It was a temporary stop until I found a house to buy.

I know—I've just said how tight money is and how worried I am about the future, but I had made the decision I was going to buy a house because I had to do something to give myself some stability. And there are now noises that we'll be getting a settlement before the summer is out. The NHL can't afford to blow two seasons. No one can. And owning property is an investment.

I have a budget of $800,000 and I've asked my broker to show me some homes in Laurel Canyon in the shimmering hills of West Hollywood. Laurel Canyon was made famous by the music scene of the 1970s with the Doors and Joni Mitchell and CSNY and Bob Dylan and all those who wanted to be just like them calling the place home. Laurel Canyon has its own trippy energy, perfumed by the incense burning from all the cool little cottages that dot the neighborhood.

What I got was a Spanish-style casa hanging over the Canyon, with a giant deck that overlooked the City of Angels. I loved it. I had already decided I was going to do the forty-minute drive to the Kings' practice rink in El Segundo and the twenty-minute drive to Staples Center where we played our games. I mean, you have to drive everywhere in LA anyway, right? Luc Robitaille was the only other King who lived outside Manhattan Beach, and no King has ever lived in the hills of Laurel Canyon. I had a feeling my teammates would think I was trying to make some kind of statement—they lived within a six-block radius of each other. I was wrong about that. The Kings were very happy to have me there because they now had a place to crash after a late night in town. Who wants to drive to Manhattan Beach when you can stay with me? I guess I have a chip on my shoulder even when it comes to real estate.

Once I moved to Laurel Canyon I started to hang out with a new group of friends who lived there, or nearby. I was becoming particularly close with a young couple, Elisha Cuthbert and Trace Ayala. I was introduced to them by my friend Cody Leibel, who was living the kind of life of excess that you read about in lifestyle magazines or LA novels. Cody had become known around town as a "whale." A whale is a guy who rolls into a club or restaurant or casino and drops big cash—I mean, big as in $100,000—in a few hours. If you think money can't buy friends, you've never met a whale.

But Cody is not your typical whale. That is, he's not a self-absorbed, entitled jackass. He's a very personable guy, and because of his whale wattage, he's become friends with a number of celebrities, including Trace and Elisha, and Trace's best friend Justin Timberlake, who also lived at the top of Mulholland Drive.

Trace had been dating Elisha for a few years, and they were now engaged. They lived together a few streets away from me, just behind the Chateau Marmont. I spent a lot of time hanging out with them, cooking BBQ at their house or mine, watching Justin record at the studio, and hitting the nightclubs—the kind of passing-the-time-LA-stuff that you do when you're all in your mid-twenties and life has not yet let you know how fast time actually passes.

The house party is also an LA social event, and I went to one at Paris Hilton's house that summer which turned out to be memorable, and expensive.

Paris lived in a 1920s Spanish-style casa, perched just above the Sunset Strip on North Kings Road and decorated in "Haute Paris" style—photos of her everywhere, a stripper pole in the living room, and, of course, a swimming pool out back.

When we arrived and were introduced, Paris couldn't believe how perfect my ass was (yes, this is the alternate universe that LA can quickly become). She wanted to know how a man could have such a perfect ass without the aid of some sort of butt implant, which was then starting to gain popularity in LA. And yes, I was wearing clothes.

So in the spirit of scientific inquiry, Paris wanted her assistant to slap my ass to see if it was real. I told her, sure, no problem, but in return, I would get to slap the female assistant's ass as well. It was a deal.

So I let the assistant slap my ass and before she could conclude that it was indeed as nature made it, I pulled my hand back, and instead of slapping the assistant's ass, I gave a healthy, firm, and flirtatious slap to Paris's ass.

I didn't realize how fragile she was, and the slap—trust me, it was not anything close to an NHL love tap—kind of stunned her, and her eyes started to well up with tears.

It was as if the upstart peasant had just struck the queen of France.

Her assistant open-hand slapped me across the face. I laughed this off, and apologized to Paris, when suddenly, in mid-apology, I get slapped again by the guy she was dating at the time, who must have realized that he looked like a complete pussy and was drunk enough to have the balls to swat me.

I remember laughing and thinking to myself that this had really gotten out of hand very quickly all because of my hockey ass, then suddenly I hear a *thump*. Trace had jumped to my defense and thrown a right hand off the side of Paris's boyfriend's head and was now grimacing in pain. I knew where this was going next.

So, seventeen hours later, I'm sitting in the hospital emergency room with Elisha when the doctor emerged to explain to us that the surgery on Trace's hand had gone well, and that the cast would need to be on for six weeks to let the screw in his thumb set properly.

I really think that the $12,000 Elisha had to spend on Trace's surgery was the beginning of the end of their relationship. I think it scared her to realize how all the financial responsibility was probably going to land on her, and that eventually being Justin Timberlake's best friend did not pay the bills. And that she wanted a guy who was more than the best pal of a celebrity.

This is when Elisha and I started to fall in love without even really knowing it.

Even so, I head to Memphis to hang out with Trace and his family on the Fourth of July weekend. To see the heart of America on the most patriotic weekend of the year was a beautiful thing. As a professional athlete you're sheltered from the middle class, even though almost all of us are from the middle class. We stop camping and become snobs—I mean, anything less than four stars in a hotel constitutes camping. Our reality becomes foggy from the fast ride we're on and we don't remind ourselves where we came from, or that we could be back there pretty damn soon if things don't work out.

So a weekend like this was a welcome change from my high-speed LA life. We spent some time at Justin Timberlake's family home, and seeing one of the biggest stars in the world being so comfortable in his small town, dancing around a fire and eating BBQ with his family and best friend, is something I'll never forget. He lived on planet Earth, and his family is the reason why.

But it does bother me to think about Trace opening up his family and friends to me knowing in my heart what was coming next. Part of the reason why Elisha and I were coming together—aside from our strong physical attraction—was that we came from the same place. It's funny. I used to avoid Canadian women, and now here I am in LA, all excited that my girlfriend knows about the Tragically Hip and Coffee Crisp. It was kind of like having a secret language. And the fact that she was beautiful and smart and had a great sense of humor and loved hockey didn't hurt either.

Elisha broke off her engagement to Trace soon after the punch at Paris Hilton's house, and he moved out, but nothing physical had happened between us. I was stopping by her house more than usual, though, and we had a group of friends who would hang out, have dinner, watch *Who Wants to Be a Millionaire* on TV, or go see a movie. I enjoyed the group, but I wanted to be alone with Elisha, and it was obvious to both of us what was going on. We had our first kiss on the walkway in front of her house, and when we looked at each other after the kiss, she laughed and said, "They're going to have a field day with this." We both knew that. But forward was the only direction that we both wanted to go.

———

On July 22, 2005, the NHL lockout officially ended after we voted, pretty much overwhelmingly, to accept what the league was going to give us. I voted to end it, because at that point we were all just waiting for the league to make us an offer so we could get back to work. But it had all come at a cost.

The lockout itself cost the league about $2 billion in lost revenue. Players who were under multi-year contracts before the lockout had their salaries rolled back twenty-four percent, which was a major hurt. NHL teams could each spend $21 million to $39 million on players the following season, which made the NHLPA's rejection in February of the league's offer of a $42.5 million salary cap—an offer that would have saved the season—even more painful.

Our new contract also guaranteed that we would receive fifty-four percent of the league's revenue, but in the past we got closer to seventy-five percent. I remember reading about the settlement, and a quote from a labor lawyer in New York, who'd worked for the NFL and NBA unions, stuck with me. He called our deal "the largest setback for players that I've seen in collective bargaining."

It had been a hard time not just for us, but for people who worked in arenas at our games, both off and on the ice. Referee Bill McCreary, who'd put me in the penalty box a few times, installed kitchen cabinets to pay the bills during the lockout. Stéphane Provost, a linesman who'd officiated more than 700 NHL games, was painting houses for $10 an hour during the months when we should have been playing for the Stanley Cup.

And as I predicted, there were older guys who would hang them up, and some of them were Hall of Famers. Scott Stevens, Ron Francis, Al MacInnis, Mark Messier, Adam Oates, Igor Larionov, Steve Thomas, and Felix Potvin all retired, not in a blaze of glory as they should have done, but in a ditch of greed dug by the owners, and by the NHL, and by some of us. As for Cheli, he worked even harder to expose all the backroom dealing that had gone on during the lockout. He was tireless. The rest of us were just tired.

Before the regular season even started I was already in trouble. We were playing an exhibition game against Phoenix at the Staples Center, and it's early in the second period. My teammate Jeremy Roenick takes a pass from Alex Frolov when the Coyotes' Denis Gauthier slams Roenick into the boards so hard he has to leave the game with a concussion. It was at least the tenth concussion that Roenick has suffered, and we all know the problems that head injuries can cause you down the road.

"I think it indicates the state of our game, the lack of respect, especially in the pre-season," Roenick said at the time. "It is uncalled for, it is ridiculous, it is one of the reasons our game isn't as good as it once was."

So, when I was on TSN, one of Canada's sports networks, a couple of days later, I spoke up on behalf of my teammate. And I said this: "I think it was typical of most French guys in our league with a visor on, running around and playing tough and not back[ing] anything up."

The problem was the word "French." It was as if I'd insulted every single soul in the great province of Quebec, when all I really meant was that if you're wearing a visor you're sending a signal that you're not ready to fight—which you're going to be invited to do if you crush a star like Roenick. And back then it was mostly French Canadians and Europeans wearing visors. Maybe I could have put it better, but the NHL's vice-president of hockey operations, Colin Campbell, called me up and said, "Listen, we know how some of these guys are, but you can't say it, Sean. You can't always say what you're thinking."

So I said sorry. But I still think that if you wear a visor, and don't fight, then you don't run guys.

A couple of months later I was in trouble again. We were playing in Phoenix, and I collided with a Coyote and went down. There was no penalty called on either of us, but a day later, the NHL fined me $1,000 for diving. Basically, someone in the league offices was calling me a liar and a faker. Now, guys will sometimes dive. But hockey players, and fans, take pride in our game's difference from soccer. (The joke is, soccer players pretend they're hurt, and hockey players pretend they're not.) I'm pissed off if I get a penalty, but I'm even more pissed off if I get a penalty long after the game is over. And I let my feelings be known to an *LA Times* reporter. For that, Colin Campbell fined me another $1,000 for my "complete lack of respect for all those associated with our game."

I was even more annoyed when I found out I couldn't appeal this injustice, thanks to the work of our brain trust at the NHLPA in further eroding our rights in the new CBA.

It was clear to me that the NHL had a bull's eye on my back, and would use this "lack of respect" argument to get me somehow, somewhere. What I didn't respect was having someone watching me on a TV thousands of miles away tell me that I'd taken a dive. Things happen fast in hockey, and if a guy trips you or hooks you or elbows you in the head, it's quite likely that you'll go down. And sure, part of my game is to suck the other team into penalties, and so I have gone down a little quickly on occasion, but it's such a subjective penalty, and this time I didn't dive. For the league to get inside your head and say that no, you really embellished the offense is a classic "blame the victim" strategy.

I know that there are certain guys I have to fight in the NHL and that there are certain times when I have to fight them. It's November 2, and we're playing in Dallas, and I make another one of those calculated decisions to fight tonight. Steve Ott is a player similar to myself, a guy who came out of the

OHL a couple of years after me, but the difference is that he was chosen twenty-fifth overall in the NHL Entry Draft. He can play and he can put the puck in the net, but he's got a nasty streak, and I'd say he's the third-most hated man in the NHL after Gary Bettman and me. Ott would take a baseball swing two-hander with the intent of breaking your wrist, for example.

I knew this fight would happen the moment I saw the schedule, and I also knew that this would be a strategic fight where I would try and get the first punch in. I start the game well, getting a goal early in the first. Halfway through the third, we're up 6–2 when the puck goes over the glass and I give Stu Barnes a little shove after the whistle. Right on cue, Ott comes over and we're off. We wrestle a bit to get loose, and I throw one. Ott throws one back and misses. We dance like this for a bit and my helmet comes off, and then I get Ott's helmet off and land a couple more. Then the linesmen come in and break us up.

Hockey players try to get helmets off so we don't hurt our hands punching a helmet. But I think punching a head hurts more than hitting a helmet.

The moment those gloves hit the ice everything goes quiet and everything slows down. You don't think about anything else during those ten, twenty, thirty, forty seconds. Everything surrounding you and your opponent goes blurry and it's completely silent until the moment you hit the ice.

I have a move where I roll my head under my opponent's right arm, which confuses him and gives me a different angle to throw my rights from. Hockey fights are as strategic as a chess match—each time you grab your opponent's jersey you're setting up the next punch. Of course, he's trying to do the same thing, so I always try to limit my opponent's ability to hit me by ducking and weaving and bobbing back as he throws haymakers. I wait for an opening and then I strike. You can win a hockey fight with one punch, and sometimes that punch doesn't KO your opponent, but it knocks him off balance enough that you can throw the punch that knocks him to the ice and then you follow on top of him for the win.

A magical adrenaline rush fuels it all, and with 20,000 people cheering for you, it's that roar that lifts you up to the rafters. And then you are slammed down by exhaustion. I've had some fights where it took an hour for my legs to stop shaking and my heart rate to return to something approaching normal. Although I was far from a heavyweight, I understand how hard that job is on those guys. When you look at the schedule in September and know that in November you have eight games where you're going to fight another man and that he could end your career with one punch, that is the definition of stress. We have no idea how hard that job is, and I've chosen to do it from time to time, but still I stand in amazement at the guys who have to do it to stay in the league.

On December 5, 2005, the Kings land in Toronto. Elisha has arrived from Montreal where she's been visiting her parents for a few days, and she'll come to the Kings–Leafs game the next night. She snuck into the team hotel, though it wasn't a stealth mission because it was freezing cold and she was bundled up, so no one recognized her. I've made sure to book a room of my own.

At this point in our relationship we're under deep cover. Maybe just two of our mutual friends know what's going on between us. We started as friends but now it's obvious that we're falling in love, and we probably have been for months, even though nothing physical went on between us until quite a while after she called off her engagement.

Before we descend to the freezing streets of Toronto where all the eyes of the city will be upon us—this is the hockey hotbed of the world, after all—I need to make a phone call to Trace. I need to tell him what's going on before he sees it online. This is not an easy call to make, and although there is something very serious happening between myself and E, I do feel like my character is about to take a hit.

Trace has been my friend for more than a year and we've spent a lot of time together, both he and I as well as the three of us. I call Trace's cell phone and he answers. He's in Memphis. Trace and Elisha had split up two months earlier, so he's gone home to spend some time with his family and his best friend, Justin Timberlake.

I tell Trace that I'm in Toronto with Elisha and that we're together. I tell him I've broken the code between two men and try to justify it by saying it was something I couldn't control. Part of this is true, but I'm a big boy and I can control pretty much every decision in my life. I just knew I wanted to be with Elisha.

Trace asks to speak with Elisha and tells her she's broken his heart, and that he knew this was going to happen between her and me. Then he hangs up. I didn't steal her away from him. She realized that Trace was not the man she wanted to marry, and I happened to be there. I was perspective, but I wanted to be much more than that, and she wanted me to be, too.

The heaviness of that call is numbed by the adrenaline we feel being with each other, and we're about to step out to show anyone who cares that we're together. Elisha is a rarity in Canada—a successful working actress. She was on *24*, one of the biggest shows in TV history, and I'm going to be on *Hockey Night in Canada* the next night. People will notice. And little did I know then how much they would care.

After our 2–1 win against the Leafs I'm doing the media scrum and for the first time the media ask me a question about my love life. So I give the "Hollywood Answer" and say, "Ah, guys you know I don't talk about that."

But when I meet E in a quiet corner near the team bus waiting to take me to the Kings' 747, ready to whisk me home to LA for a few days' rest between gigs, I feel like a fucking rock star.

I know the increased attention that I'm getting both on and off the ice bothers my teammates. I know some of my teammates wonder why this guy who wasn't drafted and hasn't scored twenty goals is getting so much love. No one says this to my face, but Luc Robitaille gently lets it be known when he's checking in with me, which he's done since I first joined the team. When I got traded to LA he was one of the first guys to call me and tell me how much I was going to enjoy the city. He liked to send me texts, and he'd call me up to make sure I was OK. Now he was telling me that I had to manage my growing celebrity so that it wasn't too much, too soon. He'd been teammates with our GM, Dave Taylor, and said that Taylor didn't like it when you went after attention aggressively. You had to be "slow" about it.

I listen to Luc—he's friendly and supportive—but behind his words I hear the voices of my teammates saying, "I'm a better player than this guy Avery, so why the fuck is he getting this attention?" I never once walked into a dressing room carrying a magazine with my picture in it, or flaunting some magazine that had my girlfriend on the cover. But if the guys are jealous of the attention I'm getting, what am I supposed to do? Not date Elisha? I play my game on the ice just like I always have, but the temperature of the room has changed, and I know that it's going to get even colder.

Elisha was proud of me, though, and she was the warmth countering the chill that was blowing my way because of our relationship. She was very funny and she could take a joke, and she also preferred the company of guys to women. Elisha was like one of the guys in many ways. She could sit down and polish off a bottle of Jack Daniels on her own. There were times when I got up to go to practice and Elisha was still up and hanging out with our friends whom I'd said goodnight to a few hours earlier. She was a female Cheli, in a way. I loved it. She also understood hockey because she was a fan. After a tough game when I might not have played my best, she'd say to me, "I'll see you at home." She knew that I didn't want to talk about it in the car.

When I started dating Elisha she'd recently made a decision to focus on her movie career and to put television—which had catapulted her into a much higher level of fame than she'd ever known—on the back burner. I wish I'd talked to her more about acting. I would do line readings with her but I didn't understand any of it. I was so focused on my own work that I didn't pay enough attention to hers.

Elisha had an amazing work ethic. When she was doing *24* she was up at 4:30 A.M. She was always prepared for auditions, and always worked on being an actor and getting better at it. I remember going to the *24* Christmas party and meeting Kiefer Sutherland. He played hockey in an old-timers league and was a fan, but he was the type of guy who didn't want to bother me by talking about work, in the same way he didn't want me asking him about Jack Bauer. When he buckled up to have a good time, that's what he wanted to do. And he was good at it.

Usually my friend Lawrence Longo and Elisha would go to games together. He'd pick her up and drive her since she liked to have a drink before the game. She'd start to get nervous in the afternoon, a few hours before puck drop. At this point in my career my nerves are more excitement than fear, because we haven't really done anything in LA so there's not a lot of pressure on us.

There were so many times when I'd come out after a game and Elisha would be pissed off, and I'd ask Lawrence what happened and he'd tell me she got into it with an opposing fan. They had to leave a game in Anaheim once after she got into it with some Ducks fans. She was defending me and the team, and after she'd had a couple of beers she was six feet tall with the mouth of a trucker, and Lawrence decided for their mutual well-being they should escape. I have to say, any woman who is willing to stand up for Sean Avery in a hockey rink has more backbone than most guys I've played with.

By the end of the season—and it's a better season than the previous one—we're still in the playoff hunt, but on a skid. It's March 24, 2006, and we've lost four of our last five games. Vancouver, Edmonton, and Colorado are all swimming around the same playoff spot, and we were shut out by Colorado 5–0 in our last game. The tension in our dressing room is high, but tension like this in an NHL dressing room is sometimes the best remedy for a slump.

This combination of a slump and the looming playoffs means it's the one time in the year where teammates fight in practice. This is what always happens, and the team goes on to win the next game. But even though guys fight and we're on our way to working things out, our coach, Andy Murray, decides to impose a new motivational tool in practice, so when I screw up a drill he decides that the way to rally me and the Los Angeles Kings is to make us do some push-ups. I am stunned. Has Andy been taking coaching lessons from some B-movie about motivating a slacker high school football team?

My teammates are stunned as well. I mean, push-ups? When we're trying to make the playoffs? How about helping us understand the drill we screwed up? But as I said earlier, Andy didn't play hockey, so how could he really coach it? I was not happy about this stunt he'd just pulled, and I knew I wasn't alone. The guys had given up on Andy.

Our game the next day is against Nashville, who are one of the best teams in the NHL this season, and who are definitely going to make the playoffs. I'm pissed off from the moment I wake up and want to shove it up Andy's ass in tonight's game. Just how would I do this, though?

It's late in the third period and we're leading Nashville 5–4. It's been a wild game. I start out with the puck in our end and gather speed through the middle. I go wide on the D-man and at the top of the circle I take a shot that somehow ends up back on my stick, and I'm now below the goal line. I unleash a hard snapshot at Tomáš Vokoun, the Nashville goalie, just trying to hit him in the off chance I can bank it in behind him. And it works.

I skate to the corner and Mike Cammalleri skates over to give me the

celebratory hug, but he must sense that I'm going to do something different because he backs off. In one swift motion, I'm down on the ice, banging
out three push-ups.

Nobody in the Staples Center knows why I'm doing this except the
guys who'd been at practice the day before. They know it was a huge "fuck
you" to Andy. And Andy knows it too. But I never learn what he thinks
of it. Because the next day he gets fired.

Although I didn't love Andy Murray, and had precious little respect for his
coaching ability, I was in the awkward position of also appreciating his
assessment of me. He must think I'm valuable to the team because he has
me in the lineup, and all you can ask as a player is to get a shot. Then you
have no excuses.

I mean, how would I coach me? If I had a guy who worked hard all the
time and expected his teammates to do the same and called them out
when they didn't, and also got in trouble with the league for shit he said
and did, would I try to change him? I like to think I'd channel what was
best about his game into a force that would help the team. And I would
do it with a light touch, because guys like me are always hardest on ourselves, and don't need a coach to keep pointing it out. Guys like me need
a coach who will teach us stuff that makes us better players, and Andy
Murray was not that guy.

So while I'm confident in my ability to keep bringing value to my team,
I'm also nervous that the new guy may not like me. But then, everyone is
feeling this, because who fires a coach this late in the season when you
have a shot at the playoffs? I mean, you might think I'm always blaming
the coaches, but this time management went even further. I know now
that LA's ownership must have told Dave Taylor he could fire Andy but
only if he hired an "interim" coach and didn't sign him beyond the end of

this season. Because if the Kings didn't make the playoffs there would be a house-cleaning in management, and maybe in the dressing room, too.

Dave Taylor obviously didn't have many options, then, because what kind of coach would take an eleven-game tryout, on a team that had plunged so far, without a contract for the following year? A coach with no job and no leverage, that's who.

John Torchetti was from Boston, and to be fair to the man, he'd played in the Quebec Major Junior Hockey League and toughed out a few seasons as a winger in the minor pros. He'd also been behind an NHL bench, as an assistant coach with Tampa Bay and Florida, and two seasons earlier he was a mid-season (or late season—just twenty-seven games left) head coach replacement in Florida. They did not make the playoffs.

He had been behind the taxi wheel during the lockout, yet another example of what guys had to do to get by. He was hungry, and he was likely very inexpensive, and he also had NHL experience. He was the perfect sacrificial lamb for the Kings' brain trust. We'd be a Disney movie if Torchetti's inspired leadership had us raising the Stanley Cup.

I liked John. I mean, he was doing his best considering the circumstances, and even though we were all relieved by the fact that he was an interim coach and unlikely to come down hard on us, or mess with the lineup, we also knew that we could be an interim team if we didn't step up and give the playoffs our best shot. Torchetti had to inherit Andy Murray's assistant coaches, Mark Hardy and John Van Boxmeer, and it turned out that it would be the assistants who would be the trouble.

During practice before our third-to-last game, when we still had a mathematical shot at the post-season, I got into a "fuck you" match with Mark Hardy.

Honestly, I don't even remember what happened, even though all the reports have said that I refused to participate in a drill, which is complete bullshit. Everyone was miserable and tension was high and everyone was stressed to the max, so I might have questioned the point of whatever drill

Hardy thought we needed to do with three games left in the season, games that we had to win.

Hardy kicked me off the ice and the next morning told me that I wouldn't play the final three games of the season. I wasn't being suspended by the team or the league, I just wasn't playing. I was scratched. Mark Hardy had found his scapegoat, and so I sat in the stands for the game we had to win against Phoenix. We rose to the occasion by losing 3–0. We were out of the playoffs.

The old boys' club in the NHL is filled with yes men, and if you're deemed an old boy it's assumed you're an upstanding citizen—no questions asked—until you say something that the old boys don't like or you do something they can't sweep under the rug.

The latter is what happened to Hardy. Years after our dustup he apparently got hammered in Washington, DC, where he was staying in a hotel with his family, and stumbled back to the hotel and crawled into bed with his twenty-one-year-old daughter. Then he did something that she obviously did not want to happen, so she called the police and had her father arrested. He was charged with sexually assaulting his daughter, although the charge was later dropped for "want of prosecution."

And Mark Hardy has a better reputation than I do.

The Kings removed Dave Taylor as GM of the team in April, shortly after our death spiral, and, as pro hockey is so good at doing, reassigned him to another position within the organization. A bunch of scouts and player personnel were also fired or reassigned. I'm not going to stress about the new GM and who he's going to hire as the new coach because I had a strong season and had statistically improved from the previous season.

Nevertheless, the new GM, Dean Lombardi, summons me to a meeting in his office in May. Lombardi played college hockey, then went to law school, became a player agent, and crossed the street into management when he joined Minnesota as an assistant GM in 1988. He went on to do some good things as GM in San Jose, and now he was here, looking at me like I'm an interesting experiment.

Dean is a straight-talking guy who respects his players. He understands that each one of them is different and that part of a great team are the personalities that make up its DNA. I like him. We talk about how I'm an effective player and how his expectations for my play this season build on what I've done so far on the ice. His concerns are all directed at my behavior off the ice—which he has not seen—but he thinks if I correct my "off-ice adventures," then I'll also be more controlled on the ice. He doesn't cite anything specific, and I listen to him in surprise. I've never had a DUI, I've never been late for a game or practice, and when I did get arrested for playing music too loud the charges were dropped. Even so, people in the hockey world who've never met me think I'm a major problem once I'm let loose on the public.

Realizing that Dean thinks I might be a psycho-killer about to attack LA, I ask him to please do me a favor and check in with some of my friends—Matty Norström or Luc Robitaille or Jeremy Roenick—for a character reference. I know they'll speak well of me (or at least fairly well) because they don't feel threatened or have any jealousy toward me.

Dean listens and then tells me that I'm on a short leash (I always love it when my boss compares me to a dog) and that he won't hesitate to trade me if I'm not fitting in with his team. And then, even though he's a "man that stays out of the spotlight," he decides to inform our friends in the media that he's putting me on "double secret probation." (You might recall another Dean—Dean Vernon Wormer in the film *Animal House*—talking about double secret probation, which is what he put the Delta Tau Chi fraternity on when regular probation didn't cut it.)

Years later Dean Lombardi would have a player accused of smuggling drugs across the Canadian border, and a player accused of beating his wife, and another player caught trying to bring ecstasy and cocaine into a Vegas pool party. All three players would be charged or suspended or both within the year. Yet it was me who earned double secret probation. I guess it worked so well with me that he figured he never needed to do it again.

That summer there was a new music festival happening in George, Washington (yes, that's a real place, about 150 miles southeast of Seattle), so Elisha and I and Lawrence Longo rented a forty-four-foot RV—the largest you can rent with a regular driver's license—and loaded it with supplies for the sixteen-hour drive to "the Gorge" in George. Lawrence's girlfriend, Kim, came with us.

We pile into the RV and I put that baby in drive, and using old-school road maps which cover the front dashboard, we head down Sunset Boulevard to Highway 1 and then head north on the scenic route, which will take us along the Pacific coast and through the redwood forests into Washington State.

The landscape is stunning, with trees stretching into the heavens like nature's skyscrapers and the blue Pacific surf crashing against the rocks below. I've never been to this part of the world before, and now I see why people who come from here are so hard to impress when they arrive in parts of the world less blessed by nature.

Yet while the forests of Oregon are indeed awesome to behold, the drive up a two-lane mountain road is not easy for a forty-four-foot RV to navigate, and the drive back down is even harder. But Elisha is game for anything, and when we stop she is the first one to get out of the motor home and fill it up with gas and pull out her own credit card. She's proud of being self-sufficient, and I'm proud of her generous attitude toward everyone and everything. There's nothing like traveling on winding narrow roads in a rented RV to put someone's character into perspective, and

I realize more than I have done just how fine a person Elisha is, and how lucky I am.

When Lawrence takes over his share of the driving, Elisha and I try to get some sleep in the back bedroom of the massive RV.

Now I haven't talked about my real addiction, other than my sweet tooth. I'm addicted to cleaning. I clean my sneakers after I wear them outside. I change the laces in my skates before a hockey game. I wash the dishes before everyone is even done with dinner and I vacuum the apartment two or three times a day.

Lawrence, on the other hand, is a tornado, leaving a trail of destruction in his wake, so I have to give the RV a quick clean before I can possibly expect Elisha and myself to have any chance of falling asleep. Finally we lie down and we're just drifting off when the RV swerves to the right and taps the guardrail. The roads are tight, so I let this slide. Then we tap another guardrail, but it's a bit bigger tap this time.

Elisha gives me the look to go have a chat with Lawrence and make sure he's concentrating. When I get to the front, Lawrence is in the driver's seat, smoking a joint with a bottle of wine nearby while Kim is trying to give him a blow job. If he wasn't already swerving all over the road and she could actually do the job at hand (pardon the pun) I'm afraid he would have taken that RV over the edge and it would have been goodbye to all of us.

But my intervention worked. We made it to George, Washington, in time to see the Tragically Hip, and we got really lucky at the incredible five-star hotel directly next door. E was tough and she could have roughed it, but we would have been crazy not to take this room. And I don't think we could have lasted three minutes—let alone three days—bunking in an RV with Lawrence Longo.

14

FROM LA TO NEW YORK

As we start the 2006–07 season we get a new coach in Los Angeles, and it's like getting a new boss anywhere: the first thing that comes to mind is the question "Are they going to like me?" There's always the chance that the new guy will want to clean house, and if he cleans me out, it won't be because I didn't give Marc Crawford my very best effort.

Everyone calls him "Crow." He looks a bit like one, with intense eyes and perfectly gelled hair, and in profile he has a kind of cunning crow-like beak. He's played for the Vancouver Canucks, he's done a lot of time in the minors, and he won a Stanley Cup as head coach in Colorado, though given the all-star lineup on the bench I think Lawrence Longo could have coached that team to a Cup, even while he was in full RV relaxed mode.

Crow last coached the Vancouver Canucks, but got fired after the team never made it past the second round of the playoffs in his six seasons with them (in fact, they never made it past the first round three times, and never made the playoffs at all twice under Crow). In the world of pro sport recycling, it was Crawford's lone Stanley Cup in 1996 that made him our bench boss a decade later.

Crow has a reputation as being a bit of a crazy man. He was the coach for Vancouver when Todd Bertuzzi sucker-punched Steve Moore—allegedly at

Crawford's command. And as I get to know Crow, I can absolutely believe he told Bertuzzi to go take Moore's head off as payback for Moore's hit on the Canucks captain Markus Näslund a few games earlier. So Bertuzzi attacks Moore in a game in March 2004, and winds up ending Moore's career. (Moore sued Bertuzzi for $68 million in damages. The suit was settled in 2014.)

Crawford's Vancouver reputation doesn't do him justice. He really is nuts: he loses his shit on the bench like no other coach I have ever seen. He kicks guys in the back when they're on the bench and he's unhappy with them, and he grabs guys' jerseys and pulls them inches from his face while he's screaming with ferocity. I mean, the veins are popping out of his neck.

This is new to most of us. Anytime Andy Murray tried to yell like that you'd be tapping the leg of the guy beside you in a "hey don't miss this pussy trying to actually scare us" kind of way. Andy Murray was a joke when it came to the intimidation department. Marc Crawford scares the shit out of me at times.

We're six games into my new season with Marc Crawford and things are going great. I have one goal and three assists and I'm playing more than fifteen minutes a night. Before tonight's game against Detroit I spend some time sitting on our bench at the Staples Center looking at the fresh ice and the empty stands and I have Steve Yzerman's words running through my head about just shutting up and playing hockey. In every game I've played against Detroit since I was traded to LA, I've been too pumped up and not focused on the little things. I was more focused on taking a run at Cheli or beating Draper in face-offs. Tonight, though, I settle in and play a focused game. We lose, 3–1, but I score our only goal.

As the season wore on, we lost more than we won. Crow's constant screaming at us created a different kind of toxic environment from the one Andy Murray had created. Murray was the high school math teacher trying to bombard us with information he didn't understand while Crawford was the wild-eyed gym teacher who'd once heard the roar of the crowd, and figured if he roared loud enough at us, then we'd respond.

There was one time I left him speechless, though, and that was during a practice. Halfway through he's screaming at us about this drill we'd fucked up. I'm not paying attention to his "explanation" because I can't listen to him anymore.

We were doing a break-out drill where you go into the opposing zone at speed and then come back out a few times, and on the last break-out you dump the puck in. I had the puck and because I hadn't been listening I dumped it in too early, right into the corner of the rink where Crawford was standing, watching the drill.

He didn't see the puck coming and I watched it heading toward him in slow motion. It smacked him right on the forehead. It didn't knock him out but it knocked him down. His stick and gloves went flying, and there was blood flowing from his head onto the ice. He knew it was me because the last thing he saw was the puck on my stick. He couldn't kick me off the ice because the medics were hauling him off it, to sew him up. But he gave me the death stare as he skated off, and I knew that one way or another, I wasn't going to be here long.

I'm also getting tired of Los Angeles. I mean, there are only so many days at the beach. Yes, I did love the city, but as that season wore on I wasn't excited by its possibilities. I was bored by the routine of the place, the endless sunshine, the same talk in the locker room of grabbing beers at Harry O's after the game or buying a new boat for the cottage in Muskoka or the latest thing the wife/girlfriend/mistress did with your money that is both a boast and a gripe and is always tedious.

Still, by the All-Star break at the end of January 2007, everything is going well with my season. I'm playing more than fifteen minutes a night under the lash of Marc Crawford, and he pretty much leaves me alone. The team, though, is awful. We've won sixteen games so far, and lost thirty-four.

We're in twenty-ninth place out of thirty teams, and last in the Western Division. Fuck me, Andy Murray had us playing better than Stanley Cup–winning genius Marc Crawford. It's depressing to be playing well and losing so much.

Brendan Shanahan has signed with the New York Rangers and loves it. The team and city have been a rebirth for him. After nineteen years in the NHL he says he feels alive playing before a true hockey crowd at Madison Square Garden. And, of course, there's New York City awaiting you after the game.

Shanny is meant to play for the Rangers. He looks so good in the red, white, and blue jersey—Clark Kent with a little more edge. Shanny is like the woman who walks into a room and instantly gets everyone's attention. He drinks the best wine and wears the best suits and can cross his legs in a way that makes him look even smarter and richer than he is.

After our final game before the All-Star break—a 3–2 loss to Phoenix—I hustle to LAX for my red-eye flight to New York. I'm going to visit Elisha, who is in New York shooting a movie called *My Sassy Girl*, but I'm also going to see Shanny. The Rangers aren't playing well this year either, and because of the season I'm having, I know Shanny is confident in planting a seed with Glen Sather about making a trade for me.

Elisha was tired from long days of shooting, so on my first night in town I met up with Shanny for dinner at Dos Caminos in the West Village. He was with a few guys from the team, and it was awkward, as it almost felt like an audition. My reputation with the rest of the league at the time was not very good, so even though the legend that is Shanahan is vouching for me it's almost like I still need to be vetted by the mob.

"Just keep it simple, Sean," Shanny told me. "Drink a beer or two, talk about nothing, laugh at the right time, and the guys will be able to say you're normal. That's all we want." Shanny's strategy was to softly introduce me to some of the players on the team so that when he broached the topic with Sather or with coach Tom Renney he could say, "Some of the guys met him the other night and thought he was a good guy."

In truth, the guys weren't tough on me at all. There were a few young players there, like Jed Ortmeyer and Ryan Hollweg, along with Matt Cullen and the Rangers PR guy, John Rosasco, who was an important voice when it came to talking to the Rangers management. JR had a lot of influence on Glen Sather and he and Shanny were buddies. Shanny coached me with his eyes from across the table to make sure I said the right things.

I would have said just about anything to stay in New York. The energy of the great city's streets was exactly what I was craving. Initially the glitter of Hollywood had attracted my attention, but now the bullshit scene of fake friends and "what can you do for me?" attitude was wearing thin. Now I wanted some of New York's grit. I wanted to walk down Broadway through the hordes of tourists and say that I lived here.

Elisha is working fifteen-hour days, and I'm not seeing much of her. When you date someone who works and travels as hard as we do, you understand the sacrifice. We went to dinner once while I was there.

I talked about how much I loved it here, and she listened. At no point did she say, "Well, that wouldn't be good for us." She was aspirational like me, and she said she'd love to work in New York, and do a play on Broadway, but her schedule was locked for the next year. Mine, as a pro athlete, was not, in that I could be traded in the time it took to make a phone call. She definitely felt that it wouldn't be easy if I got traded to New York, because long distance is never easy. But we were both confident that if I did move east, we could make it work. We certainly wanted to make it work.

I flew back to LA focused on playing well. And hoping that by doing that, I'd get the call to come to the center of the world and become a New York Ranger.

———

It didn't take long. On February 5, 2007, I'm in a Macy's department store in a mall in Tampa, Florida, with my mother and my grandmother, who lives sixty miles down the road in Sarasota. Mom has flown here from Toronto to spend some time with me because it's easier than getting out to Los Angeles, and maybe she's here because of mother's intuition. Shanny has told me that he's had conversations with Glen Sather about making the deal happen.

Tomorrow we play Tampa Bay, but when I packed my bags for this road trip I put a little extra gear into the mix—two extra suits, extra underwear, my lace-up boots, and my leather jacket, in case I was going somewhere colder.

While we're hanging out in the mall, my cell phone rings and on the other end of the line is Dean Lombardi. Usually this is the worst phone call a pro athlete can receive because it means your life is about to be turned upside down, but I'm ready for it. We're programmed to say good-bye to our friends and teammates at the drop of a hat. It doesn't matter if you've been with them for six years or two weeks—you live always ready to be on the move. The news is always a blow, and you feel a surge of emotion at having to leave. But this time the call is different.

Dean comes straight to the point: he tells me that I've been traded to the New York Rangers, and he gives me Glen Sather's phone number. He tells me I have to get in touch with Slats to organize my trip to New York.

My call with Glen was like any call you have with him (as I would learn): direct, to the point, and quick. "We're happy to have you," he said. "Get here as soon as possible, mix things up and get our guys going."

My life path is about to change, and the disappointment that my mom and nana feel about me having to fly to New York tonight turns into pleasure when they realize how happy I am. We take a taxi back to the hotel so I can get my bags and head to the airport. I kiss them goodbye and walk off to a new beginning as a Broadway Blueshirt.

15

I LOOK GOOD IN BLUE

When you start with a new team, there are so many moving parts that you usually don't remember much when the dust settles. But this time, I remember everything. My senses were on high alert, just as I imagined they would be when I pulled the Ranger jersey over my head for the first time. It felt like a second skin. The blue matches my eyes, and red is my favorite color. And the Rangers have restored the hockey cosmos to its proper order: they've given me No. 16. The number I wore until I made the NHL. I take it as a sign that I'm in the right place.

Seeing Shanahan in the dressing room feels good. This is the first time I've seen him since the trade, though he texted me once the deal was done to say "Get ready!" He's his usual suave self, as if this is just another day at the office, but I think I detect a wink. Seeing Jaromír Jágr there makes me kind of starstruck. He comes up to me and shakes my hand and says, "Nice to meet you." Before the trade Jágr asked New York management why they needed to trade for me, because he thought I was a goon. After our first game together, he said he wanted me on his line.

The game is across the Hudson River in New Jersey, and I'm getting my first taste of how different road trips are when you play on the East Coast as opposed to the West. In New York you can take the bus to games in New Jersey, Long Island, and Philadelphia, and everywhere else in the East is a short flight away. Even Florida. Playing on the East Coast can literally add years to a player's career.

My first game was to be across the Hudson against the Devils in New Jersey. I was fired up the moment I hit the ice for our warm-up. A weird thing always happens in hockey when a new guy arrives with his new team: he scores a point in his first game. It happens so often that no one is surprised by it.

Tom Renney is our coach and he throws me out on the power play, and just like that I have my first point as a Ranger—I get an assist fifteen minutes into the first period, a little more than a minute after the Devils open the scoring. Game on.

In the second period, a new game begins, one that will play out for my entire career as a Ranger. I snag a turnover at center and then turn up ice, stickhandling around a few Devils. I take D-man Colin White wide and make a nifty move to the inside and it's now just me and the Devils goalie, Mr. Martin Pierre Brodeur.

I don't have much room after I beat White, and Marty plays it perfectly, like the Vezina-Hart-Stanley Cup–winning goalie he is, taking most of my angle away. I bury a shot in his chest and actually try to pull up before I get to him but we both go down. We get to our feet and Marty pushes me with both hands and I remember thinking, "This fucking guy, I actually tried to pull up," and I plow my stick into Marty's solar plexus. You might say that the Devils fans instantly saw me as Public Enemy No. 1, and one of the greatest New York Ranger feuds was born with our friends in the Meadowlands. The night was February 6, 2007, and my new mission— after taking Manhattan—was to find out every personal detail on Marty Brodeur that I could get. For the next time we met.

All I really knew about New York was that it was a place I wanted to live—but I had no idea where. The handful of players who stayed in

Manhattan all lived on the Upper West Side because of the easy access to the West Side Highway, which was the route to the Rangers' practice rink about an hour's drive north of the city near Tarrytown, New York, and where the team's owner, James Dolan, whose family used to own Cablevision, kept his fleet of airplanes and helicopters.

Every NHL team has a guy that handles team travel, hotels, and meals on the road, as well as helping players find a place to hang their hat. In New York, Jason Vogel is the go-to guy for the Rangers, and the Knicks and he helped me with the hunt to find a furnished apartment to rent for the remainder of the season.

Despite Jason's friendly warnings, I wound up choosing the worst place a person could live in New York City: Times Square. The place is a total assault on the senses—from the streets constantly jammed with people going to Broadway shows and the tourists getting their tongues sunburned from walking around with their mouths open in astonishment to the neon signs and video screens that light the place up like it's high noon when it's actually midnight.

Even so, this choice was about me staying on theme, which was to absolutely immerse myself in New York City. What better place to live than the center of it all? So I moved into a furnished one-bedroom apartment sixteen floors above the M&M'S store in Times Square. It was as far from LA as I could get.

I didn't have a car in New York, so I relied on carpooling to practices with Jed Ortmeyer and Ryan Hollweg. They were gritty, hard-nosed Rangers who were both good guys. Hollweg was a California kid who liked to party hard and to play video games and guitar in his spare time, but he worked his ass off at the rink. Ortmeyer was from Omaha, and had played for Red Berenson at the University of Michigan. He was a grinder as well, with the work ethic of a champion. He drove to the practice facility in Tarrytown in his black GMC Denali, and since both guys were usually as tired as I was from being out the night before, the ride wasn't exactly Fury Road. It was a very quiet forty-five-minute trip coming and going, because after practice, we all just wanted to get back home to go to sleep.

On my fourth day living in Times Square, after treating myself to some local cuisine—my first New York pastrami sandwich from a classic New York deli—I was pickpocketed on my walk home. Welcome to New York.

Once I'd recreated the contents of my wallet—which included a three-hour detour to the Department of Motor Vehicles, a true New York initiation—I purchased a new wallet that was attached to a chain which clipped onto my belt loop. But I had to admit, I was starstruck—I even loved getting pick-pocketed in this city.

What I do not love is where things stand with me and Elisha. Not good, in short. Elisha is great, and she's a Canadian girl, so she gets hockey. She understands the game and the players, and she knows that this is a big step up for me, and she couldn't be more supportive. But her life is in LA and mine is here. And from the moment I got to New York it's been like being in a bullet train. Non-stop New York. I was totally focused on succeeding here. As much as I loved Elisha, I knew I wanted to stay in New York for the rest of my life. Elisha and I have about two months left in the tank at this point, and our phone calls become less frequent as we both stop sacrificing sleep to make up for the time difference between us. When we broke up it was over the phone, and Elisha had contempt for me because she thought I was bailing on the relationship. And in truth, I was bailing, before things got really bad between us. I needed to follow my New York dream and Elisha needed her life in LA. Of course, karma would soon come back to punch me in the face.

On February 9, 2007, I made the ten-minute stroll from Times Square to the Garden to play my first game in Manhattan against the team I was supposed to play against when I got traded here, the Tampa Bay Lightning. I feel like it's the Stanley Cup Final because I'm on top of the world.

The old dressing room at MSG was so small and cramped that you could touch the ceiling. The trainer's room had three tables and a cold tub/ ice machine in the back. The guys who worked helping with laundry and hauling water bottles and moving sticks from the dressing room to the bench were real New Yorkers. These guys were Teamsters who also worked on movie sets in the city, and they talked with heavy accents like they were straight out of a Scorsese movie. "Fuck you" was a term of endearment from these guys.

The hallways of MSG were lined with photos of the legendary performances the place had seen over the years: Zeppelin, the Stones, Aretha Franklin, Steve Martin, Sinatra, Messier in 1994, Joe Louis, George Harrison, Billy Joel (sixty-five times), the 1976 Democratic Convention, the Jackson 5, Wrestlemania, Ali vs. Frazier (three times).

The moment you walk into the Garden, a feeling starts to tingle in your veins, like the buzz of it is going to lift you up into the air. This is no longer a place where I come to play in once a year or every few years. This is now home.

Holy shit, this is special.

About halfway through the game, I take a Michael Nylander pass from the half-boards. I take a single stride as my bottom hand slides up toward my top hand, and the flex in my Easton snaps the puck off my blade into the top corner past Johan Holmqvist for my first goal as a New York Ranger. We're now up 4–0 on the Lightning, and the crowd starts the A-V-E-R-Y chant. MSG is chanting my fucking name. This is the big time.

A week later in Carolina we win 5–2. I get two assists on the power play, more than sixteen minutes of ice time, and we've won three in a row. It's an away game, but I know they're chanting back home. In New York.

On February 17, we play Philadelphia in our barn. They're a traditional Ranger enemy, and it's the first time that I square off for a fight at center ice. I'm thinking Ali vs. Frazier, and of course, Frazier was a son of Philly.

We're ten minutes into the game when Todd Fedoruk of the Flyers goes berserk, elbows Jágr in the head, trips Petr Průcha as he skates behind him, and takes a run at pretty much everyone. Crazy. Shanny goes after Fedoruk and there's a scrum and I emerge from it to find myself face-to-face with Mike Richards, and it's on. It's a long fight, and I get some pretty good ones on Richards, and when it's done I throw my hands up on the way to the penalty box. The building goes fucking nuts, and here we go again: A-V-E-R-Y.

On February 18, we beat Chicago 2–1. That's four wins in our last six games.

On February 20, against Marty and the Devils, I receive a penalty for goaltending interference. Yeah, I was starting to like tormenting the guy.

On March 3, against St. Louis, we're down a goal with just under three minutes to play. I bust up the ice and take a drop pass three feet inside the blue line and then bury a slap shot just under the cross bar to tie the score. We win in the shootout.

On March 5, we're playing the Islanders. We have seventy-one points and the Isles have seventy-six, and we're currently in the last playoff spot which means nothing if we don't keep winning. We're eating the pre-game meal and I ask Shanny how come he's not nervous. He laughs and says, "I only get nervous for games in June." This is the first time in my career I'm actually afraid to lose a game. I want this to keep going so we make the playoffs. I feel that this is the first time in my NHL career that I'm "all in" because this team is my team and this city is my city. Whatever it takes, I'll do it. We win 2–1 in the shootout. It's our ninth win since I arrived and the city, which misses nothing, is starting to take notice.

There's a headline in the *New York Post* (which will take a keen interest in me over the years): "A-VERY Good Player . . ." And underneath it: *"Glen Sather has used his magic touch with the recent Sean Avery trade . . ."*

My mom and dad are very happy that I'm in New York, because my mother loves the city and it's only an hour from Toronto by plane. My dad, Al, finds New York too big and noisy, but he brings along his best friend Roly Evelyn to ride shotgun. He's known Roly since he was in his early teens playing golf on the course that Roly's family owned in Scarborough, Ontario. Roly was also one of my biggest fans and would go with my dad to my games in Detroit, Ottawa, Buffalo, Nashville, Montreal, and New York, even making a trip out to LA once for some weekend games.

Roly understood the game on the ice as well as off, and the off-ice game is something that athletes rarely talk about. It's what happens after the game, and specifically after a loss. Players always have guests at games, either home or away, and these guests usually consist of close family and close friends. Then it's a pretty big drop to the next category, which is the "friends of friends" who manage to gain entry to a roped-in waiting area at away arenas and a place they call the "Green Room," the "Wives Room," or the "Players Lounge" at home.

This room is not green and it always has a girlfriend—and sometimes a mistress—and a group of wives sitting at tables dressed in their fancy clothes, chasing kids and balancing the insecurities that come with being a hockey wife and where you fit (or don't fit) in the hierarchy. After a loss, most players are miserable. The last thing we want to do is bullshit with the brother of your mother's co-worker who lives in Colorado, especially if we were a minus-2 in a 6–0 loss.

It's almost impossible to fake it but guys do; they're putting on their best frozen smile and exchanging some painful small talk about what it's like to play in the NHL. I've never understood why people don't read this situation better. Could the thrill of talking to an NHLer who's just had the worst game of his life be so powerful that it kills all reason? I mean, can't they see that this player would rather have taken a slap shot off his foot so he'd have to spend extra time in the ice bath after the game and not be able to hit the Green Room before the bus pulls out?

Most rock bands get on a bus after a concert and drive all night to the next city for the next show the following day, but pro athletes travel on custom 747 jets that have their favorite beverages waiting for them (depending on the next day's schedule, and whether you just won or lost). Well, your drinks will be there regardless, but you can't exactly drown your sorrows if you have a game the next night and a tough game-day skate ahead after the loss you just helped make happen. But you can always try.

We also have gourmet hot meals—win or lose—and we watch movies, or play cards, or read, or listen to music, or watch game tape, or chew painkillers or tobacco to pass the time because it's such a tough way to travel.

Dad's friend Roly was the best at letting us get on our way, but he also knew when to pull out his bag of jerseys to get signed for his friends back home. In New York, he even knew how to ask Henrik Lundqvist to sign a shirt, which can be a dangerous request depending on Hank's game, but Hank always had time for Roly.

Roly knew how to point out a play that I made that didn't show up on the score sheet but was important to being a good NHL player. Roly was also a tonic to the stress my dad, Al, would feel if I wasn't getting enough ice time or I'd been screwed by the referees calling off a deflection goal I'd scored because I had a foot in the crease. Al was beat up worse than me after games because of the emotional roller coaster he put himself on from the warm-up to the final whistle. Roly was always there to make sure they got home safe and sound, and that they hit the road on a full stomach, because nobody liked food more than Roly. He always knew which arena had the best French fries or pretzels.

Roly died a while back, and I'm thinking of him now. It's a cliché, sure, but it's not when you really feel it: I need to spend more time with the people I love.

After a loss to Ottawa—2–1—on March 13, I feel like I need to blow off some steam. We're heading into the home stretch here, and we're two points out of the last playoff spot, with twelve games to go in the season.

So I take a taxi to the part of NYC called Clubland. It's the area on the far west side of Manhattan where a lot of the music and strip clubs with cabaret licenses are found. Even though my Rangers teammates call the most famous arena in the world home, they don't hang out at the real New York hot spots. The guys are more mainstream, but I'm looking to walk on the wild side.

Bungalow 8 is the most exclusive club in New York. I walk up to the door and two of the biggest men I've ever seen are standing there with a velvet rope in front of them. I'll learn that you know you're at an NYC hot spot when you walk up to it and there's actually nobody in line. I approach the men confidently, as if I've been here a million times, and I ask the giant on the right if I might speak with the owner.

He laughs and says, "You mean Amy?"

Yes sir, Amy it is.

"She's busy," he replies.

At this point I know the owner isn't coming out, so I lay my cards on the table. I've learned that humility is one of the most important qualities for success (unless you've just scored a goal at MSG). "Gentlemen," I begin. "My name is Sean Avery and I was just traded from the Los Angeles Kings to the New York Rangers, and I know Bungalow is a legendary spot, so I decided to come by myself and would love to come inside and have a drink." And I'm in.

When I walk through the doors, I'm in a room that resembles a California bungalow. There are palm trees everywhere and murals depicting poolside scenes, and it's small and intimate.

I see Heath Ledger at a table chain-smoking with a few models . . . the Olsen twins at another table also chain-smoking with a bunch of their friends . . . Colin Farrell chats up a pretty blonde and Sienna Miller hangs with some really good-looking friends who are swearing more than a group of guys in a locker room.

The mammoth man at the front door asks if I can hook him up with some Rangers tickets so he can bring his daughter to a game. I tell my new friend named "Disco" that he can come to any game he wants, and I give him my phone number so I'm just a text away.

I didn't think it was going to be this easy, but I'm starting to understand New York City and how much less social bullshit there is here than in LA. Disco introduces me to the Queen of New York Nightlife (she didn't give herself that title) and the owner of Bungalow 8, Amy Sacco, and I shake hands with this lively blond lady who has a voice like a Zamboni engine.

Hockey players did not typically hang out in Amy's bar, but any Jersey girl knows who the Rangers are and Amy is a Jersey girl. Amy became a self-proclaimed Rangerette and started coming to games because I was hanging out in her bar. She took it upon herself to turn the New York Rangers' green room into a revolving cast of A-list models/actors/directors/actresses. At any time you could see the likes of Paul Haggis, Gerard Butler, Scarlett Johansson, and Sienna Miller paying homage to the Blueshirts in the green room.

Amy became a close friend and a golden ticket. Eventually I was one of the few guys on the planet who could walk up to the door of Bungalow 8 and walk right in no matter who I was with or how I was dressed. As a matter of fact, this very thing happened one night when Brendan Shanahan had found his way into the Bungalow after a game and for some reason I was already home.

After the second text from Shanny calling me out for being home already, I walked downstairs to my car, which at that time was a matte black Audi S8 (faster than a Ferrari but a mature four-door), and pounded down 10th Avenue, running red lights until I was double-parked and inside Bungalow. Shanny broke out in laughter when he saw me walking through the crowd à la *Goodfellas*, still wearing my bathrobe.

New York is the city that never sleeps, and since the day I arrived I've been on call.

One night Amy connects me to Mary-Kate Olsen, one half of the infamous twins who starred in *Full House* for eight seasons, starting from when they were babies. MK is very smart and she loves music and socializing over cocktails and cigarettes. We hit it off and talk fashion and music and finally around 4 A.M. we both walk out onto West 27th Street a little worse for wear.

The funny thing about this story is that I actually became very close with her security guard, Bill Durney (and remain so to this day). Along with his partner, Dale, Bill had taken care of Mary Kate and Ashley since they were little girls. Everyone slags on these girls, but they're Hollywood success stories and have grown up to be successful business women. Not many child stars end up as normal and successful as they have done, and considering these girls' fame and fortune, they've made it through the fire not only alive but very, very well.

I also met Scarlett Johansson, who had begun her beautiful, blond ascent into the starry ether that was the home of the A-list actors, and Amy Sacco introduced me to her the same way: as the star player for the New York Rangers. I always got a little embarrassed when she did that, but she knew what she was doing and it was OK because it was Amy.

And thank you, Amy, because Scarlett pulled out a joint and asked if I wanted to join her in enjoyment of same, and so we went to Amy's private office in Bungalow 8 which was normally off-limits unless Clooney or Pitt needed some privacy.

Privacy was also part of Amy's genius. She never blabbed to the media about who or what happened in her club, and the giants guarding the door were so smooth at lifting that velvet rope that I'm willing to wager the

NYPD—who were dying to get a look inside—never did because those savvy doormen would clock an undercover cop at fifty paces.

Scarlett and I enjoyed the joint and made small talk—yes, I had spent the night with the Stanley Cup, and she had spent the night cheering for the Yankees, but she still liked the Rangers—and we were feeling the vibe of the "groovy cool" music DJ Uncle Mike was spinning for the club, which drifted through the closed door of Amy's lair. I could see that Scarlett wanted something in that moment, and I don't think it was me in particular, but she leaned in and we kissed.

We sort of just flowed back out to the club to sit and enjoy the music pumping through our bodies. NYC nightclubs play the music so loud that conversation becomes difficult, so we chilled and smoked a few cigarettes. I liked her, and I did the same thing I did when I met Rachel, at least in spirit. I gave her a bit of unexpected sass. I got up from the table and extended my hand to her and said it was a pleasure and I think she's a very interesting woman (this always confuses women because they immediately question whether I think they're pretty enough). I gave her a kiss on the cheek and walked out. I never asked for her number.

We went out a few times after that night and it was always set up by Amy, telling me she was going for a drink with Scarlett and I should come. I smile every time I think about Amy Sacco.

On March 16, 2007, we play Atlanta. We lose in a shootout, which means we still get a point. And I score again. The next night, we play Boston. It's St. Patrick's Day, and in New York City that means everyone is Irish for the day and there's a massive parade up Fifth Avenue and booze everywhere—it's like Mardi Gras crossed with New Year's Eve. Tonight, the luck of the Irish was certainly with me, as I had one of those games where everything bounced the right way. Every fourth shift I seemed to come off the ice with a point.

It's my first four-point game in the NHL and it feels like I'm flying.

I realize on this night that I'd played too hard over my career, and what I mean by that is that I played holding my stick too tight. I always wanted to play so very well for my team and for our fans and for the hot girl I'd invited to the game, but I didn't have the carefree attitude that most "pure" goal scorers have been blessed with. When I get in tight on the goalie and have some time to pick my spot I've been rushing my shot, and invariably bury it in the goalie's chest. Easy save.

But tonight I'm loose and seeing everything on the ice, and patience runs through my blood. The lights are brighter and the fans are louder and while I may have had an assist from lucky St. Patrick, I know that I've worked all my life to be in this place. It's a huge moment for me as a person and as a player. I know that New York has had a big influence in this transformation. I don't think that how I played before was wrong, because it got me to this point. But I was gaining a new confidence in myself and my game because now I realized that not only could I play at the highest level, I was also a pretty good player.

On March 21, the guys in orange and black from the City of Brotherly Love come to town, and I am in a hospitable mood. This is the most comfortable I've ever been in my own skin since I can actually remember, and my life in this city has inspired me to raise the level of my game to a place that excites me. *If you can make it here . . .*

I score my fifteenth and sixteenth goals of the season tonight and we send the Flyers back to Philly on the wrong end of a 5–0 game. It's one that they'll remember, as my teammate Colton Orr showed everyone in MSG tonight why he is hands down the toughest guy in the NHL, and easily the toughest man I've ever played with or against.

The Flyers' Todd Fedoruk picks up where he left off against us a month ago, and resumes his maniacal freight-train routine, trying to run our guys through the walls of MSG and onto 7th Avenue (which is actually six stories below ice level). We knew that this was going to happen, and Colton

Orr knows his job, so he's ready and waiting because he's keenly aware that if Shanny has to step in again, then he's probaby looking for work elsewhere. He would have been losing sleep over the fact that he hadn't been out on the ice the last time Fedoruk went apeshit and Shanny had to handle it.

So Fedoruk nails four guys before Colton gets on the ice and puts a stop to it. They exchange a couple of punches, and tussle a bit, and then Colton lands a ferocious right to Fedoruk's jaw. I was standing five feet away on the ice when Fedoruk took the best punch that Colton has ever thrown, and it's the only time I've ever truly believed that a player just died in front of my eyes. I swear I thought he was dead.

Fedoruk is lying on his back with both arms bent at a ninety-degree angle and they are convulsing slightly. MSG is dead silent. New York fans can be hard on visiting players, but I've also seen them give standing ovations to stars like LeBron James on his fifty-point night against the Knicks. They appreciate excellence.

They also have compassion, and now they're in shock as the paramedics and doctors surround Fedoruk and the stretcher is wheeled onto the ice. I look at Colton sitting in the penalty box, a huge ice pack on the hand that just did that to Fedoruk, and I know by the look on his face that he thinks he may have just killed Todd.

One moment you want to kill a guy and the next you're being escorted to a mock prison cell wishing you'd taken just a little off the finishing punch. I don't wish the job of NHL heavyweight on anyone.

The whole arena and both benches exhale in relief when we see that Fedoruk is conscious, talking, and has movement as he's carted off the ice on the stretcher. Although Colton did come back to play for a few more seasons in the NHL, this fight really affected him, and he was never the same after it.

It's the end of March and we're battling with nine other teams to secure a playoff spot. To give you an idea of how tight it is, today, March 25, sees us sitting in the fourteenth spot in the NHL with eighty-five points. Sixteen teams will make the playoffs, and we have a three-game road trip ahead of us. Tonight's opponent, the New York Islanders, are currently out of the playoffs, and yet they're only two points behind us. We're all laser focused to make sure that we're not going to lose our spot.

My roommate on the road is Colton Orr. Even though Colton is the toughest player in the NHL, he's a real teddy bear off the ice—if a teddy bear had paws that look like he put them through a meat grinder. Off the ice, he keeps to himself a lot, going to movies alone and not really hanging out, but I figured that was just fine, because as long as the Rangers needed a tough guy, then Colton Orr had a job in the NHL. We complemented each other, but were in competition. I stirred things up with my agitating and now Colton protected the talent from abuse by our opponents.

Colton has some demons, and sometimes he's too honest with everyone around him. I say that because honesty can leave you open to people with ulterior motives being able to use that honesty against you. For instance, Colton had been sober for a while, but when we were in Montreal a while back he went out and tied one on. A well-known punk of a Montreal drug dealer brought him back to our hotel room in the middle of the night and demanded money from me, money he said Colton owed him. Colton was out of it, and this guy was trying to rough me up, but he picked the wrong guy. I had both my hands around his neck and slammed him against the wall and told him he was leaving now and never coming back. He agreed.

The next day, Colton sat the entire team and coaching staff down and told everyone about his slide from sobriety. I know he felt he had to do it, but I certainly wasn't going to tell anyone, and I could see that some of the guys didn't take this information the way he meant it to be taken. They just looked at him as weak.

But tonight, in another "must win" game, Colton scores our first goal of the night and his second goal of the season and the guys on the team are jumping up and down on the bench because we're so happy for him. Colton makes all our lives easier because just having him dressed and in the lineup protects us. No one wants to leave an arena the way Todd Fedoruk left it.

Colton's goal is the only one we score in regulation, and the game goes into OT. Michael Nylander wins it for us in overtime.

Our next game is in Montreal, and the Habs are another of the teams swarming around the same playoff spot as we are. They're three points behind us. In my opinion, Montreal is the hardest NHL rink to play in, not just because of the ghosts of all the greats who have worn the *bleu, blanc, et rouge*, but also because I made a comment about French players wearing protective visors running around and taking shots at guys and from that day forward I was Public Enemy No. 1 in Montreal.

In truth, though, the Canadiens were the only other NHL team that showed any interest in me, and they even invited me to their training camp, but I picked the Wings because I knew Kris Draper. So I always had a soft spot for Montreal. As I said before, I enjoyed playing the character of the villain, but that didn't automatically make it easy. The way I got motivated was partly through my desire to win, and a lot through the people yelling and screaming at me to fail. They fueled me and I played into it and that's how my engine ran.

In Montreal we would walk to Bell Centre and autograph seekers would hound us for autographs—not kids but the professionals. I would tell them to *"va-t'en foutre"* (which means "go fuck yourself") in the hope they would tell their friends that it was all true, I was the biggest scumbag on skates. I enjoyed messing with them.

We lost in Montreal that night, 6–4, and now, with five games left in the season, we pretty much have to win them all if we don't want to be golfing come the playoffs in April.

On the very last day of March, we play the Flyers in Philly. We open the scoring three and a half minutes in, but the Flyers tie us twenty seconds later. Two minutes after that I feed the puck to Matt Cullen, and he pops it to Ryan Callahan, and we get the lead and never give it up. We won that huge game 6–4, and I played more than eighteen minutes.

On April Fool's Day we play our biggest game of the season at MSG against the Toronto Maple Leafs. We have eighty-nine points and still occupy the fourteenth playoff position, and Toronto has eighty-seven points and aren't in the playoffs at all. Yet. This season is going to go right to the very last game. Toronto scores first, and then I tie it with an unassisted goal, my seventeenth of the season. I get an assist on our fourth goal, and then I score my eighteenth—again unassisted—on our way to a 7–2 win over the Leafs.

Oh, and near the end of the first period I had a fight with Darcy Tucker that wound up with me on top. I have a Gordie Howe Hat Trick with a goal to spare.

The sweetest sound is the eruption of MSG with the A-V-E-R-Y chant after I score both goals. I've captured the hearts and minds of the New York Ranger fans. These blue-collar cops and firefighters and Teamsters love my "no fucks given" attitude. I'm representing the workers of New York, and hard work is respected more than flash in the world's greatest city.

It's April 5, and Montreal is in town to play us. It's our second-last game of the regular season, and Montreal is two points behind us and chasing a play-off berth. Because of my whole new level of game, I'm playing on a line with the great Jaromír Jágr.

He was not on my favorite-player lists when I was growing up because Brett Hull took up all of that space, and I didn't realize what a machine this guy was until I played beside him. He is easily the strongest player in the NHL—able to outmuscle anyone and protect the puck as he works his magic. After he and I assist on our third goal and we meet in the pile to hug and high-five, I realize for a second how small I look beside a mountain of a man like Jágr. But then I shake it off and pretend I never saw myself in this mirror.

He was crazy when it came to superstitions. When he went on a hot scoring streak, he wouldn't cut his fingernails or toenails. And some of his streaks were pretty long. It must have been painful to skate that way, especially if he ever took a shot off the toe. I've seen guys who cut their nails pull their toenail out of their sock after getting a blast in the foot, but that was Jags. Superstition in the NHL is really more about routine than anything else—you do the same thing over and over, and you don't want to break the routine because it could disrupt your game. Not cutting your nails, however, was in a class by itself.

Jágr was a big kid in a big man's body. When he wasn't playing or practicing hockey he watched cartoons and ate cereal and slept a lot. I mean, he slept fourteen hours a day minimum.

We won the game against Montreal 3–1, and other teams chasing us lost, which helped us squeak in. We're going to be in the playoffs.

I realize my life is now the best it's ever been and all of a sudden all the pains of a long season go away. I'm logging nearly twenty minutes a night, and we're going to take on Atlanta in the quarterfinals for the 2007 Stanley Cup.

After the last game of the regular season I'm feeling so confident and happy that I want to celebrate. So I decide to expand my nightclub repertoire, and pick the Beatrice Inn, which, true to my nature of taking the hard way, was actually the most difficult club to get into in New York City.

Angelo and Todd were roommates who also ran the door to the Beatrice, and part of their job was to read the face of every person trying to gain entry to the basement of this West Village apartment building, which was kitty corner to the Cubbyhole, New York's famous lesbian bar. You couldn't buy your way in, and if you looked like you were going to hit on every woman in the place, that wouldn't work either. You just had to give off the vibe that you belonged inside.

Banking on my success at Bungalow 8, I walked up to the door of the Beatrice and asked to speak with the owner. I can't remember if Todd or Angelo was the one who actually went inside and brought Matt Abramcyk out. When he looked at me I could see the confusion and excitement on his face, because Matt was a born-and-bred New Yorker and a diehard Ranger fan who still wore his Starter jacket from the sainted year of 1994, when his favorite player Mark Messier ended the Curse and brought the Stanley Cup back to town.

New York loves winners, and the city expects its sports teams to win every game and every championship, but even when they don't, the love doesn't die. When the Rangers won the Cup in 1994 it was not only a win for the city but also for hockey, because it put the game back in the spotlight, even though New York has always been a hockey town. The Rangers are as respected and loved as any team here because they're part of the sports fabric of the city. People still talk about Greschner and Duguay and the hot models they had on their arms in the 1970s, and about Messier and Madonna in the 1990s, and now they talk about me.

The Beatrice was so exclusive—no, check that, so curated—that they would not automatically admit a Yankee, Met, or Knick, and certainly no visiting players. Actually most professional athletes would not fit comfortably inside because the ceilings were just under seven feet.

Matt had been to a few games since my arrival in New York and he knew exactly who I was. He walked me into the Beatrice and it was like being backstage at a Victoria's Secret show, as that's the only other venue where

I've ever seen so many models in one place. The front part of the room housed the bar and six different seating areas, and the Pink Room was a very small—maybe six-by-six-foot—room which opened onto the bar so that you could order drinks without having to leave the room. This was handy if you were the new celebrity couple trying to be undercover on the couch in the corner (just to be clear, the Beatrice was the worst place you could go to be undercover).

It was open every night of the week, and a little after 11 P.M. the place would fill with models and young celebrities and fashion designers and downtown hipsters. It seems like a contradiction, but the Beatrice was the type of place that drew celebrities who didn't like to go to splashy clubs. Kirsten Dunst and Josh Hartnett and Sophia Coppola all liked the Beatrice. It was a safe space for young "New York Hollywood."

The back room was a five-step walk-up with banquette seating built around the perimeter of the entire room. On busy nights you couldn't see the other side of the room because the cigarette smoke was so thick. That's where the music happened. Chloë Sevigny's brother, Paul, was the DJ. She was there a lot, too.

Usually when you meet the people who own clubs, it's simply a business relationship: you spend money and they take care of you. The relationships that I found with Matt at the Beatrice and Amy at the Bungalow were special. I was connecting with people on this small but mighty island, and it was connecting with me.

And I was having a fabulous time. Sure, I was on a Stanley Cup–winning team my first year in the NHL, but I didn't get to play in the playoffs because I was injured. I know it's a cliché to say that you should never take the post-season for granted because you never know if you'll get there again, but it's true. It feels like I have been in the league for ages since that championship run with the Red Wings, and that five seasons later I'm in my first true playoff series. And I'm getting part of the credit for that, since the Rangers have been 17–12 since I arrived from LA, and have moved up from twenty-first place in the NHL into the Stanley Cup playoffs.

I've always played well under pressure, and it invigorates me, but the feeling as we fly to Atlanta is much different from what I'm used to because usually the pressure comes from something that I said. Or from something that I did to a team we're about to play again, and it's the forty-second game of the regular season.

This pressure is what a guy's career is made of, and how you respond to it is what leads to glory and praise and more zeros before the decimal sign on your paycheck. All the guys on the plane are aware that how we perform in the playoffs is what management will use to determine a player's value. If you have a bad playoffs, or "disappear" in the tighter, harder game that the post-season dictates, it's not the end of the world. But the only way you can stick around in the league if you have a crap playoff run is by scoring a lot in the regular season, because regular season goals still hold a lot of value. And there are some guys who always just shine in the playoffs, like Shanny or Stevie Y.

I look around, and this plane ride to Atlanta is exactly the same as every other plane ride I've made in the NHL. There are guys around the card table losing money to each other, guys watching movies on their computers, guys catching up on texts to their mistresses (you can use your phone on the team plane), and the training staff are all passed out in deep sleep, catching some hours before the grind begins the moment the plane touches down in Atlanta.

The flight is long enough that guys change out of their suits into sweatpants and kick back with wads of chewing tobacco tucked inside their lips. I never understood why guys are allowed to chew tobacco before a game or in between periods to take the edge off, and yet I'm not allowed to light up a cigarette. (I would do it in the shower so the smoke didn't bother the guys.) Guy Lafleur used to smoke a pack a day, and Scotty Bowman said Lafleur would smoke a cigarette or two between periods. I'm not saying I'm

Guy Lafleur, but seriously, sometimes the double standards of the NHL get to me.

But I'm not going to let them do that now. I'm going to chase the best ashtray ever invented. The Stanley Cup.

I'm really fucking nervous before Game 1. The run that I helped the Rangers go on to make the playoffs is not enough—it got us here, but it's now history. We need to win four here, and then move on to the next twelve wins needed to hoist the Jug.

Ilya Kovalchuk is Atlanta's best player and I'm going to play against his line during the series. He has no idea how much he's going to hate me when this is over. Kovalchuk is one of the most gifted scorers the league has seen in the last twenty years. He's also one of the first Russians who has a nasty edge to him. He doesn't like to get hit and he's wicked with his stick. He's a big guy—six-three and 230 pounds—and he has to fight for space because players are getting bigger and the rink is not, and so the game is getting tougher to play. Kovalchuk is a superstar and he's a hothead, and he brings a lot of emotion to his game. And that gives me a huge opening to do what I do.

During my first shift I slash him hard in the back of the legs—where there's no padding, and where it hurts. I do it each time I'm on the ice with him. He's in shock because nobody has ever done this to him. After each whistle I skate beside him telling him that he's a soft fucking Russian who will never win because it's too hard. I mess with him, adding that losing the series is OK with all the money that he has.

We win the first game 4–3 and I lead the team with seven shots on goal.

On my sixth shift of Game 2 I get to the blue line and dump the puck into Atlanta's end, but it takes a funny bounce off the glass and moves ninety degrees into the empty net. Atlanta goalie Johan Hedberg is standing behind the net where he was anticipating my dump-in, and now he has the kind of look on his face that you might see if you'd told him he was being sent down to play in a Swedish beer league. We have that critical first goal, and I remember how such a fluky goal totally destroyed the confidence of the Vancouver Canucks when I was playing with Detroit. We swept them four straight after we scored from center ice.

But my assignment, Kovalchuk, scores to tie the game early in the third period, and it stays that way until there's just over four minutes left in regulation. I get a bouncing puck on my stick inside the middle of the right circle in Atlanta's end, and I can see Marty Straka heading for the back door. I'm going to fire the puck to him.

It's amazing to think about how fast we process information on the ice. We even see things before they happen based on patterns—it's real-life NASA space-perception testing right here in an NHL game.

In the last possible millisecond I see Shanny skating to my left, and so I fake a snap shot and pass across my body right onto his blade and he fires it across the line for a goal.

We're going back home to MSG up 2–0 in the best of seven series.

I'd be lying if I didn't feel good about this latest "fuck you" to everyone who says I can't play.

I didn't think the atmosphere at MSG could be any more electric until Michael Nylander scores our first goal thirty-two seconds into Game 3. It's like the roof is going to blow off. Nylander also scores our last at 15:54 of the third period to give himself a hat trick and cement our win—7–0 over the Atlanta Thrashers, who are pretty much done. I mean, they had to win this game and we smoked them. The cherry on top is that Ilya Kovalchuk finally blows his lid at my continual stealth attacks on him and he drops his gloves. Before I know what's happening he throws a heavy Russian right hand square off my nose. My eyes fill with water, and as I skate to the penalty box wiping blood from a broken nose, I smile because I've taken one of the best "pure skill" players in NHL history off his game and rendered him useless. The guy who scored forty-two goals in the regular season has only scored one so far. I promise him that he won't have another goal in the series.

Before Game 4, John Amirante, who has sung "The Star-Spangled Banner" at MSG since around the year I was born (1980), is coming down the home stretch—*"Oh say does that star-spangled banner yet wave/O'er the land of the free, and the home of the brave?"*—and I think I'm having an out-of-body experience because it seems as if the whole arena is moving. I mean, the people, the walls, the rafters—everything is swaying with the anthem.

I know—when the camera pans the guys on the ice and the benches during the national anthem, it looks like they're doing the "I gotta pee really bad" shuffle from skate to skate, or are deep in some Zen-like trance, or are actually praying. It's all true, but there's no way you can tune out the anthem, and I love hearing "The Star-Spangled Banner" as it rises to its conclusion: the land of the free and the home of the brave. How can you beat that?

You feel the surge of emotion from the fans after the anthem and it carries you onto the ice, assuming the ice doesn't crumble like some CGI glacier and we all fall through and splatter on the tracks of Penn Station below us. I swear this building is moving.

The Thrashers strike first, but we tie it a minute later. They score again midway through the second, but with a little more than two minutes left in the period, I dish to Shanny and he scores and Atlanta is done. We add two more in the third and we've swept Atlanta. We're feeling as confident as a team can feel.

Of course, the beauty of the NHL playoffs is that you need to win sixteen games to win the Cup, so no team wins the greatest trophy in sports because their opponent had a bad Sunday afternoon. You can go from high to low as the playoffs progress, and we went from the high of our sweep of Atlanta to considerably lower a couple of weeks later as we went into Game 6 against Buffalo. We were down 3–2 in the series against the Sabres, and preparing for our must-win Game 6, when Shanny received a life-changing email. We were sitting in a hotel suite that the Rangers had reserved for the players to receive treatment, watch games, play cards, snack, and talk shit the way most teams do while they kill time between playoff games. "To prevent distractions" is what they call it.

Shanny's email was, for me, a major distraction. He was being invited to the Met Ball—which is the fashion world's Oscars—by *Vogue*'s famous editor Anna Wintour. A *Vogue* editor's kids went to school with Shanny's kids, and his school drop-offs became a chance for the Upper East Side moms to swoon at the Clark Kent lookalike. Even so, Shanny showed me the email and asked me who she was.

I think in 2007 that I was one of the few—if not the only—professional athlete who knew who Anna Wintour was because I had been reading *Vogue* since my days with the Kings. I was in shock. Why the hell did Shanny get this email and not his fashion fanatic teammate? Sure, he looked great in a tux, but so did I.

I begged him to email *Vogue* back and ask if it would breach the fashion world etiquette to bring his teammate Sean Avery as his date. They wrote back that usually a date is not permitted, but this time, they would allow it. I was ecstatic.

Of course, the Met Ball was scheduled for the same night as Game 7 against Buffalo.

Before Game 6, I was nervous. The entire team was on edge, and you could have heard a hair from Jágr's mullet drop in our dressing room. My body was banged up, and because this was my first playoff grind on top of the eighty-four-game regular season (due to the trade, I played two more than the usual eighty-two), I was tired mentally and physically.

By no means did I want to lose Game 6 so that we could attend the Met Ball, but I used it as a crutch, something that would soothe the sting of defeat that I believe we all felt was coming our way. Buffalo was simply a better team.

All our gung-ho momentum from winning four straight over the Thrashers crashed into the reality that was the Buffalo Sabres. They had won the Presidents' Trophy with 113 points—nineteen better than us— and had dispatched the Islanders in the first round of the playoffs four games to one.

They finished us off in six. Aside from the first game, which they won 5–2, the others were all one-goal games, with a couple going to overtime.

I take this loss personally. I think we went out because I didn't know how to block shots. No one had ever taught me, which is not surprising when you consider that most of the assistant coaches I had—the guys responsible for teaching shot-blocking—had never played pro. I wasn't afraid of blocking shots, but because I didn't have the technique, I looked timid. I didn't know how to properly position myself in the shooting lanes to take down some shots, and that ended up being the difference.

I'd played the best hockey of my life since arriving in New York, and the victory against Atlanta had been the kind of professional experience that makes you think you can do anything. And even after we lost Game 6 to Buffalo, at home, 5–4, our fans gave us a standing ovation, because they believed we'd done our best. And yet part of me knew that I could have played better. I realized now, after this devastating loss to Buffalo, that I still had a lot to learn. But I took to heart a piece that appeared in the *New York Times*, in which our coach, Tom Renney, said about me: "Pound for pound, I don't know if there is a tougher, more engaging player in the game than that guy right there."

I knew the Met Ball would be filled with every famous actress and model in the world, and I also knew that two New York Rangers would stick out like a sore thumb—but a very well-dressed and interesting sore thumb.

I pulled out the black Prada tux that I bought two weeks after arriving in New York because I'd expected to be attending many black-tie affairs in the city that never sleeps, though this was my first. Our black Town Car pulled up to the steps of the Metropolitan Museum of Art and all I could see at the top of the stairs were flashbulbs.

Now, I'm used to media attention at this point in my career, but walking up those stairs felt like taking the last 100 steps to a summit that I'd only dreamt of, and when I got to the top and saw that the wall of photographers was literally two stories high, I nearly fell back down the steps. Which would not have been the elegant entrance that I had dreamed of making into this world to which I desperately wanted access.

My legs started to shake. I'm telling you, hearing 20,000 screaming fans inside MSG with my career just one bad bounce from ending had nothing on the nerves running through my body as we approached Anna Wintour and Michael Bloomberg, the mayor of New York, who were greeting each guest as they entered Cinderella's ball.

I extend my hand and try to keep it from shaking as I move to pump the hand of the editor-in-chief of *Vogue* (just like in the movies, she had an assistant whispering each approaching person's name into her ear), and I make my first impression unforgettable by saying, "Pleasure to meet you, Mrs. Bloomberg," and then shaking the mayor's hand and saying, "Honor to meet you, Mr. Wintour."

I can't believe I just did that. It's like I was watching myself say the wrong lines in a play.

Shanny, as always, steps in to fix it. He apologizes to Anna Wintour and the mayor of New York City and says, "Sorry about my friend . . . he was very nervous to meet you both."

They laugh.

The Met Ball is also called the East Coast Oscars, and it was filled with movie stars like Cate Blanchett and Renée Zellweger and Cameron Diaz. Rihanna was there, and so was Alicia Keys, and so were Melania and Ivanka Trump, though back then they were just part of the wall of famous faces who drifted by. There were supermodels galore, including Gisele Bündchen and Christy Turlington and Hilary Rhoda, the woman whom I would one day marry. We didn't meet that night, as I was so in awe of it all; I was watching a movie—one that I happened to be in.

I shook my head in wonder. In a few months my life had changed. Now New Yorkers were chanting my name at MSG and yelling it out from car windows as they drove past me on the street, and here I was at the toughest ticket event in New York City—by invitation. Well, invitation once removed, but I was through the magic door. And now that I'd seen life on the other side, this fantasy world of creativity and beauty and success, I wanted to see more. I had to figure out how I could stay a while longer.

16

THE AVERY RULE

At the end of July, after my success with the Rangers, I was feeling good about the future. My salary the previous year had been $1.1 million, and after the way I'd landed in New York and inspired the Rangers (and myself), I was looking for a long-term deal that would give me a nice cash bump and reward me for what I'd contributed to the team.

If they didn't agree, then we'd have to go to arbitration, which is not what anyone wants because it means that there's going to be a lot of mud thrown in your general direction.

But the Rangers wouldn't budge, so we had to go to arbitration.

The day before my arbitration hearing, I did one of the dumbest things I could possibly do. I sent my new friend Larry Brooks, hockey beat maestro of the *New York Post*, a copy of the Rangers' position arguing why they thought I should only be entitled to a $200,000 raise.

Larry wrote: "For in seeking to give Avery just a $200,000 raise over the $1.1 million he earned last season, the Blueshirts simply hammered away at one of their most important players in an astonishingly shortsighted, penny-saved-pound-foolish attack."

Leaking this confidential document was certainly against the rules, and our team's boss, Glen Sather, probably had a feeling I was the one who leaked it. Glen had seen it all but I'm sure this was a first for him. Some of the things he liked about me—my intensity, my fierce hate for the opponent, my "not give a fuck" attitude—were also some of the things that would get me in trouble.

The arbitration hearing was in Toronto, and by the end of the longest day of my life I was shaking and had sweat seeping through my suit jacket. While Glen sat silently and chomped on an unlit cigar, I had to listen to Cam Hope—the husband of Glen's assistant, whom he'd made his assistant GM—trash-talk me.

Sather was the boss and called all the shots, so why wouldn't the secretary's husband be AGM? But Cam Hope did all the dirty work in the arbitrations, and the thing that sent me through the roof was that he'd never played hockey. He was a lawyer from Edmonton who'd been involved in the Canadian Football League Players Association, so he knew something about athletes but he knew shit about hockey. And in the end he got a taste of his own medicine when he called Glen's bluff in his own contract negotiation. When he said he'd walk if he didn't get the cash, Glen said "Get a good pair of walking shoes." He's now GM of a junior hockey team in Victoria, but he was the asshole who told me that New York, despite what they'd said in public, now didn't see me that way at all.

I was devastated. It hurt to hear this, and it was also a bald-faced lie. Larry Brooks defended the truth in print: "Apparently forgotten were all the testimonials delivered to Avery from the Rangers' hierarchy last spring when the winger was repeatedly lauded for the intangibles he brought to the team both on and off the ice upon his Feb. 5 acquisition from the Kings. Apparently forgotten as well were similar testimonials delivered by teammates including Jaromír Jágr, Brendan Shanahan and Henrik Lundqvist."

It's a cruel aspect of the way the game—sorry, the business—works, but it seems to be very much in the spirit of the times. Factories close because the same stuff can be made cheaper in China, jobs-for-life get outsourced, promises are broken, people suffer, and yet the management keeps ticking along doing just fine, paying themselves fat bonuses for their skills at shaving layers off the bottom line.

As a professional athlete, you're trained to think of yourself as an individual who brings the best that he can to the team. Each player adds something special to the mix. That's how teams are built. The Rangers could not find some dude in India to do my job, but they certainly made it sound as if it was truly painful to have to pay me to do what I did for them. As if I was conning them.

The arbitrator awarded me a salary of $1.8 million for the upcoming season, so you could say that I won. Yes, that's more than most of the world makes, but the NHL is not a charity. And I didn't really win at all, because everyone loses in the bitter conflict of arbitration, and not many relationships come out the other side of it as solid as they were when they went in. I mean, it's impossible. But that was the business I was in, and today, if I ever wound up being a GM, I'd probably think the same thing that Sather thought about it all. "It will toughen him up a bit" was his take on arbitration.

Even so, it was worst day of my life to date.

Still, I knew that I wasn't planning on leaving New York, even if the Rangers, in a fit of revenge for my arbitrated salary increase, decided to trade me to hell. I knew I would still live here in the off-season, so I needed to buy an apartment. My first NYC apartment.

I'm still a New York rookie and don't really understand the lofts of Soho yet, so I look a little further north. When I walk into 444 West 19th Street I know that this is home (I'd also later discover that this was, so far, the furthest downtown any Ranger had ever lived. Now they all live in Tribeca). I also know that my aesthetic has changed and that I'm no longer into the Cali hippie Laurel Canyon vibe (a lot of which has to do with the fact that I'm not in Laurel Canyon). I'm into a full-blown *American Psycho* kind of existence and I have two months to renovate 19th Street so that it's ready for me to take Manhattan when training camp opens in September.

Let me be clear with the *American Psycho* reference. Patrick Bateman appeals to my sense of organization, and that's it. For me, routine is everything. Consistency gives me the ability to focus on my job of hockey, and being organized also gives me the luxury of time—and of saving time so that I can always get rest.

When you open my bathroom vanity and you see triple of everything—toiletries, towels—you think, hmm, *American Psycho*. When you open my closet and see ten black T-shirts that are exactly the same you think, hmm, *American Psycho*. It's the same thing with shoes, leather jackets, and trousers—this machine is being built to maximize time. There's no question that a few ladies have walked into my apartment and taken a deep breath, probably thinking "What have I got myself into?" until I quickly explain my theory of efficiency, which makes me sound even more like Patrick Bateman. Jesus, maybe I am Patrick Bateman. Except for the homicidal maniac bit.

Over the summer the Rangers signed Chris Drury, Scott Gomez, and Wade Redden to monster contracts. All this, of course, while the guy who'd done quite a bit in a short time to help make the Rangers a team that you wanted to play for was still stinging from a pummeling at arbitration.

Gomez signed a seven-year deal with the Rangers worth $51.5 million. Drury was cheaper, getting a five-year contract for $35.25 million. Redden signed for six years and $39 million.

And I had to sit in a stifling room in Toronto and hear how I wasn't worth an extra $600,000 from the team that had just blasted $125.75 million into the hockey salary universe.

I started the 2007–08 season determined to show the guys in the suits that I was one of the most valuable players on this team. Everything that I'd accomplished in my short season with the Rangers was going to pale in comparison to what I could do for them over eighty-two games in the red, white, and blue jersey.

We opened with a 5–2 win against Florida, and while I didn't register any points, I played more than eighteen minutes and helped us win. In our second game of the season against Ottawa, we were less than eight minutes into the first period when I was circling out of our zone with the puck. I'd already had a skirmish with Ottawa's tough guy Chris Neil less than a minute into the game, and we both got two minutes for roughing.

I was protecting the puck so I didn't see Neil coming, and he nailed me with a shoulder-to-shoulder hit. The pain shot through me as if he'd plunged a knife six inches into my ribs from behind. And that's it for me.

I have a Grade 3 sprain of my acromioclavicular joint, or AC joint, which is the joint at the top of the shoulder. In other words, it's a bad shoulder separation and the pain is like someone is drilling into my shoulder bones.

I beg our trainer Jim Ramsay for a bottle of Vicodin, and he gives me two tablets. I look at him in disbelief. That's not even going to get me out of the building. Through my nagging—and I mean a lot of nagging—he eventually doled out some more. Years later the issue of subscription overdoses has become a hot topic because the number of deaths happening to former players has increased tremendously, and that's because so many guys have become addicted to opioids. I think it's because the players are all much bigger, faster, and stronger as a result of superior nutrition, superior genetics, and the supplements and training programs we use. This is topped off by the protective gear we wear, which is like a weapon in itself when you're moving at speed. I mean, getting the hard plastic of an elbow pad in the face can easily knock you out.

And yet our brains are still the same size, and the organs inside our bodies are the same size as they were in 1875, when hockey first started to be played indoors. The difference is that the impact and force trauma in today's game is exponentially greater.

In the old days, a player could drink a bottle of Jim Beam to numb the pain, but not now. You need drugs, and the more you need the more tolerance to them you develop, and the worse the injuries become.

So all of this adds up to why the rate of serious injury to athletes has risen. And the only way you can fix this problem is to change the rules of the game, which have to evolve with technology. Otherwise technology is going to kill sports.

But instead we blame the trainers. How is a trainer supposed to say no to my request for pain pills when I'm lying on the floor of a dirty locker room dry-heaving because my shoulder hurts so much? So the trainer gives the player the drugs he's asking for so that he can get through the game and go back out to sacrifice his body for himself, his family, and the fans of the city he loves.

I missed eighteen games with that shoulder injury, which is my longest NHL injury to date. Being injured puts you in a very lonely place as a professional athlete. You see the injured players at practice, watching the guys play the game they cannot play for the time being, and sometimes they come on road trips, though they usually stay behind. Sometimes the healthy players start to resent them. "This fucking guy doesn't miss a paycheck and gets to enjoy his family time while I play sixteen games in thirty days." It's a natural feeling for players to have and it gets really bad if the injured player's teammates don't think he's working as hard at rehab as he should.

Because statistics are the barometer to measure how an NHL player gets paid, it's human nature for players to work the system. Let's say a guy has a great first half of the season—in forty games he scores sixteen goals, and adds thirty-four assists for a nice fifty-point total at a time of the season when it's always easier to come by points because you're not banged up or worn down.

But then, from games 41 to 69, his production drops, and when he gets hurt in Game 70 his stat is 1.4 points per game. He would be smart to milk his injury to the end of the season so that he'll finish with the higher points per game total—that way, when contract negotiations start in the off-season, his agent has better bargaining power. You would be surprised how often this happens, and although athletes are not usually great with math, we understand the angles you need in negotiations. We call the players who milk their injuries "Band-Aids."

It's the end of November and Shanny takes a slap shot and hits me in the left hand in a game against Dallas and I'm out again. I'm acting like a real baby because I feel like Shanny should have scored on some passes I've given him the last five games, and I've told him so. The guy has fifteen years on me in the NHL and he knows the long-term rhythm of the game much better than I do, but even so I share my opinion that he should be working harder. Then I don't speak to him for a week.

Even though Shanny is not pissed at me, this bad bounce has now led to me being injured. It was an honest mistake and hockey players would never blame another teammate for a bad bounce. But still, I'm annoyed by it all.

I've also had problems with this left wrist ever since I had a fight with Darcy Tucker earlier in November, and to be honest, it bothered me last year, so maybe Shanny has done me a favor. They tell me I won't be out long, and, as I don't want to do any more damage, I decide to go for the surgery.

Because of all the credit I received after the trade last year for turning the team around, and because this season the Rangers are 9-4-1 with me in the lineup and 4-5-1 without me, that evil little thing called human nature pokes his head out again. When a player is out of the lineup he wants the team to win sixty percent of the time and lose forty percent of the time. Nobody has the balls to say this except me, but it's true, and it's because when a hockey player is injured his self-worth is low. He doesn't feel wanted or needed because a team's mentality is "we need to push ahead with whatever we have." The only thing that keeps the injured player from going insane is to have his team lose so that he feels wanted. It's just human nature. Even so, good teammates who are out because of injury want their team to win more than they want to see it lose.

These thoughts don't consume me since I'm working my ass off to get back into the lineup because my drug is the jersey. My drug is MSG. My drug is New York.

The day after Christmas we're playing against Carolina and I get a bogus call for interference in front of the net when I tap a Carolina D-man's stick out of the way so that it doesn't deflect a puck into my face. There's a scrum, someone takes a punch at me, and then Andrew Ladd is after me. But the linesmen have him, and they have me, too. Even so, I get a good right hand in (I'm being careful with my left) and break the orbital bone in his left eye. You never want to injure another player, but that's what's going to happen until they change the rules. I get tossed from the game, but we win 5–2.

I loved loved-loved-loved getting in on a hard forecheck. I would time my arrival to hit the defenseman just as he's about to touch the puck to try to get it the hell out of his zone while I'm careering in at him full speed and looking to tattoo him into the end boards.

I also love to taunt defensemen on face-offs, so they know that no matter how quickly they think they can play the puck out of their zone, I'm still going to hit them hard. It's similar to defensive linemen talking to the quarterback before every snap in football, announcing their imminent plans to make him part of the turf.

Tonight it's March 10 and we're in Buffalo. Once again, as the playoffs loom, it's a tight squeeze in the standings among a bunch of clubs. We're comfortably in the middle of the playoff-bound teams at the moment, with eighty-one points, but the Sabres have seventy-four and are, at this moment, out of a playoff spot.

We're almost halfway through the second period with the game tied at one when I'm racing for the puck with Buffalo D-man Nathan Paetsch. It's been dumped around the end boards from left to right and I hit him with perfect timing and he flies from the goal line to the back boards and I think he's dead. The puck goes bang, bang off the boards, and ends up on my stick behind the net. I put a perfect backhand pass onto the stick of No. 68 and Jaromír Jágr buries it in the back of the net.

It was the best bodycheck of my career. We won 3–2 in a shootout

On March 29, 2008, I was feeling pretty great. My body had healed from injury and surgery, and we were in a much better place in the standings than we had been this time last year. I was looking forward to the playoffs.

We had a practice that morning, and when I stepped out of the elevator and saw the look on the face of my doorman, I knew something was wrong. Usually if I was on Page Six of the *New York Post* he would say, "Don't worry, big guy, Page Six just showing you love this morning," in his heavy Queens accent. But today he just handed me the *Daily News* and I almost shit my pants. My knees gave out and I had to lean up against the desk in the front lobby of my 19th Street apartment building, for there was my picture in a Rangers uniform under the headline "THE RANGER and THE MADAM."

"Rangers hockey star Sean Avery's name and private cell phone number are in the little black book of Manhattan madam Kristin Davis," the *Daily News* crowed.

"Avery, 27, a trash-talking enforcer who has dated a string of models and actresses, is listed as a $500 client of brothel Maison de L'Amour."

Now, if there's one thing that I didn't need to pay for it was sex. Or let me qualify that: every man pays for sex somehow—some with vacations, shoes, dresses, emotional vulnerability. It's called being in a relationship, and those forms of payment are what we all do, one way or another. But paying for a hooker is not my thing.

I was shaking for the entire hour and change that it took to drive to the practice rink, and as soon as I arrived I walked into Glen Sather's office to apologize and to explain very clearly that I had nothing to do with this.

Glen had his feet up on his desk and was chomping on his customary cigar. He told me, with a twinkle in his eye, to weather the media storm and it would go away, for there was nothing the New York media liked better that to prove each other wrong.

After practice, the reporters and photographers were waiting for me, and I just laughed and said to the cameras, "I can promise you that if I ventured into one of these establishments I wouldn't use my own name."

A couple of days later, my pals at the *New York Post* came to the rescue.

"Busty accused madam Kristin Davis is icing a report that New York Ranger star Sean Avery was a customer of her high-end escort service.

"'I personally spoke to her, and she confirmed that she has never had any contact with Sean Avery in any shape or form, Davis' lawyer, Mark Jay Heller, told The Post yesterday."

The *Post* took delight in saying that I was going to sue the *Daily News* for hundreds of millions of dollars as I had free agency coming up, but really, I found the fact that I'd wound up and then not wound up in the little black book of a celebrated New York madam to reveal just how much I'd gotten into the imagination of the city.

We make the 2008 Stanley Cup Playoffs with ease, and our first-round opponent is across the Hudson River in New Jersey, which is almost as good as a Subway Series. It means that I get to sleep in my own bed (and not the one at the brothel . . .) for the entire series, which we'd like to end as quickly as we can.

Our record against the Devils this season has been fantastic. We played them eight times and won seven, with one loss in OT, which was our last game against them. While that's not exactly the way you want to go into a playoff series where ties are decided in full overtime periods, we like our chances.

The atmosphere in the Prudential Center, this cavern of a new rink in Newark, is hostile, but that's because half the crowd are Devils fans and the other half are Rangers fans. In the last game of the regular season I was all over Marty Brodeur. This time my speech to him was easy, and true: I was standing on top of the crease telling him what a disgrace he is for falling in love with his sister-in-law.

Just so everyone is clear here, he started to fuck around with his wife's brother's wife, and eventually left his wife for her sister-in-law. Consider that for just a second. You leave your wife, the mother of your kids, for her brother's wife? That's so twisted on so many levels that it makes you dizzy trying to unravel the layers of betrayal.

So please tell me where in the "Hockey Man" rule book it says that I can't tell this guy he's a fucking dirtbag every time I see him. It's excessive, yes, but we really aren't here to make friends. I want to win the Cup, and this guy—no matter what plane of hockey godship people think he lives on—is in my way.

A few minutes into the second period I make a patient, and if I do say so, pretty damned skilled backhand pass to Scott Gomez, who is flying up the middle. He fires a hard pass to Shanahan on the right wing and vintage Shanny takes two steps and fires a laser that slides under Mrs. Brodeur's ex-husband.

It's 1–0 and I skate by Marty to remind him that that's my first assist of the series and I ask what section his fellow home-wrecker is sitting in so I can blow her a kiss. He leaves me guessing, the rogue.

We're up 2–1 in the third period when Gomez takes a puck over the Devils' blue line and goes wide around both D-men but runs out of room because Brodeur comes out so far to challenge. At the last second Gomez looks over his right shoulder and sees me cutting down the middle of the slot. I'm in the sweetest of spots, alone in front of the gaping net, and he lays the puck in the crease for me to pound home. If there was any doubt, Marty knows my name.

In Game 2, every time I come near Marty's crease he taps the back of my legs and I lose balance, a few times dangerously close to falling on him. But I do not turn and whack him back. My discipline is spot-on during the playoffs and I really am like a different player. I've grown as a professional, and New York has made it happen. I can just play the game I love, and drive my opponent nuts by doing just that.

Of course, my reputation precedes me, and I need to be careful not to let Marty suck me into a penalty, especially going into a game tied at zero in the third period. I'm thinking about how I can avoid Marty's little tricks, and then I come up with the solution. Nearly five minutes into the third, and twenty seconds after Jágr puts one past Marty and gives us the lead, the puck finds its way to the tip of my blade as I'm standing in the slot. And with a one-timer I snap it just under the cross bar.

The Devils score later in the third, but my goal stands as the game-winner. We're going back to MSG up two games to zip, and I already have two goals in the series. I'm pretty sure Marty is rattled when he heads home to his sister-in-law . . . I mean wife.

Game 3 is at MSG and it's a madhouse. Our fans were loud in New Jersey, but in their home barn, they're mighty. Shaking-the-joint mighty.

We're tied at one and it's early in the second period when we wind up on a five-on-three power play. Jaromír Jágr is on the right point and Shanahan is on the left, with Gomez and Drury each on their respective back doors and me in front. I can't take a penalty here, and I know that the refs would love to call one on us because five-on-three is a pretty serious advantage, especially in the playoffs.

This means I need to improvise. Hockey is a game of instincts and vision, of being able to stay one step ahead. My job is to screen Brodeur, but he's behind me.

Then it hits me. I will simply turn around and face Marty. The moment

I put my hands in Marty's face I realize that this is incredibly smart. As in, a moment of genius.

Standing the normal way to screen a goalie is ineffective because all the goalie needs to do is look around me, and I don't have eyes in the back of my head to see which way he's looking. I also can't protect myself from his whacks to the back of my legs.

So I stand facing Marty, and the crowd starts to go crazy. Marty puts his hands up and takes a swipe at my face with his glove hand, so I put all my weight on my heels and lean back to avoid the contact. One of the referees, Don Van Massenhoven, skates inches away from me and tells me to cut the shit or he's going to give me two minutes. A ref skating to a guy standing in front of the net on a five-on-three and then talking to him while the play is still live is unheard of, and he wants to give me a penalty for this? I yell back at him "For what?"

I'm staring into the whites of Mr. Martin Brodeur's eyes, which are starting to turn as red as the Devils logo on his chest. Chris Drury skates over now to my left side and sort of whispers in my ear to stop because Van Massenhoven is going to give me two minutes, and I still don't know why I would be getting this penalty. All the while I have two of the hardest shooters in the NHL taking slap shots that could shatter my spine or break my ribs or crack my tailbone and smash up any other bone in my back that I don't know about, so that should put any dumb statements about me doing this for show to rest.

I don't get a penalty, and about fifteen seconds later Gomez makes a quick pass to my waiting stick and I bury it between the legs of Mrs. Brodeur's ex-husband. MSG goes absolutely insane: nobody has ever seen anything like this—including the NHL.

And so the next day they officially amended the NHL rule book— without consulting the owners, or the NHLPA, or anyone, they just did it—so that I could never do this again, even though nowhere in the rule book was it illegal. But now it was. I was actually flattered that they called this rule book rejig "The Avery Rule."

Colin Campbell, the NHL's director of hockey operations, announced it to the waiting world. "An unsportsmanlike conduct minor penalty will be interpreted and applied, effective immediately, to a situation when an offensive player positions himself facing the opposition goaltender and engages in actions such as waving his arms or stick in front of the goaltender's face, for the purpose of improperly interfering with and/or distracting the goaltender as opposed to positioning himself to try to make a play."

We ended up beating New Jersey in five games, and in the traditional handshake line at the end of the series Marty pulled his hand away as I stuck mine out. The unsportsmanlike gesture just proved what I had been saying about him, when I wasn't scoring goals on him. Not a class act, on the ice or off it.

We felt very confident going into the semifinals against the Penguins. We'd played them eight times during the season, and had a 5–3 record against them. So we felt more than able to win four games against them now.

And then we go and lose the first two. We need to win the next one at home, or else it's going to be a very steep climb out of the hole. I mean, at this point in NHL history, only two teams have come back from being down three games to zip in the Stanley Cup playoffs. The Leafs did it against Detroit in 1942, and the Islanders did it in 1975. Against Pittsburgh. Maybe it's an omen.

We play Game 3 at MSG, and as ever, our fans are giving us a boost. I'm skating full speed on the offensive zone forecheck and have my target locked in: it's Hal Gill, the Penguins' six-seven, 250-pound D-man. He actually sees me coming and braces himself, so he steps into the check and we hit each other straight on, full blast.

The wind gets blown out of my chest and it feels as if I've just torn my abdominals. In the first intermission I walk into the trainer's room and ask

Jim Ramsay and our team doctor, Andy Feldman, to give me the good stuff—more Toradol.

I play the rest of the game and get an assist in the second period, but we can't beat the Penguins and now we're down 3–0. After the game I'm exhausted. I can hardly pick my head up and all I can think about is getting into the cold tub. About a minute into my cold tub session it feels as if someone just came up behind me and stabbed me in the shoulder. I call Dr. Feldman over and tell him what's going on and he immediately tells me to get dressed. We're going to the hospital.

I feel so weak walking into St. Vincent's in Greenwich Village that they immediately run a CT scan and MRI. While we're waiting for the doctors to read the tests, the pain gets really bad so they hit me with Dilaudid, which is a morphine derivative that treats moderate to severe pain. It doesn't sit well, so I start projectile vomiting.

This was a blessing in disguise because now I'm puking blood and the room looks like I've just committed mass murder. I'm covered in blood, too, and the doctors now know I'm bleeding internally. It turned out that my collision with Hal Gill had lacerated my spleen, and I spent the next five days in a room in the basement of St. Vincent's. The only way they can find the laceration is by hoping that it pops its head out and sprays my insides with blood while they have the scope inside me, and after a few tries they finally found it. I would live to fight another day, but my season was done.

The next morning, James Dolan, the owner of the Rangers, and Glen Sather, the GM, came to see me. My close friend Lauren Flynn was asleep on a chair in the corner of the room, and Lauren had brought our mutual friend May Andersen along. May is Danish, and a world-famous model. I was in a ton of pain during the night and the ladies took turns giving me ice chips because I'd never been so thirsty in my life but every time I drank something I'd throw it up, which in turn would make me even thirstier.

May fell asleep in the fetal position at the bottom of my bed and the night nurse had put blankets over her, so at first glance you couldn't even tell she was there. The look on the faces of Slats and Mr. Dolan when they walked into the room and May popped her head out from under the sheets was legendary. I mean, you couldn't have staged it better. And now I realized it also really hurt to laugh.

17

THE SUMMER OF *VOGUE*

While sitting in my hotel room between Games 3 and 4 against New Jersey, I wrote a letter to the woman I'd called Mrs. Bloomberg when I first met her at the Met Ball, asking the celebrated Anna Wintour of *Vogue* if I could be an intern during my upcoming off-season.

I had started reading *Vogue* in LA, and dove deeper into the fashion world after I moved to New York City, just really by paying attention to all the amazing ways people put themselves together in this city. And I still read *Vogue*, and *GQ*, and anything, really, that would help me understand what I was seeing.

My personal style had always been important to me, starting with my first pair of Nike sneakers, which I got on my ninth birthday. I'd coveted those shoes as soon as I'd first seen them, and looking back at how important they were I regret not keeping them as a memento: Air Pegasus 1989.

I remember my first T-shirt from Chip and Pepper, and I also remember the first time I met Pepper at a house party in LA, after I'd given his wife a cigarette and started to inappropriately vibe with her, not knowing she was married and certainly not to my favorite clothing designer and maker.

I started to read *Vogue* for a few reasons. I was actually into the story-telling, as the magazine isn't just pages of glossy paper with pictures of pretty women in expensive clothes. I realized this when I opened a story shot by Annie Leibovitz, and although I didn't read books that often as a child, flipping through the pages of this story engaged me, and I wanted to know what happened next. It was a magical story being told with clothes and a supermodel. It was visual art.

I also used *Vogue* as a kind of social media tool. I was tired of the conversations that had surrounded me for the last eight years in NHL locker rooms, ones that would usually consist of cars-pussy-food-drugs-money-watches and more money, so I carried my monthly copy of *Vogue* onto the team plane tucked under my arm, with the cover very visible, as a sort of subtle "fuck you" to my immediate society.

The circles in which I was socializing in New York were much different from the ones in Los Angeles. In New York, people talk about interesting things, and in those conversations, because I didn't feel as worldly, I needed something to separate me even more.

What better way to do that than to learn everything I could about fashion? I could walk into a party and tell a woman exactly who made her bag and what season it was first shown in. I was blowing people away—especially the gay guys. And as soon as you get the gay vote you have a shot at any woman in the room. Which is not why I was doing it, but it didn't hurt.

And yes, meeting babes was also part of the reason for sending my letter to Anna Wintour, though my love of fashion was the prime mover. I heard back from her through the proper channels, and once I'd recovered from my lacerated spleen I was to go through *Vogue*'s version of training camp—a series of meetings with different people at the magazine to see if I was worthy, and why I wanted to do this. I didn't blame them for wanting to test me, and because I was the first athlete to try to do this, everyone needed to make sure that I was sincere.

I met Laurie Jones in her office at 4 Times Square. Laurie was *Vogue*'s managing editor, and had also spent twenty years at *New York* magazine.

She's this tough Texan with an acute bullshit meter. I explained to her that I really loved fashion and wanted to understand it more and to learn about the business from the inside. I promised that I'd do all the same stuff as the regular interns, showing up on time Monday through Friday and working as long as I had to in order to do whatever they wanted. I would make minimum wage, and check in with her each week to tell her what I'd done.

Ms. Jones seemed satisfied by what I had to say, and so she picked up the phone and called Sally Singer, who was a senior editor, and asked if she was ready for me.

Sally was softer than Laurie, and my intimidation was quashed the moment I walked into her office. She explained that she wanted me to shadow specific editors. We agreed that I'd have a thirty-day internship and that it would start on Monday at 9 A.M. I was as excited as if I'd just made the team after a tough camp, the difference being that the team would give me a uniform. Now I had to figure out what I was going to wear on wear at my first day at *Vogue*.

When I walked into the office that Monday morning in May at 9 A.M. sharp with a tea in one hand and the *New York Post* in the other, I could feel all eyes on me and everyone asking the same question: what the hell is this New York Ranger doing at *Vogue*? There was confusion and interest and excitement rippling through the halls at 4 Times Square, and I felt it too, like you do when you join a new team. Will I fit in? Will I be able to pull this off? But the added twist is that while I know how to play hockey, I've never played on a world-class fashion team.

One thing that I'd have to pull off better was my own fashion sense—for my first day at *Vogue* I wore slacks, a checked shirt, and a patterned tie. I mean, the checks and pattern did not go together, and all the *Vogue* people knew that and soon enough I would, too.

My first mission is to take care of "the Closet," which does not look like the one in the movies, but its function is the same. It's the fashion nerve center of the place, a small office with minimal shelving crammed with garment racks of clothes, and shoes everywhere. I'm helping to organize it with two other interns known as Voguettes.

Voguettes are the interns tasked with carrying clothes across the city and around the globe so that the well-traveled editors have all the tools to create stories and images that will command millions in advertising dollars. Voguettes are usually from wealthy families, but they're hard-working and cute—never hot, but always cute. They're well-read and have great manners, and have chosen to sacrifice their social lives, love lives, and family lives so that they can be a part of the magazine they've dreamed of working for since they were teenagers. I found it fascinating to see the dedication the staffers at *Vogue* have. These women work for low wages and they put in grueling seventy-hour weeks. Let me tell you, most men could not finish one week at 4 Times Square.

The gossip buzzed through the building on my first day, with people wondering if I was leaving pro hockey for fashion, or if I was part of some elaborate reality TV prank. At lunch I further confused everyone by heading to the cafeteria and filling my plate with a mountain of food, which stood in stark contrast to the meager salads consumed by the girls of *Glamour–Teen Vogue–Men's Vogue–Self* (other magazines in the building).

I couldn't have been happier. Back home in Pickering, my mother, Marlene, was proud of my detour from the predictable pro-hockey player summer path, though my father, Al, was a little surprised by it. He took a ribbing from his golf buddies about me, the tough NHL agitator now swishing through the corridors of fashion. Though he's a man of few words with me, he did ask me if I was trying to tell him I was gay. I laughed and told him it was exactly the opposite: I'd found a summer gig doing something I loved in a workplace filled with beautiful women where I was the only straight guy. He smiled. He got it.

———

A black Town Car picked me up one morning at 6 o'clock from my place on West 19th Street, and forty-five minutes later I was on the set of my first *Vogue* shoot. The only time I'd been on the set of a photo shoot before was when I was playing in LA. I was the subject, and the great Bruce Weber shot me for *Vanity Fair.*

For my *Vanity Fair* shoot I flew to Florida and we did some shots in a hockey rink in suburban Miami, and then we went back to Bruce's home on Ocean Boulevard in Hollywood, Florida, which is easily the coolest house I've ever seen. It's a one-story modern masterpiece with a glass wall that opens up to connect the inside of the house to the white sand beaches outside.

Bruce had me eating out of the palm of his hand, posing in my tighty whities on the beach and in the pool, surrounded by more golden retrievers than people. It hit me that all his photo assistants looked like college football quarterbacks, sculpted from granite, tanned, and not wearing all that much.

I leaned in to my publicist Nicole and said, "Are you seeing what I'm seeing?" By the size of the smile on her face I guessed that she did. I mean, I've been in locker rooms with twenty naked guys watching two naked guys wrestle and nobody for a minute thought it was gay. Because your life as a pro athlete means that you're always surrounded by athletic guys in various states of undress, the Bruce Weber shoot just seemed like a locker room. Until the moment I realized that I might be the only straight guy on set. No one hit on me or anything, but it was a funny realization because sometimes, if you're not looking, you can't see the obvious.

Today's photo shoot for *Vogue* has nothing to do with me in my underwear and everything to do with Narciso Rodriguez, a veteran designer favored by A-list celebrities and more importantly, by the editors of *Vogue.*

We're shooting at a beach club on Long Island which looks like it hasn't had a coat of fresh paint in half a century. Raquel Zimmermann, a Brazilian goddess, is the supermodel of the day, and I study her up close. She's a perfectly proportioned five-ten, with long sculpted legs and perfect breasts and shoulders like a world-class swimmer and long curly blond hair. She's perfection when it comes to beauty, and she becomes even more beautiful when seen through the eye of a lens.

Claire Danes is also in the shoot. She's a complicated soul which makes her a true talent on screen and stage, and while she does not have the body of a supermodel, she still captures the camera's fickle eye with her pouty, intense, intelligent seduction.

I try to stay focused and perform the odd jobs I'm assigned, such as helping the catering crew find a table to set up lunch and picking up garbage to keep the set tidy. Everyone from Claire to Raquel to the stylists is confused by my presence. I'm wearing black shorts, a black T-shirt, and black desert boots, and I have a $25K Rolex on my wrist and look like I should be playing hockey. But I'm an intern at *Vogue*.

I soon made a fashion statement of my own. Because the heat and humidity make NYC a hot and swampy mess in spring and summer, I had my tailor turn the pants of my suit into shorts, and I wear them along with the suit jacket over a white dress shirt. I beat the heat and still look great doing it. As I walk into 4 Times Square, almost every single person who passes by me does a double-take, and by lunchtime the cafeteria is buzzing with talk of my suit. I had men from all the different magazines coming up and complimenting me on my idea and asking if I think they can pull it off. You can pull off anything if you're confident, except maybe a checked shirt and patterned tie. (Actually, my most embarrassing moment at *Vogue* came in the cafeteria, too. As I walked toward the checkout with two plates of beef Stroganoff, salad, bottles of water, and Jell-o for dessert, I noticed Hamish Bowles out of the corner of my eye. Hamish is an extremely dandy fashion man and one of the most powerful people at *Vogue*. While noticing him I didn't realize that the "wet floor" sign was right below my feet, but when I did, my natural instinct was to avoid it, and I slipped. And so I watched in the slowest of slow motion my tray of food land a foot in front of me and ranch dressing paint the front of my black T-shirt and vest. The worst part was that when I stood up and gave a bow—which would usually be followed by a round of applause at MSG—I was met by a very deafening silence.)

Vogue editors are in charge of overseeing the stories that fill the pages of each month's issue. They are often women from affluent families who went to private schools in Connecticut and then to Ivy League colleges. A lot of them have husbands in private equity, and they summer in the Hamptons. They run themselves ragged and are truly slaves to fashion, and sustain themselves with Marlboro Reds and green juice. They're very talented, but they must please the Queen herself, Anna Wintour, whom some underlings have called Nuclear Wintour due to her icy personality.

The Devil Wears Prada was a very successful novel and movie based on the life of an Anna Wintour assistant who was tasked with impossible jobs, like securing an advance copy of the latest *Harry Potter*. These assistants aspired to become *Vogue* editors someday as well, and one of the unbelievable perks that came with an internship was sitting in on editorial meetings where all the editors would update Anna on new ideas for next month's issue and review pictures from the most recent shoots.

Everyone was nervous in these meetings in which Anna would sit at the head of the table with her sunglasses on and a cup of Starbucks in her hand. One of her two assistants would be taking notes, and I'd sit in a chair off to the side, trying to control my sweating so it wasn't obvious how nervous I was.

I can't remember anything specific that was reviewed during my time there because all I could think about was whether Anna was sizing me up behind her shades. When she didn't like a picture or idea she would sit in silence, and the editor presenting it would disappear through a hole in the floor. Not really, but they probably wanted to, and then Anna would immediately move on to the next idea. It was a tense room, but it was very effective in getting the edition sorted out. There was no debating back and forth—you just kept moving forward until the boss was satisfied because hers was the only opinion that mattered.

One of the legendary editors at *Vogue* was André Leon Talley, who had worked under Anna Wintour since 1983 and was one of the few gay African-American men in such an influential position.

After I had written my letter to Anna Wintour I invited him to come to see us in a playoff game against Pittsburgh, and he agreed; I was to arrange everything with his assistant. I was shocked when the assistant informed me that I'd need to send a car to Talley's home in Westchester, which would drive him to the game, take him to dinner after the game, and then drive him home. This was years before Uber existed, and I knew this adventure would easily set me back $1,000.

After our warm-up, the Rangers media man Jason Vogel grabbed me outside the locker room with a look of panic in his eyes. "We have a problem," he said, "your friend André can't fit in the seat."

André was six-six, and though Anna Wintour had initiated an intervention about the man's weight in 2005, three years later he was still pretty substantial. I wondered if we'd have to seat him in the penalty box, because there was certainly room for him there. Jason was one step ahead of me, though, and had already put André in a plush fold-out chair in the handicapped section of MSG, which was actually one of the best seats in the house.

The sight of this gigantic black man in a full-length fur coat sitting alone in majestic splendor was not hard to miss from the ice level, and it had the guys laughing every time they looked up into that section. It was as if some exotic African royalty had come to MSG to bestow his blessing upon the Blueshirts, but he seemed to be enjoying the spectacle of which he was part.

After the game, we'd made plans to go to dinner at the Waverly Inn, which was the hottest restaurant in NYC. I didn't dare make André wait around while I did media and showered, and had the car take him to the restaurant immediately after the final buzzer.

When I walked into the Waverly, Karl Lagerfeld, the most famous fashion designer in the world, was at our table. It's always hard to stop sweating after a game even when you've showered and changed, and once I saw Karl, dressed, as always, as if he was mashing up an 18th-century tableau with a vampire movie (high collars and sunglasses), my nerves went into high gear and I was dripping away.

I didn't say much and listened hard, but Karl's thick German-French accent and the speed with which he spoke made it almost impossible for me to understand him when meeting for the first time.

During that dinner I saw a lot of people whom I knew socially, and the cool ones just gave me a nod and kept walking. There were a few who wanted to stop to talk, and so to avoid disrupting my dinner companions, I'd get up from the table to speak to them.

I had no idea that this is apparently hitting the absolute bottom in table manners, and the next morning I get word that André is beyond furious with me and can't believe I would get up from the table while he was there. Apparently I was supposed to ignore everyone who tried to say hello to me because who could be more interesting or powerful than the people at the table? So, ignoring your other friends is considered polite in the fashion world.

One day during my internship I was asked to go to LA to help an editor named Katherine McNeil with a few different shoots she had, and this task filled me with pleasure and a little worry, as I was flying back to the city I'd loved once and then left, in my new incarnation as a New York Ranger fashionisto.

The Black Eyed Peas are one of the biggest pop bands in the world and *Vogue* was shooting them. They were using an LA-based crew and stylist assistants, and I didn't know anyone on set, but I could feel that everyone was confused by my presence. It's not like everyone stops and introduces themselves at the beginning—just like they didn't on every NHL team I played for except the Rangers—and there are a lot of fast-moving parts.

Everything was running smoothly until will.i.am started to give Katherine a hard time about the clothes options. He didn't want to wear anything that *Vogue* wanted him to wear, and insisted on wearing his own clothes. He was being diff.i.cult as they did a light test, and eventually walked off the set with his publicist, leaving Katherine in tears.

As he walked toward me I rose out of the shadows and stepped in front of him. "You don't know me," I began, "but my advice would be to think twice about walking out of a *Vogue* shoot that has you starring in it. And you can also break the news to Fergie that her *Vogue* shoot won't be happening."

He didn't say anything, he just looked confused, and his publicist tried to move them along. I wasn't budging, and will.i.am could see that.

"Once word gets out that you bailed, you will have more than problems from *Vogue*, and in my humble opinion, I don't think that's something you want."

I wasn't trash-talking him, but I used the same sense of authority that I used when getting into someone's head on the ice, and now he looked worried. I stepped out of the way and he and his publicist walked past, with the publicist giving me the death stare.

It was an interesting lesson for me. When a celebrity acts like they're a celebrity, all of a sudden they lose that power of seduction. It was certainly the first time a *Vogue* intern had stepped into an NHL enforcer's role on a photo shoot, but it worked. will.i.am came back to Earth from his lofty perch in the stars, and we made it through. After that, I could do no wrong in Katherine's eyes.

As I said earlier, part of the reason I did this internship was to meet some babes, and ideally, one of the ladies being shot for the magazine. Walking through the halls of *Vogue* was always an adventure, and because I was one of the few straight men in the office, I think I was the object of the odd crush. I liked this attention, and would go out of my way to do little things, like buying the girls lunch in the cafeteria or ordering a Town Car for them when I overheard a summons to head downtown with those dreaded black garment bags. Anytime you see a pretty girl carrying a black garment bag in NYC, you know she's an intern for a fashion magazine.

I really tried to behave myself while I worked one month as an intern, since I was representing not only *Vogue* while on set or in the studio, but also the New York Rangers.

The one big difference between the NHL and the fashion world is the lack of rules. When it came to sex/drugs/music/opinions, the fashion world really didn't have any rules, as long as what you were doing or saying had style. I loved it.

Steven Klein is one of the most famous fashion photographers in the world and today he is shooting a story for *Vogue*. I'm on set not because I'm needed there but because I want to see the great Steven Klein work, and this is another perk when you're a famous intern.

As they fixed a light during the third look of the day, Steven Klein suddenly stopped in the middle of a conversation he was having with two models and just stared at me. He stared for quite a while, and then leaned into the girls and whispered something to them.

Four hours later, I was behind the wheel of my Audi waiting for the incredibly sexy model who'd been at Steven Klein's side for most of the day. After Steven whispered whatever he said about me to her, she, too, suddenly couldn't stop staring at me, and after lunch, while we were both sneaking a cigarette, we agreed to an early Friday evening dinner at the Mercer after the shoot wrapped.

By Sunday morning, I was finally back home after a weekend with her, one which took a turn for the better around 1 P.M. on a Friday, all because of a whisper and a look. Someday I'm going to open a small café in Soho and call it "A Whisper and A Look." It will definitely sell copies of *Vogue*.

July 1 is about a week away, and that's the day I become an unrestricted free agent, which means that if I don't sign with the Rangers before then, I can sign with any team in the league. Nothing is going on with New York, who have put a lowball offer on the table, and the mix of my emotions is intense. At one moment, I'm angry at the offer from the Rangers. I almost died for this team just a few months ago, and the arena chants my name on a regular basis, and the damn team has won with me in the lineup and lost when I'm not there. I also had the stats over the last two years to get paid more than the $2.5 million a year that the Rangers want to pay me.

Pat Morris, my agent, said he was going to get me the most money that he could, and then I could decide on my next NHL jersey. Pat felt Glen made that below-market offer because he didn't believe that I would leave. Was he right?

Running through me is a cocktail of excitement and dread, because I'm about to make more money than I ever dreamed of making, but I know that it's going to be somewhere other than New York. It would mean leaving the one place I finally felt was home, the place where all my hard work was finally being respected and rewarded. Or was it?

One night during the negotiations, my close friend Matt Abramcyk, at that time the owner of the Beatrice, came by my apartment and said he wanted to go for a ride to Tribeca, so we jumped in his Range Rover and headed downtown. You can feel the energy shift when you cross over Canal

Street into Tribeca (the Triangle Below Canal). It has cobblestone streets and beautiful lofts, but it's still pretty empty in Tribeca in the summer of 2008. We pull up in front of 77 Warren, a Vietnamese restaurant that's now gone out of business and where, rather sadly, the tables are still set. It was a total surprise because Matt had said nothing about going to check out a potential restaurant.

The moment I walked inside I saw exactly what Matt saw: with its brick walls and battered hardwood floors we could turn this place into a non-sports-bar sports bar, the Rangers locker room, circa 1968.

Matt and I had kicked around the idea of opening up a bar or eatery together during some of our late nights at the Beatrice, and because of the uncertainty of my NHL future I am looking for ways to anchor myself in this city I love. And seeing this place made me realize that the time had come: I was about to get into the hospitality business.

Around the same time, I'd also started to hang out with this beautiful model, whom I'd noticed during the off-season a few years back while we were both working out at Equinox West Hollywood, which is full of buff and tanned LA girls. You would never see a look like this woman had, which was a mix of natural beauty and grunge. When we met again in New York, Noot Seear and I had a connection that had been brewing for years.

Noot was from Squamish, British Columbia. On July 25, I landed in Vancouver with Noot and we headed up the majestic Sea to Sky Highway, past her hometown and onward to the ski resort of Whistler. We were going to attend the first-ever Pemberton Music Festival.

To get there, we took a helicopter from Whistler to Pemberton (it's about a seventeen-minute flight), and flying over those snow-capped Coast Mountains, emerald lakes, and incredibly dense and powerful forests made me feel humbled. It was the perfect place to be at that moment, suspended above paradise just as I was suspended between NHL teams, awaiting my professional fate.

The festival was held around the base of Mount Currie, elevation 8,500 feet, and as we descended in the chopper we could see the festival below, with cars on the narrow highway backed up for hours, trying to get in. We landed in the backyard of a ski chalet across the street from the festival, which had been set up as a party house for the bands to hang out in, so it was stocked with drinks and food and spots to relax in splendor.

I was now used to first-class treatment at festivals, partly because I'd started attending them at the beginning of the push, with Bonnaroo and Coachella. But now I was here with a supermodel and we were in our home country of Canada and I was starting to become very well known in the land that gave the world hockey.

This weekend was another piece in the creation of my character in the NHL. The legend of Sean Avery was becoming stronger in a league that very much discouraged individuality. At Pemberton, I'm surrounded by 20,000 drunk Canadians, and half of them seem to have an opinion of me, the common take being something like, "There's that crazy fucker Sean Avery." Soon enough they'd be calling me a motherfucker.

The music was excellent—the Tragically Hip were there, along with about fifty other bands—and I ended up having an incredible weekend, watching Noot dance like the true hippie she is, and watching a barefoot Jordin Tootoo drink more beer than I thought was humanly possible. Tootoo was there with his former Nashville teammate Scottie Upshall. This was the first time I'd ever met either of them off the ice, and they were great guys. I became friends with Scottie because of our mutual love of music. Tootoo vanished from the party scene once he got sober, and I'm glad he came out OK on the other side.

And then the festival was over, and I was flying back to New York. I had this feeling on the plane that I couldn't shake: that I'd soon be on another plane taking me away from the city I loved.

18

SEAN DOES DALLAS

I knew I was going to be moving when a call came in from Pat Morris. The Chicago Blackhawks and Dallas Stars were the front-runners for my services, now that the Rangers no longer seemed to think I brought value. Or at least, less value than they were willing to pay for. As I said, they had a strange attitude toward money and me, happily shelling out for guys who brought much less to the team than I did and yet always grinding me. I still don't understand why.

My pal Brett Hull is the co-GM in Dallas, and we have a relationship that goes back to Detroit—I mean, I lived in his house and drove him to practice and my friends nearly killed him with their dope cookies. Brett knows how effective I can be on the ice and off it. He tells me that Dallas is committed to winning, and is going to spend some money to do that. Hully told me that I would like Dallas—good people, fun town, which is all true. It just wouldn't end up being my type of fun.

The one thing that neither of us knew was just how deeply ingrained in NYC I had become. Dallas won me over with a four-year, $15.5 million offer, and for that, I was happy to move to the Lone Star State, though not in much of a rush, as I actually delayed the press conference introducing me as a Dallas Star for two days because I was apparently doing something more important in New York. So important I can't even remember.

The congratulatory calls started to flood in, and although I was extremely happy that I'd finally been recognized by a hockey team which had made a pretty clear statement about how much they wanted me, I also knew that the team in the place I called home didn't want me as badly.

I did the appropriate dance with the media and gave the standard bull-shit lines about signing with a contender and Dallas being a great hockey town, but I knew that it wasn't. Dallas is the land of the Cowboys, and even after the Mavericks' maverick owner, Mark Cuban, brought an NBA championship to the city, it was still a football town and a Friday Night Lights state.

I remember telling my friends that I couldn't wait to get a big house with lots of bedrooms for everyone to visit, but in truth, I was thinking about how many days I had left in NYC before I needed to pack up and head to Texas. When I finally made it to Dallas for the press conference, I planned on doing everything, including finding a place to live, in two days. I needed to get back to New York already.

After going to see a third rental property in Dallas, I couldn't handle seeing another home filled with pink-themed children's rooms and country-style kitchens. So I found a concrete building near the American Airlines Center that was filled with New York–style lofts. I can get a five-bedroom, 4,500-square-foot apartment with concrete polished floors for $3,000 a month, which is about $17,000 cheaper than I'd pay for it in downtown Manhattan. I sign the lease and head directly to the airport to fly back to New York. I'm not as happy as I thought I would be after this money dream come true.

NHL training camp for the 2008–09 season opens on September 15, which means players arrive in town the day after Labor Day. I'm having a hard time booking my flight and getting on the plane, but I finally do it on September 9, and I'm one of the last guys to arrive in Dallas, which doesn't look good, especially after the large financial vote of confidence Hully has given me.

Everything is different in Dallas. New York is hot in the summer, and even has a neighborhood called Hell's Kitchen (so named because of ancient bigotry, but I like to think of it as being because of climate change), but here in the middle of September, Dallas feels like Hell's Furnace. Everyone drives, everywhere, and Mexican is the food of choice. I love Mexican food, but not three times a day.

Dallas people love their guns and do not love gays. Dallas people love to drink booze and they take it a bit too far, and I've seen a lot of far, so am in a position to judge. The women of Dallas are also remarkable, redefining the notion of casual. A Dallas *belle* at a football game means fully done hair and makeup, but replace the high heel with a flat and the denim blouse with a Texas Tech sweatshirt. I can't really tell what these ladies look like, because in public they have on more war paint than Mel Gibson's troops in *Braveheart*. Putting on and taking off their makeup must add hours to their days, but Dallas, like LA, is about surfaces.

Brad Richards moved into my building near the AAC, and from time to time he'd catch me in my apartment with the lights turned down and some candles burning as I listened to the best thing I found in Dallas by a Texas mile: a 1972 Magnavox record player in mint condition. In the world of pro hockey, listening to music by yourself with the lights dimmed and candles burning is something only guys who are outside the herd do. And I'm doing it from the start.

I had fought the Stars' captain Brenden Morrow a lot prior to being his new teammate. He didn't like me before I walked into the dressing room, and he liked me even less after. He didn't like the attention I was taking away from him when I signed. He'd married his former teammate Guy Carbonneau's daughter in 2002, and because he was the team leader, that meant she was tasked with being the leader in the wives' room, though fortunately she didn't have to set the standard for her mother-in-law, as Carbonneau retired in 2000.

Mike Modano is the hockey king of Dallas, which is sort of like being third-string on the Dallas Community College football team in terms of public awareness. No one has chanted his name at MSG.

Modano has certainly had a Hall of Fame career, and is very close with Brett Hull. I have an uneasy feeling when I think about Modano keeping things together in the dressing room, because this team is made up of a lot of guys who have that Texas "I'm No. 1" thing going on. Marty Turco, the goalie, is another Dallas big shot and he doesn't like me either because of my taunting of Marty Brodeur, who as far as I can tell plays for a team 1,500 miles away.

I do not mix well with this group.

Except, to my surprise, Steve Ott. Steve is a similar player to me, and while he hasn't had an impact on the league like I did during my time in New York, he's still very good at what he does. Nothing is off-limits for Ott, and he'll say almost anything to get a guy off his game. He's the one guy I thought I definitely wouldn't get along with. I like Brad Richards as well. So, two out of thirty-nine. If I was playing Texas Holdem with that hand, I'd fold.

It's over 100 degrees in Texas and I'm hot all the time, and when I'm hot I sweat. So I dust off one of my short-pants suits for a trip to Los Angeles and head for my seat at the back of the team plane. I know it's going to take everyone a minute to get used to the look, but maybe it will actually catch on with some of the guys in this cauldron of a place. The next thing I know, the other co-GM, Les Jackson, tells me I need to go home and change into something more manly, and that the plane will wait. Yes, the Dallas Stars couldn't handle a guy in a suit with short pants, so they spent thousands of extra dollars in rental fees for an airplane while they waited for me to change. I've never seen this happen before, but then again, I'm the first to ever try it. Did I mention I looked great?

I think I arrived in Dallas to a very passive-aggressive reception because of my relationship with Brett Hull. Some of my new teammates felt like Brett had showed some favoritism that I didn't merit. Well, that's exactly what happened, and if I were running a team, I'd try to sign as many players I could who I had a previous relationship with and who I knew could step up and help the team. I'd want to know as much as I could about my players, and if I'd not only played with a guy but lived with him and we hadn't killed each other, I'd sure as hell take a shot at getting him when he was available.

I didn't do a good enough job mourning my break-up with New York. In sports you don't get to take as much time as you need to get over a relationship with a team. You're expected to forget about it in hours and get on with the next one as soon as you pull on the new jersey. Everyone knows that if you don't take enough time after a tough break-up, and if you get into a rebound relationship, it never lasts. I think I'm in a rebound relationship with Dallas.

And fuck do I miss New York.

Going from MSG to the American Airlines Center is like the rock star playing sell-out crowds in the capital of the world one day, and then playing the state fair where fried butter is a delicacy the next. It's like coming down off Adderall. I feel tired and depressed and anxious and irritable.

I hate it here.

I hated it from the first game.

I missed taking the subway to the arena before the game in my fresh-pressed Prada suit and my scuffed-up boots. I missed walking through the crowded restaurants, passing tables filled with people who were there because they were the best at what they did—from supermodels to fashion designers to actors to bankers to filmmakers, and even to the Teamsters who hauled our gear. I missed getting into a yellow cab and pulling up to the Beatrice Inn after a game. This was my life and now I'm in Dallas eating BBQ ribs and watching a bunch of rich kids pretending to be cowboys throwing darts while tacky blondes drink martinis and talk about their upcoming trips. To New York.

On October 20, I played my first game back at MSG, and we're in town for five whole days because we're also playing the Devils and the Islanders. And it's Fashion Week in New York, which means some fun stuff will be going on day and night, in addition to all the rest of the fun stuff. In case I needed reminding.

I decided I didn't want to stay in the team hotel in Times Square, so I booked a room at the Mercer in Soho. The Mercer is my favorite hotel in New York, six stories of elegant Romanesque revival in the heart of one of the city's most interesting neighborhoods. It's the sister hotel to, ta-da, the Chateau Marmont in LA.

Brad Richards also wanted to have some freelance fun and joined me downtown with a room of his own. Technically this was not allowed, but as long as you show up to the rink on time it really doesn't matter.

I know Richie has made his mind up that he's getting out of Dallas when his contract runs out with the Stars, and he has his sights set on signing with the Rangers, so he wanted to see what the city was really like. It was the perfect opportunity to show him around a bit, and not at the tourist spots that you'd see when you came as a visitor.

Usually you land in a city and spend most of your time in the hotel when you're not at the rink, and then before you know it, you're sitting on the plane getting ready to land in the next city. Life on the road is not that glamorous, but that doesn't count when you're in NYC.

We beat the Rangers 2–1 at MSG. I'm a pro so I did what I'm supposed to do. I put on my Sean Avery character face, and went out of my way to get into goalie Henrik Lundqvist's space, and talked shit to the talented young Brandon Dubinsky in warm-up. I wasn't happy. Beating the team that I still wanted to play for was not a great feeling.

Richie is a good guy, a smart guy, and he was a total professional. He'd been focused on being a great NHLer for a long time and now he was starting to enjoy himself a little bit more. Still, he was naive about what fame as a professional athlete could bring you. After the game, Richie and I took two dates to dinner at the Waverly Inn, and when we got back to the Mercer I lit a fire in the wood-burning fireplace in my room and we all went down to the lobby for a drink. Fifteen minutes later the fire alarm goes off, and as hotel guests start filing into the lobby the hotel manager approaches me and says, "Mr. Avery, you lit a fire in your room but forgot to open the flue." I wanted to set New York on fire again, but not literally.

Being back in town gave me the chance to check in with Matt Abramcyk and our new sports bar in Tribeca called Warren 77, which was coming along nicely. One of the reasons we ended up in Tribeca was that the rent was still manageable, and a restaurant's lease is what makes or breaks it. We'd have soft lighting with dark colors like hunter green, and the banquettes would be the classic red pleather with some pretty special art on the walls—some Diane Arbus, and a Warhol of Gretzky that I loaned the bar. I was really excited about this world I was creating outside hockey, and was confident that it would yield some security for when I hung up the skates. I knew I would be living back here in New York no matter what.

But on I went with Dallas. I think the first real turning point that marked the beginning of my end with the Stars came on November 1, 2008, in Boston. I've never seen two players turn an arena upside down like Steve Ott and I did that night; it was just one of those games that's nasty from the start. There were 146 minutes of penalties in that game—I had twenty-one, Ott had eighteen—and the Bruins tried to get us suspended. They said the timekeepers who sit in the penalty box have never heard such disgusting language or obscene talk in thirty-five years of NHL hockey.

Being an effective agitator is about being original, so I took that as a compliment. They forgot to mention the two train wrecks of girls who somehow got down to the penalty box area and started calling us faggots and asking us if it felt good to fuck each other's assholes.

We felt obliged to respond.

I always found it interesting when women wore jerseys with player names on the back to the game, as these ladies had done in Boston. We asked them: "How does your boyfriend feel knowing that his girlfriend would blow Phil Kessel after the game in his fucking car?" One of the girls' boyfriends came down to try talking shit back to us. So we asked him if she was allowed to blow Kessel so long as she brings home an auto-graphed stick. He lasted about seventeen seconds then bailed ten rows back up to his seat. He knew what we said was, if not literally true, then at least her fantasy, and he didn't want to go there.

It was a nasty game from the get-go, with chippy play and questionable hits and just a miserable kind of vibe in the barn in Boston. We lost 5–1, and I scored our only goal.

After the game, Mike Modano actually said that we'd created a circus and he had no interest in playing in a game that was as rough and testy an environment as the one caused by Avery and Ott.

From day one of my time on Dallas, Modano was pissed off that they were paying me that much money, and he was pissed off that he wasn't making more. He was also coming to the end of his career and didn't like people who didn't roll out the red carpet for him as they once had. He was one of those supremely talented players who didn't work hard in practice and didn't backcheck and was as soft as a baby's ass. He didn't lay his body on the line for the team. He was also very close to Brett Hull, and since Hully and I were also close, I think he was a bit jealous.

I knew my Dallas days were numbered.

———

"Hockey's Evil Genius." That's what the *Hockey News* called me when they put me on their May 13, 2008, cover with devil's horns and a mustache and goatee drawn with a Sharpie over my face. So before we landed in Calgary on December 1, 2008, the Canadian media had been hyping this big game against Calgary because of my growing reputation in the NHL, combined with the fact that Elisha Cuthbert, my ex-girlfriend of a year and a half, had started dating Dion Phaneuf, the "star" player of the Calgary Flames.

I had certainly been in love with Elisha, but the fact that she'd moved on with her life after we split—as I had done—and was dating Phaneuf was not the least bit upsetting. What bothered me was that the Canadian media not only thought that this was actually an interesting story line, but that they also thought it was an acceptable story.

As well, there was a perfect storm brewing because I was miserable in Dallas—except for a brief surge of happiness every second Friday when we got paid and my paycheck was even bigger than I'd imagined because Texas has no state income tax. But the pleasure of the paycheck was fleeting.

I wasn't having fun.

Cameras—print, TV, cell phone—were waiting in front of our hotel before we left for morning skate. I walked out to get one of the best things Canada has to offer, a coffee and doughnut (or two) from Tim Hortons. The media horde immediately started asking me about Dion. I am astonished that the news day is so slow that this is the story they want to follow: how another NHLer is dating a woman I used to date. They really want to make this seem like some kind of bitter rivalry between me and Phaneuf, so I'm thinking, OK, maybe there's a way to play this so I get inside his head before the game. But it's just a vague thought.

Cameras were inside the arena and following my every movement in our morning skate, and now I'm annoyed. There are things going on in the world that are way more important than this—I mean a million times more important—and I'm kind of embarrassed for these guys that this is what they wake up in the morning to do.

I get off the ice and the media is standing in the dressing room in a huddle, just waiting for me to invite them over. I walk into the trainer's room and the guys are all laughing about how I have become The Biggest Story in Calgary, and then it happens: I say, "I just want to comment on how it's become like a common thing in the NHL for guys to fall in love with my sloppy seconds."

I have no idea why I used that term other than it's the most relevant slang I could think of for the situation, and my aim was to poke Dion Phaneuf before the game and get him mad at me. Brad Richards had said, "You won't do it . . ." Excuse me, but was that a challenge? So I walked out of the trainer's room and into the dressing room and spoke to the media and the rest is history.

Of course, it didn't seem that way at first. I got dressed and could feel that my teammates were playing it off like it was just another sound bite in an eighty-two-game schedule. I got on the team bus to go back to the hotel for our lunch and pre-game nap, and then it started . . .

Guys' phones are buzzing and pinging and when I walk into the lunchroom, all eyes are on me. Everyone already knows, including the coaches sitting at a table eating and looking at me like I've just ruined Christmas.

I can hardly eat. I can't stop thinking about what I just said, and what the suits at the NHL are going to bring down on me now. It was trash talk before a game, and what's the worst that can happen? The NHL will fine me and that's the end of it.

I walk into my hotel room and turn on the TV and I'm on every channel. And just like in the movies, the phone rings and on the other end is my friend and my boss, Brett Hull, who says, "Holy shit, you really did it this time." The great thing about Hully is that he always said what he thought, and by now, I was thinking the same thing.

We knew each other well enough that when he said, "Get out of this shitstorm ASAP—just pack up and fly to New York and we will figure this out," we both knew my time in Dallas was over. He hadn't suspended me or anything like that. He was trying to protect me from what we both knew was about to happen. Though it was worse than we imagined.

As I sat on the tarmac waiting for my flight to leave for New York, I felt shame and relief. I felt like shit for embarrassing Elisha, which was certainly not my intention. I was in love with her once, and it didn't work out, but she's a great person and we had a wonderful year and change together. Just to make it clear here, I am very sorry for causing her any distress at all. That was never my intention. I was just trash-talking Phaneuf. But I missed the target.

I also feel a heavy burden of shame and disappointment in myself that I let my childhood idol down. Brett Hull was a guy who did nothing but good things for me when he didn't have to do anything. Other than my parents, nobody has done more for me than Brett Hull, and now I'd embarrassed the team he managed in a way that could affect his life.

On other hand, I was so relieved to be on a plane home, back to the place that feels safe and that inspires me every day. It's funny how, even more so today, if I haven't done my workout-shower-shave-and-then-dressed by 9 A.M. I feel so guilty and embarrassed because by 9 A.M. in NYC the streets are filled with people who've been on the grind for three hours, and I think if they see me walking to the gym at 9:30 it makes me look weak, like I have nothing to do. It's a bit crazy, but I love it.

For the next few days, my comments were the talk of the sports world—more so than if I had murdered someone (NFL), beaten my wife (MLB), been drunk and brawling with the public (NBA), sometimes with guns (all of the above).

I had many conversations with my agent, Pat Morris, and the NHLPA about just what the fuck I was thinking, and of course I hadn't been thinking, I'd been reacting. All our conversations were about interpreting the rules, in case Dallas wanted to void my contract, which they couldn't do. They could suspend me, but we all thought it would be for a game or two as a kind of public relations gesture. I mean, I hadn't put a guy in the morgue. But no, the NHL suspended me indefinitely, "in accordance with the provisions of By-Law 17 and Article 6 of the NHL Constitution for conduct detrimental to the League or game of hockey." They set a hearing date where I would throw myself on the mercy of Bettman and his court.

And I had little support from the Stars.

"I completely support the league's decision to suspend Sean Avery," Stars owner Tom Hicks said. "Had the league not have suspended him, the Dallas Stars would have. This organization will not tolerate such behavior, especially from a member of our hockey team. We hold our team to a higher standard and will continue to do so."

Marty Turco got in on it, too. "It's just so disappointing for guys who have been around here for a long time and have taken a lot of pride in how this organization has been perceived. The disrespect of this morning and other things over the course of the season have been extremely disappointing for us. It's a slap in the face."

Even John Tortorella said I was an embarrassment to the league, a comment that would soon be a very rich piece of irony. But right now, this was the perfect opportunity for everyone who hated Sean Avery to crush me. You'd think I was a repeat offender of some crime, but actually I had not been suspended by the NHL prior to this incident.

Despite what my agent and the NHLPA said, there was still some talk that the Stars were going to try and tear up my contract. But I knew the NHLPA would never let that happen, because setting that type of precedent would change sports forever. I mean, if they could rip up my deal because I said something vulgar then the owners might as well just put us all on golden leashes because no contract would be safe.

I had my friend Billy Durney, head of security for the Olsen twins, pick me up at my West 19th Street apartment and drive me to the NHL offices and walk me into the hearing, just in case anyone was out front to cause me a problem, but mostly to put on a show.

Basically, the NHLPA said that my only shot at escaping the guillotine was to kiss the little man's ring, the little man being the second-most hated person in hockey after me, Gary Bettman. I told Brett Hull to stay in Dallas and let me do this, because I wanted Brett to distance himself from me as much as he could. Brett is a loyal motherfucker and really doesn't give a crap what anyone says about him. He'd also scored 700 NHL goals and was NHL royalty, so he came with me.

We walked into the fancy conference room at NHL headquarters and everyone took their seats. The NHL's minister of justice, Colin Campbell, played the clip of me saying what I had said to the media in Calgary. He must have played it twenty times. He played it in slow motion again and again like they were trying to find the second gunman in the JFK assassination.

The NHL had at least a six-pack of lawyers in the room, and they walked us through all my prior incidents. There was the recent game in Boston (I scored a goal, made some hits, got in a fight) and the time I scuffled with Darcy Tucker in warm-up, and the time I called out visor-wearing French players for running guys, and the time I told Brian Hayward that he was a hack when he played and a hack on TV after he said he'd like to see me beaten to a pulp. (That's right—a TV commentator advocated extreme violence against a professional athlete.)

I mean, in the history of the NHL, there had been far worse things than this, but that wasn't the point. They wanted me gone.

It was a kangaroo court. These guys had been blowing hot air, and the only way I could get out of here with a job in the NHL was to blow some back. The difference being, what I said was true.

Cue the music. I talked about being the small kid on the team, the guy who was always told he was too short to play in the NHL, and how, when I finally made it after clawing my way in, I started to become a man who had interests away from the rink, catching up on all those things that junior hockey takes away from you.

I told them I liked to read, and to listen to music at home and at concerts, and that I liked art and design and fashion. And because I liked these things and was different from your typical NHLer, I had endured years and years of abuse from NHL fans and opposing players. They called me a "faggot" and held up signs in visiting arenas that called me a fag, and when I'd bang on the glass and point out the offending signs to the game officials, they did nothing.

Cue the tears, which were real, because I was feeling frustrated by this sham of a hearing in which I wasn't being heard. But I told them that certainly, yes, the words I used to taunt Phaneuf could have been chosen better.

Then I tried to flip the script on the NHL, and blame them for not protecting me against this abuse directed at my assumed homosexual preference (even though the women I dated were regular tabloid fodder). Did the NHL suspend star Eddie Belfour when he had to be pepper-sprayed in a Dallas hotel and offered the cops one billion dollars? What about Kevin Stevens, who was arrested with crack cocaine and a hooker? What about Dany Heatley, who was convicted of vehicular homicide after killing my friend Dan Snyder? What about all those players who called Willie O'Ree, the first black man to play in the NHL, the N-word?

Nothing.

I was trying my best to not get the death penalty. As I walk out of the NHL offices I have no idea what fate awaits me.

And then I get the call. I've been suspended for six games and sentenced to thirty days in a Malibu, California, rehab facility. Hold on a second—did they just say rehab? What the fuck could I possibly be going to spend a month in a rehab facility for? I hardly ever drink, and other than the occasional joint, I don't do drugs. Is this a joke?

No. The NHL's council of wizards have determined that I have anger issues, and so I will go to rehab for "anger management."

19

DOWN AND OUT
AND BACK AGAIN

The few days I had to wait before flying to Los Angeles—business class, paid for by the NHL, but still, to rehab—were just like waiting to go to the Big House. I had lost my liberty—just for a month, but even so, I was worried that I would lose my livelihood. And what would await me in rehab? People who should be there, most likely. Unlike me.

I land in LA and my old friends Lawrence Longo and Cody Leibel pick me up at the airport and we all head to In-N-Out before we make the drive to Malibu. We're cracking jokes and the mood is light. I'm not really nervous. My fate has been decided, so now it's time to embrace the ride.

We wind our way into a canyon in Malibu and I think about the first time I came to this part of the world, to Chris Chelios's beach party, which seems like an age ago. Finally, we pull into a driveway—no gates or barbed wire—and park in front of a beautiful house with a pool in the backyard. I gave the guys a hug and they drove off.

Rehab has a name and it's called the Canyon. It opened in 2004, and it's big—a 4,000-square-foot main house with clusters of cottages spread over 240 acres. It has a cool view of the surrounding Santa Monica Mountains and the Pacific surf beyond. There are two eight-bed facilities, one for women and one for men. You have a roommate, but the rooms are big, have fireplaces, four-poster beds, and sheets with a very high thread count. And so it should be a little deluxe, as it costs $58,000 for a thirty-day visit.

I can tell that the people running the Canyon—very professional and welcoming—are confused by my situation, since they don't run me through the normal search before check-in. It's 10:45 P.M., and as it's been a long day, I head to bed.

My roommate is already sleeping. He wakes up in the middle of the night, coming down from whatever substance has landed him here, and is jumping up and down on his bed. I have to try to calm him down until staff can arrive. He's older, pushing seventy, and he's won Emmys and an Oscar, and I didn't know who he was until the fourth day when one of the workers told me. He was in for an addiction that he'd been trying to manage for many years, and he was certainly a calming influence on me over the next while. Why I'm here, I still can't figure out.

Life at the Canyon is all about routine. I wake up early, around 7 A.M., and have breakfast. The food is great except there is NO sugar and that is something to which I am definitely addicted. I have a trainer from 9 A.M. to 11 A.M. every morning in the gym. Then I take part in group therapy and it's heavy shit—crack addiction and sexual abuse cases.

I share my story and everyone looks at me like I'm making a joke of this place. No, I wasn't raped by my uncle from ages four to fourteen, and no, I don't cut or starve myself. I'm not an alcoholic and I've never tried cocaine, and I'm taking up the place of someone who might really need to be here, like the people in my group. Was the NHL out of its mind? The only contact I have from the outside world is via NHLPA doctors, who observe the process. I knew that I was going to have to do my time here, but I also knew that once all the smoke cleared, it would all work itself out. I realized now that subconsciously, when I made the "sloppy seconds" comment, I was trying to get myself back to New York. I wanted to make something happen. I wanted to get traded. I had just picked a very hard way of going about it, and as I said, I'm very impulsive, and don't always think things through. This was certainly an awakening for me, for while I thought the reason I was in rehab was ridiculous, and demeaning to the people who really needed to be here, my journey at the Canyon did help me to understand myself better as a person.

The focus of treatment, mindfulness, ends up being a wonderful tool that I still use. Mindfulness is about controlling your impulses, using your breath, just hearing your breath as you inhale and exhale. And just remembering to breathe. It really works.

I have been in the Canyon for twenty-one days, and Christmas is a week away, and I'm starting to lose it. I feel that the people who are here really need to be here, and I feel sorry for many of them, who have none of the outside support that I have. But I am done.

Dr. Dan Cronin, who is a clinical psychologist and the NHL's substance abuse expert, and Dr. Brian Shaw, the NHLPA's guy, are the joint decision makers in this process. I think both psychologists know I'm at my breaking point and that I'm starting to think about packing my bags despite the potential consequences. I think both guys know I've done everything they asked during my time here, and clearly I don't have a problem that would put my health at risk by leaving early. So they cut me loose.

On my way out the door I'm hit by a cool blast of reality. It's clear that I'm not going back to Dallas. Modano and Turco and coach Dave Tippett (who hated me) have issued an ultimatum to Hully, and it's three against one, at least. I'm done in Dallas.

And yet I'm still the NHL-caliber player that I was a month ago, and when you take a step back and look at this fairly, you realize I didn't break the law. I made a distasteful comment, it's true—though if the NHL is worried about levels of distasteful, the execs should hang around dressing rooms more. As my plane takes off for Manhattan, I have one question bashing around inside my head: How do I get back into a New York Ranger jersey?

I know I will make this happen. And after a month in California, I need to go back to boot camp to make my NHL return a success.

Pat Manocchia is a former hockey player from Brown University who owns La Palestra, a gym on Central Park West. It's based on the ancient Greek idea of the gymnasium, and with its elegant colonnades, it is a thing of beauty. Pat trains Madonna, Howard Stern, Julia Roberts, John McEnroe, and Liam Neeson, and has a magic touch with people who need to look good for their jobs.

I need to look good for my job because sooner rather than later I'm going to get the call.

In warm weather, Central Park is a runner's paradise, but in January it's a nightmare; some paths would be better navigated on ice skates. The distance from La Palestra around the upper reservoir of the Park is two miles. Some parts of the loop are open to the major winds that whip through the canyons of Manhattan, and other than the odd winter warrior out running, the only company I have are the tips of the skyscrapers lining the perimeter of Central Park.

I use them as motivation. I've just witnessed what happens when I don't have this city. So every time it feels too cold to continue, I look at the buildings and I dig in. Every time I look around and think there's nobody here to see if I do only one lap instead of two, I look at those buildings staring down at me and I do two laps. I will not let this story have a bad ending.

I finally get the call that I've been willing the universe to make. Glen Sather wants to meet for lunch, and obviously this is not because he's hungry. Glen is sniffing out a deal and Dallas knows that they have no leverage. The only option they have is to send me down to the minors and recall me when they have word from a team that wants to claim me on re-entry.

Dallas played its hand when it sent me home, and the Stars' righteous owner, Tom Hicks, has said he doesn't want anyone of my low character on his team. (Hicks would default on more than $500 million in loans a year later; in 2011, he took the Dallas Stars to bankruptcy. In 2016, his son Tommy Junior was one of Donald Trump's biggest fundraisers. Yes, a family of top-notch character that I was a fool not to model mine on.)

I feel bad for Hully that I've put him in this situation, but Dallas management put him in an even worse one. The reality is that the team that claims me can get me at half-price, and Dallas will be on the hook for the other half. Glen Sather gets me cheaper than what he offered me as a free agent, and I'm back in New York making twice as much as I would have had I taken Glen's original offer. It's starting to look like I've pulled off a fucking miracle.

Glen Sather loves the action, and he loves the art of the deal. He loves doing things that others won't do. He's what you call a players' GM, because for the most part, he doesn't bullshit you. Glen is wearing his usual dapper sports coat with sweater and shirt to match. He reportedly makes $8 million a year, but like all rich people, he loves free stuff. He's started to get free stuff from a men's clothing company called Robert Graham, and he's rocking the shit out of these duds. He also has his signature piece—a cigar he never lights but holds in his mouth till it disappears. "Where the fuck did it go?" the guys have asked hundreds of times before.

Glen has been given the keys to the Rangers by his longtime friend, and in my opinion the best owner in sports, James Dolan. Sure, Dolan inherited his money, but he's actually aware of that and he's great to his players in terms of providing a climate that allows us to do what we do to the best of our abilities.

I know my new message is change, and I will hammer it home to Glen. I will be honest that I fucked up but that I need to get back to New York and help his team win. The amount of love I have from Ranger fans is immense, and I also have support from the face of the franchise, Henrik Lundqvist. Part of what makes Hank great is that he's a little bit oblivious to what goes on in the world around him, so he hasn't really been following my public whipping in any great detail. When I said to him, "If I can get it to the point where they'll take me back, will you stand up for me?," he said, "Yes."

Glen doesn't call Hank before he makes a move, but he and everyone else in the organization know that my relationship with the star goalie is strong. We both have a love of fashion, and we initially bonded over that. We play the game at the same level of intensity, and respect that in each other. We were also the only Rangers who had their names chanted at the Garden. And I admired the fact that he was the most well-endowed teammate I had ever seen, by a considerable margin.

I think Glen had already made up his mind before we met at Nick & Stef's Steakhouse, right next to MSG, because otherwise why would he meet me in the middle of the day in a busy NYC restaurant right next to the rink where everyone knows my name? He knew I was going to say all the right things and he also knew I was still the same guy he'd offered a multi-year deal to six months earlier. I think it was a bonus that the guy he was meeting with had changed a bit, and the only thing that was different about this convo from most of the others I had with Glen was when he noticed the new tattoo on my forearm: "*YOU/USED TO BE ALRIGHT WHAT/HAPPENED?*"

This tattoo was a reminder to use the mindfulness technique I had recently learned at the Canyon. It's a lyric from my favorite Radiohead song, "15 Step." So, thanks Gary Bettman. Rehab really did change me. Without it, I wouldn't have this tattoo. Among other things.

We agreed I would go to Hartford for two weeks and if the reports came back positive, then I would be back in a Ranger jersey. Holy shit, I'm going to pull this off.

———

To be honest, my two weeks in Hartford felt longer than my three weeks in rehab. Part of this is due to just how fast your body can get out of game shape when you're not playing, and how much work it takes to get your legs and timing back, and part of this is the fact that the Hartford coach, Ken Gernander, is a total tool.

Or maybe he thinks I am, and that's why he treats me like he has to hold his nose around me. I can see how it must seem—I'm a pampered NHLer who ran afoul of the league, got sent to some posh rehab clinic, and am now finishing my clean-up here in Hartford, and he's running a hockey team, not a clinic.

But I know that, just like the Canyon, I'm not here forever, so I make it work. It wasn't a situation where I'd beaten up my granny, so the players in Hartford and around the league were excited to play with me, or against me. Even so, I keep my head down in the dressing room and up on the ice. I play eight games, get two goals and an assist, and get sentenced to just eight minutes in the penalty box. Slats can see that I meant what I said.

Ken Gernander calls me into his office after practice one cold morning at the top of March to tell me that Dallas is putting me on re-entry, and that New York is going to claim me. Tomorrow I'll be back at MSG, so I'd better get going.

I pack my bags and turn the engine on in my Audi S8, and the roar of the fastest sedan on planet Earth replicates the sound of my game the moment I step foot on the ice of MSG.

On February 23, 2009, Slats fired coach Tom Renney. The Rangers had been on a losing skid—ten losses in twelve games—and as usually happens, the coach got the blame. Renney had a long run with the Rangers, and I liked him. He hadn't been a player, but he started out as a junior hockey coach in Kamloops, British Columbia, and had been successful. He knew how to talk to players, and he could teach us stuff.

Sather thinks the Rangers, who were in first place for a good chunk of the early season, need a kick in the ass, and that kick would be coming from John Tortorella, who piled on me for my "sloppy seconds" remark when he was working as a TV analyst after he got fired by Tampa.

At the news conference announcing his hiring, Slats had to address the elephant in the room, which was me. "I think, over time, he [Tortorella] will learn to love him [me] like we do."

It's nice of Slats to go out on a limb for me, but he isn't, not really. He's the boss, and he's telling everyone—especially Tortorella—how it's going to be. He thinks I can help the team, he's happy with my price, and that's it.

Tortorella didn't quite get Glen's message. After my first meeting with Tortorella, I knew that he meant every word when he'd called me "an embarrassment" on TV. Our meeting was very one-sided, and he wanted me to know that this was his show and I was going to become a faceless piece of the puzzle if I was going to play on his team. It was like a Chihuahua barking at a German shepherd. The little dog wants to make the big dog know that he's the boss. He wasn't yelling, he was just in a position to reaffirm his manhood in a room where you couldn't back-talk, and I would learn that he loved to do that.

I have no problem being a team player, but let's be honest: New York is a market where it's impossible to have a team of anonymous soldiers. I have a history with this city and this team, and the fans weren't chanting Tortorella's name at MSG, they were chanting mine.

I say all the right things during the meeting, and I'm willing to put the things that he said about me behind us because I understand he was an unemployed coach trying to make a living as a loudmouthed, abrasive TV analyst. Maybe we actually have some things in common. He says he's going to make me a better player, and I'm happy to go along on that journey.

I played my first game back with the Rangers on March 5, 2009. We beat the Islanders, then we beat Boston, lost to Carolina, and I got my first goal against Nashville in a 4–2 win for us.

After the Islanders game, which was on Long Island, and where the fans welcomed me back by booing me all night, a reporter from the *Daily News* asked me if I'd been nervous before the game.

"If there was any nerves coming in, I certainly got rid of them quick," I told him.

After the Nashville win, a reporter asked me how it felt to be scoring again. "Great," I said. One of the secrets of the locker room is that we want to tell the beat reporters, who we love and see as teammates, the kind of stuff they can't really print. So my fantasy answer would have gone like this:

Beat writer: Sean, you really came out of the gates flying in that first period. Can you tell us why?

Me: It's funny, because when I got to the rink tonight, I felt like shit, and when I came out for warm-up, I saw this super-hot Russian model with big, heavy C-cups standing two rows behind our bench with her agent Craig who's a personal friend and all of a sudden my legs felt like rocket launchers and I played possessed. When the puck bounced off my ass and into the net I felt like I had a real shot at her.

Beat writer: Do you think you can carry it over to tomorrow's game?

Me: Honestly, all I care about right now is getting all these stupid interviews done with and putting on my $3,000 Tom Ford suit and taking Anna with the heavy C-cups to Mr. Chow and then hopefully be done fucking her brains out by 1:30 A.M. so I can watch *Homeland* on DVR and get a few hours' sleep before morning skate.

I've always wanted to give that interview, but if I'd done it when I was playing I would have been sent to the Canyon permanently.

I finished the season playing nineteen games for the Rangers and my new coach, John Tortorella. I scored five goals, added seven assists, and served only thirty minutes in the penalty box, which is a hell of a run considering the circumstances I came back from. Tortorella put me up on the first line, and I worked as hard as I've ever worked, and we made the playoffs.

When I said I was excited to play for John Tortorella and thought he was going to make me a better player, I believed it because he said he would, and while I thought he was many things, "liar" was not one of them. Going into the first-round series against Washington, though, I was scratching my head. This coach really doesn't like me, because the better I play the less he plays me, and I've always believed my gut doesn't lie. I know what's going on here. When the team isn't playing well, he promotes me to the first line, and when they do, he buries me on the fourth. It's part of his strategy to show me in the worst possible light so that when he says to Slats, "This Avery isn't working out," it will look like he's telling the truth.

My game has lost something under Tortorella's regime. I feel tentative. We're expected to dump and chase, and the creativity has been sucked out of the Rangers game. Scott Gomez is the only player allowed to make a creative play with the risk that if he blows it, it could end up on a Washington stick. The rest of the team plays with our assholes so tight we whistle as we skate. We sit in our stalls more exhausted from the constant negativity coming from the coaches over our shoulders than from the war we're fighting on ice.

We win the first two games on the road, lose the next one at home, and then win Game 4. We're up 3–1 on Washington, and all we have to do is win one more and we're through to the next round.

Then Tortorella benches me for Game 5. It's punishment for taking two penalties in the third period in our 2–1 win in Game 4. He tells the media that I crossed an emotional line and put the team in trouble, so he's sitting one of his most effective guys to make him learn the lesson to play like a zombie.

I watch that game from the box and the Rangers lose 4–0. Washington scored less than five minutes in, and that was all they needed.

I'm back in the lineup for Game 6 at MSG—and Tortorella is suspended. While I was in the press box in Game 5, he completely lost his mind and squirted water at fans in Washington, then threw a water bottle that hit a lady in the head, and for a while, brandished a hockey stick until Jim Schoenfeld, an assistant coach, restrained him. That's right, *that* Jim Schoenfeld, the one who triggered a referees' strike by getting into it with ref Don Koharski and telling him to "have another doughnut, you fat fucking pig." If you're keeping track, the assistant coach who had been suspended for losing his cool had to restrain the head coach who was suspended for losing his cool. And I was the one sent to rehab for anger issues. But at least Schoenfeld put me back in the lineup and I get an assist on our first goal, which ties the game at one, and I stay out of the box for sixty minutes. We lose 5–3.

Now the Caps have tied the series, and Game 7 is winner take all.

We score first, and I get another assist. Washington ties it. And then, with less than five minutes left in the third period, I watch Sergei Federov raising his arms after making Wade Redden look like the worst free agent signing in the last twenty years. We lose 2–1.

We lost the series where we'd been up 3–1. That doesn't happen to good teams, especially when you have a goalie like Lundqvist in your net. Nice work, Torts.

Tortorella has a reputation as a hard-ass, but not if you know him as a player. We used to laugh at him all the time. There was always someone in the dressing room who wanted to take their skate and decapitate him or take their stick and whack him over the head with it. Marián Gáborik despised him with every bone in his body. Even Hank Lundqvist, an even-keeled Swede who was usually in his own world, thought Tortorella was a terrible manager of pro athletes.

And he can't skate and stickhandle a puck at the same time, and he doesn't realize we really don't take him seriously because of that.

I thought Tortorella was a clown, but he was hardly the first coach I didn't respect. But there were two things he did that season that made me think he was a danger to the team.

First, he referred to our fans at MSG as "idiots." He said it with hate. I wanted to stand up and bitch-slap him. What does this midget who can't even skate know about the MSG fans? How hard they've cheered for us ever since I've worn this jersey, and how hard they cheered for us the last two years in the playoffs? How they make us feel special when we walk down the street in a big city like New York? I can guarantee that I wouldn't ever bump into Tortorella on the street because he didn't even live in New York City.

And then he called our local beat writers "fucking idiots." The hockey beat writers are always there, writing about our team no matter what, win or lose. Our writers give us presence and identity in a city crowded with pro sports teams, and as players, we need it.

The confidence you get from a headline that has your name in it and an article that praises you is almost as valuable as the kick in the butt you get from an article that calls you out for not playing well and makes you realize you really need to pick up your game ASAP. And now our coach is degrading these writers as idiots. He thought these big-city writers whose profession was to follow our team and the game we played didn't have a clue about hockey. The funny thing is that Tortorella can skate just about as well as some of our beat writers.

Over the summer prior to the 2009–10 Rangers' training camp, Tortorella kept in touch with me by phone, and the calls were very weird. I actually like the idea of coaches speaking to their players during the off-season, but these calls felt more like he was pretending to give a shit about what I was doing when, really, he was spying on me.

He'd ask me whether I was working hard and getting ready for camp. He could have asked any staffer on the Rangers—trainers, conditioners, or Glen—if conditioning had ever been an issue, but no. And he also seemed to be very interested in where I was. Might I be in Paris? South of France? Croatia? He might as well have asked me for GPS coordinates. It was like he was building a dossier to prove that I was in all the places where every other serious hockey player wasn't. And nor was I. Tortorella was just trying to get evidence to make me look like a loser to Slats, when the real loser was the guy that Torts saw in the mirror.

In May 2009, I walked into the first precinct of the NYPD in Tribeca and asked to speak with the station chief. Yankees, Rangers, Jets, Mets, Giants, and Knicks are like gods with the Boys in Blue, because cops love sports and they love their local teams. It's in their DNA. I introduced myself to everyone and explained that I had a sports bar opening that night around the corner and that they were very welcome to come around and say hello.

Now, the first rule for pro athletes and everyone else is DO NOT GET INTO THE BAR BUSINESS. Of course, as a breaker of rules, I decided to give it a try, because, after all, I had Matt Abramcyk as my partner and we were going to be different. Indeed, as we designed the layout on a napkin that first time we walked the space together, we were designing a sports bar that would be the first of its kind anywhere in the world: a sports bar so chic that on opening night we had people spilling out onto Warren Street.

The crowd was a mix of fashion heavy hitters along with Yankees-Knicks-Jets-Rangers fans and a lot of downtown cool kids. Henrik Lundqvist played guitar with his band, John McEnroe was in the house, and then someone special walked in.

I was standing at the end of the bar smoking a cigarette after Hank had finished his set (we let VIPs smoke upstairs, and as co-owner, I rated . . .) when she walked in. I'd never seen a more beautiful woman in my life, and my eyes have landed on a lot of beauty. She had long legs, and a lean, toned body, and her face was perfection that God does not create very often.

I leaned over to Juan, our manager, and said, "That's the woman I'm going to marry." He didn't laugh.

Her name is Hilary Rhoda, she's twenty-two, and she's from Chevy Chase, Maryland. She's the face of one of the biggest cosmetic brands in the world, Estée Lauder, and a *Sports Illustrated* swimsuit model. She is a creature I have only seen before in the movies.

I never put the "moves" on a woman whom I find attractive when I first meet her. I always wait until our energy brings us together for a second time, and I always play it cool, that's my move. But tonight Hilary walked into Warren 77 with a mutual friend, Christina, who I suddenly became very interested in talking to, and shut out the rest of the party happening around us. Christina can see how mesmerized I am by Hilary, and like a good friend, she breaks away to give me a chance to hang with my future wife. At the end of the night, I shake Hilary's hand and tell her it was really nice to meet her. And that I cannot wait to see her again.

Later that night I send her a text—Christina gave me her number—to tell her how pretty I thought her dress was, perfect for the summer. Or the rest of our lives. I did not tell her that. But she texted me back, and said it would be great to see me again. I smiled. My life in New York was suddenly looking better again.

I hadn't been dating anyone since my return to New York, and certainly wasn't sampling from the parade of puck bunnies who circle teams from junior hockey onward. Hockey has its own slang that captures the spirit of the game—"playing heavy," which means not cutting corners in your game, "foot on the gas," which means going full tilt on the ice, and "puck bunnies," which is a kinder term for "jock sniffers," and both of which refer to groupies.

Groupies are part of any sports or entertainment culture, and in hockey they start in junior, especially if you're playing in Canada. That's when they're called "puck bunnies" and it's not really a term of endearment. You don't want your sister to be called one.

The puck bunnies go to places where players hang out, like hockey rinks, and hockey bars, which in small-town Canada is pretty much any bar in town. Some bunnies would even go to team meet-and-greets in malls. Some would go to the "get to know the season-ticket holder" party, where you'd skate with the season-ticket holders and then host a luncheon and they'd ask you questions. The hard-core bunnies would go to those events.

The higher-end puck bunnies were strategic about it. They'd suntan next to the spot where the Kings liked to play summer volleyball in Manhattan Beach, for example, and get invited to player parties.

In a small town like Own Sound, Ontario, the puck bunny wasn't as good-looking as the puck bunny in LA or New York. But then, when you hit the pros they're not puck bunnies anymore. They're just groupies.

I do not get turned on when I look into a woman's eyes and see that she is a fan, because having a fan surrender to me sexually doesn't get me going.

I like the challenge of seduction. I like planning the approach, the introduction, the small talk that I try to turn into a conversation based on the energy of mutual attraction. This is where she starts laughing because I'm funny and not because she wore my jersey as a kid.

I believe that lack of confidence is one of the main reasons athletes love jock sniffers. Before social media gave everyone instant intel on where you were and who you were with, hockey players would hang out at the same bars so that the ladies in the stands would know where to find them after games. Once I got traded to New York, I stopped going out on the road because it's all downhill after you have partied in New York and the road became the only place I could get some sleep.

Well, that's not quite true. One time when I was with the Kings we were in a Montreal bar, and the bartender, who was this gorgeous black-haired French-Canadian lady, decided we'd get more privacy in the ice box. So we waltz into the cooler aiming to heat it up a bit, and another teammate of mine was in there already, enjoying the hospitality of one of the waitresses. It was a big cooler, so the bartender just pulled me into a corner far from my busy teammate and we got busy ourselves.

My life in New York was suddenly looking better again. Falling in love with the girl of your dreams is cool. That's what's happening with Hilary, and I am playing it all fast forward. I think that being a loving husband is very cool, and being a loving father is the coolest, but that's down the road. Having a companion whom you're committed to should not end the fun.

I've had many relationships over the years, and in between them I would crank up my dating patterns and sometimes would crank them down, as I wanted to be alone. I certainly became much pickier as I got older, and the types of women I met changed when I moved to New York.

Since the opening night of Warren 77, I couldn't stop thinking about the girl from Chevy Chase, Maryland, and I finally realized why my friends and teammates made fools of themselves for women. And then I picked up the phone and told Hilary to grab a friend, and I'd have a plane waiting for her on the tarmac in Farmingdale on Long Island to fly them to Bonnaroo.

Bonnaroo was a music festival outside Nashville that a couple of friends from NYC started in 2002. My friends and I would fly to Nashville and the bus would pick us up at the airport. We'd stop at Walmart and fill the bus with supplies (water, candy, lawn chairs, AstroTurf, and enough booze for a 100-person wedding), and our access was so VIP that we'd park the bus a few hundred feet from backstage.

The first two years of Bonnaroo saw ten buses parked backstage but none of them prepared like we did, including the guys that started the festival. Over the years our bus had some famous acts cruise through for a drink: Jimmy Buffett, MGMT, Jim James, and, instead of coming in for a drink, Lily Allen, who grabbed a bottle of our Jägermeister and drove away on the back of a golf cart.

I never imagined that I might get the chance to spend a weekend with my future wife at Bonnaroo, and even if you'd told me it would cost $22K, I wouldn't have blinked. Hilary got on that plane, and as we danced together among 90,000 strangers, I had to catch myself from staring at her too much so that I wouldn't freak her out. But more than look at her, I wanted to get to know this beautiful woman. What did she think? What did she hope? What did she want? I was going to find out everything I could about her—and hope the conversation lasted for a very long time.

As the summer slid toward September, Hilary and I hung out less in groups of friends and started hanging out as a couple. Which we weren't yet, and had not even been alone together until we sat at the table of our first proper date, Mr. Chow, in Tribeca. One night in August, when I drove her home to Astor Place from my apartment on West 19th, I kissed her before she got out of the car. She kissed me back. It had begun.

As I was heading into the 2009–10 season with the Rangers, I wanted summer to never end so that I could just enjoy life with Hilary, and yet I also wanted to get back on the ice and prove to myself that I was a better player than ever. I even believed that my relationship with John Tortorella could be saved, because I was coming back to play my best season yet.

I'm also excited to have Hilary see me play. Obviously she knows that hockey is what brought me to New York, and that my success at it is what allows me to rent massively expensive airplanes and fly her to music festivals. It will be nice to have her see what all the fuss is about when we walk down the street and grown men come up to me, barely able to get the words out as they ask to shake my hand. And part of the reason I've connected so well with the fans is that New Yorkers have discovered that they never need to ask me if they can shake my hand. I consider myself a guest in their city, and hope to stay as long as I can.

Even though Hilary was a varsity-level field hockey player in high school, she's never seen an ice hockey game before. The first one she sees me play is against the Ducks in early October. I get an assist in our 3–0 shutout of Anaheim, and contrary to what Hilary thinks will happen, I do not get into a fight. I don't even get a penalty. But I can see the pride in her eyes after the game when she tells me that hockey is the most exciting sport she's ever seen. I think this is all going to work out. With Hilary, at least.

With Tortorella, I'm having my doubts. Even after being one of the top three conditioned guys in the club at training camp, I feel like I'm fighting for a job. I knew something was up when we had our media day for the Rangers to film promo packages for home games and interviews with all the local outlets, and I was an afterthought. Not front and center before the fans who chanted my name at MSG, but kind of, "Oh, it's OK, we have it covered . . ."

I had an idea this was coming because Tortorella told me when camp started that I was to stop being the center of attention on this team. I wasn't trying anything of the sort. I'd brought my personality to the team, we had won with me in the lineup, and I had connected with the fans here more than in any place I'd ever played. But the NHL discourages individuality because they like to control things, and Tortorella was cut from that controlling cloth.

He did everything in his power to deter guys from meeting their pre-Torts endorsement obligations as well as signing new endorsements. He would even put in bans on when we could do personal autograph sessions.

The reason I know this is that *ESPN The Magazine* wanted to do a feature on me, and Torts said no. I would never have known had I not gone to the ESPYs in LA and run into the editor who'd made the ask, and who told me about it. I was furious, but I had my revenge. I told Tortorella that I was going to do media that I'd already booked, and I did. As long as my media gigs didn't conflict with a game or practice, then it was my business and not theirs. It was another bull's eye on me as far as Tortorella was concerned.

And so began my daily battle of trying not to be run out of town by a little man who was scared of the power I held with the Rangers. He'd be on me for everything—he even tried to get me to stop fighting because he was so afraid of momentum that he didn't want to risk upsetting the other team and motivating them.

Tortorella was a guy who coached to tie, and hoped that Hank would be the difference in goal. We all hated it, and even a guy like Ryan Callahan, who flourished under Tortorella, hated it, because his body was falling apart under Tortorella's regime. He'd make guys block twenty shots a game, and then do it again the next night. There are days now when I look back and think I should have walked into Glen Sather's office and said, "Let's get me out of here and save us a lot of headaches," because I could see the future, but I also had this hope that I could change Tortorella's game.

I missed the first four games of the season with a knee injury and had one assist in my first game back against Anaheim, which we won 3–0. I also had 10:42 of ice time.

In the next game, against Toronto, I scored two goals in our 7–2 win and had 10:38 of ice time. Under Tom Renney, I was playing nearly twenty minutes a night. I've always been realistic when it comes to assessing myself, and I know what's going on here—Tortorella is sending me a message. I also know I should be getting more ice time than my new teammates, Chris Higgins and Aleš Kotalík and Enver Lisin, to name a few.

Every season you have new teammates who present an opportunity to form relationships that sometimes become strong bonds away from the rink long after the game has finished, but my best ones are my old ones. Shanny's now playing across the river in New Jersey and so I see him a lot, and while Norty's not in the league anymore, we stay in touch. Whenever Cheli comes into town we hang out. He likes to go to the Russian baths in the East Village, which is straight out of the film *Eastern Promises*. There are lots of scary Russian guys with Mafia tats everywhere, but no one tries to knife us in the steam room. It's probably Cheli's favorite place to go, other than his chili bar in Detroit.

And sometimes you get a teammate whose only lasting impression is something you would rather forget.

This is the case with Donald Brashear, who came in to replace Colton Orr as our tough guy. Everyone loved Colton, who had signed as a free agent with Toronto, and he was especially missed by the fans who didn't like Brashear from the start, as Brash had imprinted himself in their memories as a tough guy with archenemy Philadelphia, and most recently, Washington.

Our problem with him was simpler: Donald Brashear had halitosis, the medical term for bad breath. Brash could clear a room out with his breath, and if you were the unlucky guy sitting beside him on the bench you would immediately call for the Rangers trainer Jim Ramsay so that he could apply some Vicks VapoRub under your nose to mask the death rays coming from Brashear.

On every team I've played on there have been dog lovers, but Brashear took this to a new level. I was in the weight room when Billy, an ex-NYPD horse cop who took care of our practice rink, rushed in. He had a very dry, biting sense of humor, and he'd seen everything. He now had the kind of look on his face that suggested he hadn't see this—like maybe aliens had landed in the shower. He told me I had to see it too, so I hurried off, expecting to clock which teammate was shaving his line-mate's ass or back—which is a regular act of kindness, but nonetheless, always shocking.

This time it was much different.

Donald Brashear was in the shower, butt naked, and washing his Great Dane's balls along with everything else on that massive beast. Brashear was in a full lather and so was the dog. I asked Billy if this was the same as a father having a bath with his almost-teenage son. I know, it's an extreme comparison, but this was one of the weirdest things I had ever seen in a dressing room, and I have seen some things.

Every day during my drive to our practice facility in Tarrytown, I'm thinking about what it would mean to leave New York again, especially now that I've fallen in love with Hilary.

I've seen many teammates in long-distance relationships, and they don't work. In most cases, someone cheats, and usually it's the guy, and sometimes his girlfriend stays around but she harbors so much anger that by the time they are together and get married, they hate each other.

And because they are finally together, that probably means he's done playing. This is a recipe for disaster. You stay with this person because you're afraid of being alone, but you're not actually together in a way that lets you understand them—every ounce of their body, every mood they are in—and gives you the emotional knowledge to live together in harmony. If you're at this point, and you add the dilemma of having to find new meaning in your life when your career ends and you can no longer do the only thing you've been successful at since you were eight years old, then I can almost guarantee the marriage won't last.

And then what?

In most cases it winds up in divorce, and suddenly you have half the money you had when you retired, which is probably not enough to live on for the rest of your life, unless you move to the backwaters of Mississippi. Then it gets really dark, just before it goes completely black.

The more I fall in love with Hilary, the more I think about how much I don't want to leave her, no matter how badly hockey is going. This love is the real deal.

So is the love I get from Rangers fans. Baseball's Joe Torre put it perfectly when he explained the relationship between the New York fans and El Duque, the great Yankees pitcher Orlando Hernández: "New York fans are not easy to win over but they connected with him from day one."

That pretty much describes my experience here, one that even now can bring tears to my eyes. The energy that New York fans gave me from the very first moment was like a lifeline, keeping me close to them and urging me to do even better on the ice. It's the greatest professional gift that I've ever been given.

It's also the reason I didn't walk into Glen Sather's office and sit down, man to mentor, to ask for a trade. I had two years left on my contract after this season, but it was the addiction that I had to Rangers fans and the city and now Hilary that was too hard to break. They could send me back to the Canyon for months and that addiction would still be deep inside me. I kept thinking, "It's going to be OK, this coach is going to realize I'm a Ranger to my core and want to do my very best, and if he doesn't then it is what it is and I'll figure it out once the ride is over." But I didn't want the ride in New York to ever end.

We've won eight and lost thirteen since New Year's, and everyone is miserable under the Reign of Terror that is Torts. Our last game before the Olympic break is on Valentine's Day, and I give Hilary—and the Rangers fans—my own unique Valentine, because tonight is the only time I've ever scored on an NHL penalty shot, which I was given after being hooked while in the slot with a clear scoring chance.

The one thing that you're most nervous about with the penalty shot is that you're going to miss it—the puck's going to roll off your stick and you're not going to get any shot off. That's the fear. This is in addition to the fact that you're alone at center ice with the puck and with 20,000 people watching you—hoping you'll fail if it's an away game and that you'll score if you're at home. It's the most nerve-racking moment you can have. I mean, if you get a breakaway and score or miss, it all happens so fast you don't even think about it.

On a penalty shot, you get about a minute to think about it, and the guys from the other team are shouting trash at me like "hands of stone/ you're fucking awful/ faggot" and trying to rattle you. At this point in the NHL, the tie-breaking shootout hasn't yet started, so penalty shots are rare and they're a big deal.

The ref blows the whistle and I skate in fast on Tampa's goalie Mike Smith, fake him to the right, then swing wide to my left and he sprawls to recover. I outwait him and roof the puck over him into the net. It's the sweetest feeling you can imagine because you've scored this one all by yourself.

The fact that I scored it against Tortorella's old team, the Tampa Bay Lightning, and the fact that it was the first of our five straight goals that would give us a much-needed win, made me feel a little better, but not much.

The game had the same feeling as most games do before a break during the season, but a bit more so because we were going to be off ice longer with the Olympics. Guys' heads are more focused on making their flights to Miami or Vegas or Cabo.

Every four years the NHL sends players to the Winter Olympics, and the rest of us get a long siesta.

This Olympic break, I was going to spend time with Hilary. We went to a resort in Jamaica with my friend Lawrence Longo and my teammate Aaron Voros and their girlfriends. The place was called the Caves, and it had been founded by Chris Blackwell, the guy who started Island Records. The resort is on the north coast of Jamaica, and has these luxury cabins built on top of cliffs. It's very different from the traditional "white sand beach" Jamaica. So what's an NHLer to do during the break but a little cliff diving from twenty-five feet up?

Hilary was game for it, too, and that trip really made me see how, despite her supermodel gorgeousness, she had the soul of an outdoors girl, and loved joining into the spirit of the moment—snorkeling, cliff jumping, cave exploring, hanging in the rum bar and sampling the local beverage.

I was soon going to be thirty years old, and from that vantage point, it was my opinion that there was no reason why any professional athlete should be married before his twenty-fifth birthday. If you noticed I said "my opinion," it's because I was really getting tired of taking heat for having an "opinion," which is especially discouraged in the world of pro hockey.

I was told by everyone from the goal light judge to my agent that I should limit my "opinions," and when I'd hear this I would sometimes laugh it off and sometimes get angry and occasionally I would try to understand why nobody would ask me why I said these things. I think they didn't ask because they didn't want to hear my reasoning, just in case they agreed with me.

But Hilary wanted to know my opinion and I wanted to know hers, and that was the best thing going by far in a season that was looking increasingly bleak. She would ask me about the team after games, and always looked for the positive. When I told her that Tortorella was killing the Rangers, she accepted that as unacceptable, and asked me how I could stop him. I told her I was trying to be the best player I could be, but that he didn't seem to understand. She reassured me that even though she was biased she could see what I brought to the team, and that hearing the fans chant my name at MSG lit her up with joy. And that made me happy, too. My entire life wasn't a disaster, I was just having a rough time at work. On a very public stage. As a public figure herself, Hilary knew the pressure. But her wisdom, and her ready smile, made me believe that good would triumph.

There are some good things in my life in addition to Hilary. My sports bar, Warren 77, is considered a complete success. After games, whether we win, lose, or draw, I pull up out front and reenact the famous scene from *Goodfellas* where Ray Liotta walks to his table (all one camera shot) at the front of some hot NYC supper club and inside it's filled with diehard fans and beautiful women and high-rolling Wall Streeters and everything else in between. It makes me forget the guy behind the bench.

The food is the best bar food I've ever had and the drinks are cold and the bar is always open as long as I'm inside. And best of all, it's free for me, as we write it off as a marketing expense. We're on our way to making our initial investment back in the first year. I've shown that I can make a living off the ice once my NHL career is done.

Along the way, I've learned things about how to run a bar. Find an honest man, make him your manager, pay him handsomely, and give him a piece of equity in the bar. Cover the top of your basement cooler in glass so the Goldman Sachs guys (or whoever the rich boys are in your town) have a private place to do big lines of blow in privacy. Waitresses need to be hot single chicks who make the clients feel as if anything is possible (sometimes it is)—it's that feeling that keeps drinks and food flowing. Play a lot of Rolling Stones. Let Eddie Vedder drink straight from an $800 bottle of wine after he single-handedly destroys 20,000 people at MSG two hours earlier. Never charge a model for anything. Never charge the NYPD for anything. Play a lot of Pearl Jam. Fry your French fries in duck fat. Have Warhol paintings and Diane Arbus photos on the walls. Make sure John McEnroe comes to opening night and Page Six reports it the next day. Never charge "the Wolf," aka Harvey Keitel, and indeed, never charge ANYONE famous. Put Molson Canadian on tap. Pay your sales tax on time.

I promise that if you follow these steps and tweak them as need be to your town, you can open a successful bar anywhere from Albany, New York, to Zurich, Ontario.

We've played five games since the return from the Olympic break, and I have a goal and two assists, but the team has a record of one win and four losses. So on March 12, I'm a healthy scratch from the lineup for a game against Atlanta. We lost the previous game to New Jersey 6–3, and my plus/minus was even and I didn't take a penalty, but I guess I didn't try hard enough for the little guy behind the bench in my 10:56 of ice time.

It's obvious to anyone who knows the Rangers that I'm in a lose-lose situation. If I play hard I usually take penalties, and that also usually becomes an advantage in the end. The problem is that the moment I get involved and play the game I want to play—my best game—is the moment the little guy behind the bench tells me to "check yourself!" as if I'm about to pee on the carpet or something.

I'm back for the next game against Philly, and score two goals in our win. I am easily the best player on the ice, and I think this is the case because I'm playing for myself, and most of my teammates, and the fans of NYC. But not for the little guy behind the bench.

Ten days later we beat New Jersey in a shootout. After I screen Marty Brodeur on a Brandon Dubinsky goal that ties the game, I delay one second before celebrating with my teammates so that I can remind Marty that he's a "fucking home-wrecker" and should be ashamed of himself.

When I get back to the bench, I get an earful from Tortorella about talking to Marty, which he makes clear I'm not allowed to do as long as he's the coach. We are currently five points out of the last playoff spot, and chasing Philly. Most of the team is so nervous we can't think clearly enough to make a creative play, let alone the right play. Anyone who's not on a long-term contract and makes a mistake is told by Torts when they come back to the bench that if they fuck up again, they're going to get run out of town. Who wouldn't be squeezing the stick too tight if that's your coaching model?

I can't listen to another word from Tortorella and turn around and tell him to shut the fuck up. I've reached my breaking point with this guy. He tries to yell some more and scare me but I'm seeing red, and I think he realizes that if he doesn't back off something might go down.

Oh, and by the way, my Corsi rating is great. Corsi measures the number of shots taken while a player is on the ice—for and against. A good Corsi number says that you have possession more often than not. And my Corsi is better than that of very good players on my team, such as Marián Gaborík, Brandon Dubinsky, Brian Boyle, and Chris Drury. Just saying.

After that shootout win in New Jersey, we win five games, lose one in OT, one in a shootout, and one in regulation time, but we still don't make the playoffs. We finish one point behind both Philly and Montreal, and they get the final two playoff spots in the East.

I know the players are disappointed. The feeling in MSG in April is magic. The grind is fun, and it's all even better in May if you're lucky enough to still be playing.

And yet there's also a feeling of relief among my teammates that we're done, even if those words are never uttered out loud. It doesn't even have to be said. None of us can stand listening to the mental midget and his big goofy sidekick, Mike Sullivan.

Tortorella is a power-hungry control freak but he's not smart enough to hire a good cop, even one he could play like a violin. If Mike Sullivan had played the good cop he could still have turned around after meeting with a disgruntled player and told his puppet-master JT the details while giving the players some form of relief. Instead they're only able to bitch and vent to each other. This creates an unhealthy locker room.

In the meantime, I am going to enjoy Hilary and the summer. One of the things I love most about Hilary is her love of music, and although she is rarely not smiling, she gets even happier upon hearing a great song that she loves. And seeing her smile makes me smile, and I haven't been doing a lot of that at work.

We went to our first Phish concert at a venue on Long Island called Jones Beach. There was total pandemonium in the parking lot even before the show started and basic insanity the moment the first chord hit. I was hooked a few songs into the show, when massive funk-based freak-outs erupted among the 15,000 fans as they let go of any insecurities and danced any way they wanted. It's what I needed after being told to "check" myself once too often.

After the Jones Beach show, we were hooked on Phish and decided to drive to Saratoga Springs to see them play again.

I should also mention that most people at Phish shows are in a chemically altered state, and you could call it the secret ingredient. Because the Saratoga concert is inside a national forest, I decide it's the perfect place to trip on acid for the first time, and twenty minutes before the show starts I pop a white Altoid with a drop of LSD on it into my mouth, and make the short walk from the hotel into the venue.

Phish opened the show with a bang, the exuberant "Brother"—"*Whoa! Somebody's jumping in the tub with your brother*"—and I waited and waited and waited until a hour into the show, and then the acid hit me.

I've never felt or experienced anything like it in my life. It feels like you're in a movie, watching yourself in these amazing primary colors, with everything alive around you—even things that aren't alive. I can only compare it to a scene in *Fear and Loathing in Las Vegas* where Johnny Depp, playing Hunter S. Thompson, arrives in a hotel lobby while he's on an acid trip, and the carpet on which his character is standing comes to life . . . I must say he handles the experience much better than I did.

Phish is known for throwing curveballs at their fans by playing unusual cover songs, and that night they played one of the weirdest and most intense cover songs I've ever heard: Katy Perry's "I Kissed a Girl." Phish sent my acid trip into a whole new stratosphere, and by the middle of the song my face felt like it had melted off and my soul was exposed. My arms felt so heavy I could barely lift them to take a drag on my cigarette, and when I finally got my hand to my mouth the butt was moving like an ocean wave so that I couldn't meet my mouth to pull a drag.

The concert was outdoors, and I had to move around to shake off this beast that was hanging on me, so I made my way to the top row where the venue flattens out and looks down on the crowd and the stage. I sat and watched, trying to control my mind. Hilary, who did not drop acid, was next to me, being a good companion. To her, and everyone else, I looked like I was fine. Maybe my eyes were a little glassy, but I wasn't going to take a flying leap onto the stage. I mean, I could barely move.

People are always talking about finding themselves on acid, and I can tell you that the experience is not guaranteed to be a pleasant one. Acid is not a drug for people who are hard on themselves, and more specifically, a person like me who is motivated much of the time by fear. Yeah, I'm driven by fear that the guy beside me is working harder this off-season than I am. Right now, in the midst of this acid trip, it feels like every NHL player is definitely working harder than me. Fear and acid is not a combination I would recommend.

And so the snowball effect begins, and for the next six hours I try to wrestle this roller coaster of emotions, and also try not to walk into oncoming traffic so the roller coaster stops. And then I finally fall asleep. Hilary is cool with it all. She knows that I live an intense life, and this walk on the edge was something I wanted to try, responsibly, but it's not going to be a regular trip I make. She's not dating a junkie. She's dating a man who loves her even more each day.

20

THE LAST SEASON

On July 1, the first day of free agent signings for the 2010–11 season, the Rangers sign Derek Boogaard. Derek is six-seven and 270 pounds and one of the most feared players in the NHL. I immediately get his cell phone number from the Rangers to text him congrats and welcome him to New York. I'm happy to have him because he's the kind of tough guy who will give us a lot more room on the ice, and he has the reputation of being a much better teammate than the departed Donald Brashear.

We also signed my old friend from Los Angeles, Alex Frolov, and I wondered what new Russian beauty he was going to roll into town with. Frolov was a real ladies' man, and though I never could understand the smooth words coming out of his mouth, there wasn't a single, married, or separated Russian woman who Frolov couldn't seduce in about forty-five minutes.

And then there was Ruslan Fedotenko, who had played for John Tortorella in Tampa Bay and was so far up the coach's ass you could see his toes dangling between Torts's legs. Fedotenko was a rosy-cheeked Ukrainian who had come to play junior hockey for the Sioux City Musketeers, and as a nineteen-year-old, was billeted by a host family.

So his host mother, married with two kids a bit younger than him, fell in love with Fedotenko and left her husband for him. She hangs around the

Rangers with the other wives and girlfriends, and this is by far the most uncomfortable situation I've ever been in with a team. She's old enough to be the mother of some of the players' girlfriends. She's old enough to be his mother, too, and Steve Ott used to just light him up about it. We were all from junior towns and so we all knew the billet drill—they were your "other family" and not a dating pool. But Fedotenko is still with her, so it's all part of love's strange game.

It's funny how fast my last full season in the NHL went. And yet, at the time, it seemed to crawl. In the season opener against Buffalo, Derek Stepan scores a hat trick in his first NHL game. I set up his third goal with a superstar type of pass, a quick backhander from behind the net to Stepan in the slot, and just like that it's stretching the mesh behind Ryan Miller. It's the kind of play not even Tortorella could miss.

I finish the night with two assists, and usually when you start the season with a great game your coach gets excited and wants to ride you along with any other players coming out of the gates strong.

I do get a little more ice time, and in the third game I pick up another two assists against Toronto, then another assist against the Devils, and a goal and an assist against Atlanta. We're eight games in and I have seven points.

All my work is down low below the hash marks, which has become my specialty over the years. I've become great at protecting the puck when I can use my big Paris Hilton–approved butt to shield the puck. It's like holding a ball in your hands and keeping it from someone, twisting your body like a shield and anticipating your opponent's move, rolling your body a millisecond earlier than the attacking player. Think about the rush you get when you're the one keeping the ball away, then multiply that by a thousand and that's how I feel when I have a great shift below the hash marks.

Despite my own success on the ice, we're only playing .500 hockey. I'm not happy playing for Tortorella because I'm not really playing *for* him. I definitely don't want to keep hearing his yapping at us on the bench. I realize that if I'm going to make a move, then now is the time, because I have leverage with my play and points total. It's the best time to ask Glen Sather to move me out of New York, but I'm torn, because I still believe—just a little bit—that Tortorella is going to give me the break I deserve. On the other hand, the more I produce, the less he seems to give me.

But I'm definitely conflicted. I don't want to leave. I'm head over heels in love with Hilary. New York City makes me happier than I've ever been, and we've started construction on a second restaurant. I have a thriving business and am about to open another. So I suck it up and play on. But even at this early point in the season, I have a bad feeling about what John Tortorella is doing to this team that Glen Sather has handed to him.

I don't think Glen asked John Tortorella about whom he should and shouldn't sign or trade for. I believe Slats assembles the team he likes on paper and the guy he hires to coach them is supposed to figure out how to fit the pieces of the puzzle together. So when Derek Boogaard showed up forty pounds over his playing weight and stepped on the track for fitness testing at his first Rangers' training camp and barely finished two laps, Tortorella was already trying to figure out how to use Boogaard as little as possible.

He had almost no use for Boogaard as a player, and showed as little interest in him as a man. Boogaard had made it to the NHL because he could fight. We didn't have anyone on the team who'd fought Boogaard before he joined the Rangers, so he came in as a kind of mythic character, "the Boogeyman." In reality, his reputation as a fighter was so intimidating that he didn't have to fight all that much by the time he became a Ranger.

In his first NHL season, Boogey fought sixteen times, and in the season before he joined us, he fought nine. He'd cut his total almost in half just because guys knew what power he could unleash. Indeed, he was such a dominant fighter and had such a long reach that Georges Laraque, himself no slouch in the fight game, opted to retire from pro hockey rather than face the kind of punch that Boogaard had landed on Todd Fedoruk, shattering his cheekbone and requiring a rebuild of Fedoruk's face.

The Rangers had signed the Boogeyman for $6.5 million over four years, which is excellent money for a guy who could fight better than he could play. When Boogaard got to New York, we all knew that there was going to be a problem with him fitting in beyond his role as a fighter, because he wasn't the most skilled hockey player. There were times when he would trip over himself in practice just trying to make a standard pass. But we were sympathetic to him, because he was trying so hard.

But he did get in shape, and in a game against Washington at MSG on November 9, 2010, it paid off. The puck bounced over the Capitals' D-man at our blue line, and Boogey took it up the left wing and ripped a slap shot from the top of the circle. The puck blew past goalie Michal Neuvirth and it was Boogey's first goal since his NHL rookie season. In fact, it ended the longest goalless streak in the NHL, at 235 games. We celebrated on the bench like he'd won the Stanley Cup in Game 7 overtime. It was the happiest I've ever seen a team get for a guy scoring a regular season goal.

Exactly one month later, Matt Carkner hit Derek with a lucky punch right on the button in a game against Ottawa. Boogey landed a couple of punches of his own, but when he finished the fight he went straight to the dressing room and we knew that punch must have done damage. Indeed it had, as Derek had a concussion. He also had an aggravated shoulder injury from when he broke his collarbone in junior.

Derek also had an addiction to painkillers. The NHL knew about it, and Tortorella probably knew, too. If he did, he sure didn't seem to care. As soon as Derek was injured, a new rule came into effect that decreed that injured players who came to the rink had to finish all their medical treatments and conditioning before the healthy players arrived. In other words, Derek was effectively banished from the team.

When this rule came in, everyone was scratching their heads thinking, "What the fuck is happening here? This isn't fair." I'd never seen anything like this rule, ever. It was unheard of.

We felt terrible, and talked amongst ourselves about whether we should say something to management. We would see Boogey leaving the rink in the morning as we rolled in for practice and you could see the pain and the loneliness on his face.

This was another punch to the head for Derek, who already felt extremely abandoned before the injury (which was confirmed by the thousands of text messages he would send monthly—more than 13,000 in February 2011). Being separated from the team that was his life only isolated him even more, and with someone struggling like he was with various issues such as alcohol, drugs, depression, and his injury, it sent a very clear message that he wasn't wanted. I talked to him as much as I could. He knew he could pick up the phone and call or text me whenever. And he did. He was a very proud man, and I could tell that being away from the team was killing him, but he couldn't come out and say it. He had to be up at 5 A.M. to get to the rink ahead of us, in addition to trying to recover from his injury. It seemed to me that Tortorella was trying to make life as difficult as he could for Boogey.

Tortorella could give two shits about players who can't help him win, whereas great coaches protect their players as long as their names are on his team's roster.

I reached my breaking point with how Tortorella was treating Boogaard, and spoke to many people about it, including the Rangers assistant GM and assistant coach Jim Schoenfeld. I told Schoenfeld that it wasn't fair what they were doing to this guy, and that he couldn't handle being away from the team. The look on Schoenfeld's face said "as a former player I know you're right," but what came out of his mouth was what he was supposed to say: Tortorella called the shots. And so it continued. We hated it, and felt guilty that we could not stop the torment of Boogaard, but we played on, more for ourselves than for that lunatic running the show.

On November 14, the Edmonton Oilers were at MSG, now under the guidance of my old coach Tom Renney, who had always been decent to me. Even so, the Oilers had been taking runs at me all night. When I hit Curt Fraser with a hard, clean hit, we both went down, and when I got back up, the Oilers' Ladislav Šmid—six-four, 210 pounds—was tapping me on the shin pads, wanting to go. We were up 5–2 in the third and had the game in hand, so I didn't want to do anything to jeopardize that, but Šmid wouldn't give up. He kept following me around on the ice, tapping me with his stick, hooking my arms, and saying, "Let's fight." Since I have come to believe that, as the great war philosopher Sun Tzu said, "all warfare is based on deception," I tell Šmid to hold on until we get the puck back, and then we can fight.

He's giving me the death stare, but I can tell he's let his guard down just a little, thinking our scrap is a few seconds in the future. So I flick off my gloves and my left hand goes for his jersey just under his chin. Now I'm anchored on. The trick is to make sure you pull the other guy toward you. If you just swing like a boxer, you're as likely to topple over as he is. So you use him to give yourself leverage. I give Šmid a tug to pull him toward me, then shoot my right fist forward as hard as I can.

I timed it perfectly and hit him square on the chin. All six-four of him falls instantly and now the momentum takes me crashing down on top of him. After that, all hell breaks loose, as the Oilers want to kill me, and every guy on the ice gets into a tussle. I get tossed from the game, but we win, 8–2. Tortorella isn't happy because anytime I do something well or get the crowd on my side, he plays me less. So that was my reward from this master of coaching strategy.

My biggest fear is not being able to live in New York, and it's becoming more obvious to me that my days as a New York Ranger are slowly coming to an end. Even though I'm still producing, and had a goal and two assists in my last five games, I get the least amount of ice time of all the forwards on March 15 against the Islanders. After the game, I'm disgusted. But I still have optimism. I figure I can fix this.

I've had a few meetings with Glen Sather about it, but he didn't really have much to say. It was a tough situation for both of us, because he knew I could bring more to the team but he wasn't going to interfere with a coach's decision. It's what makes him a great GM, but then, GMs have no problem stepping in to fire the coach when the coach's decisions lead to disaster, so the principle of letting coaches self-determine is more than a little flexible.

My agent, Pat Morris, wanted to move me, but I told him to hold off because I really believed—despite the evidence—that Tortorella would have some major revelation behind the bench and I would be back in business. And I believed this because I had always been able to turn around bad situations through will and hard work. I also couldn't imagine leaving New York.

But until Tortorella sees the light, real life continues away from the rink—Hilary, and my thriving off-ice businesses.

Hilary makes me feel complete, and she says I do the same for her. I remember how when I went through the lockout with Rachel I was a mess. I was so insecure about my future that I think she grew weary trying to reassure me that it would—that I would—turn out OK. I mean, she never said that at the time, but now, from the vantage point of five years, I can see what I must have been like to live with. Tough sledding, as they say back in the old country.

I can see that I'm a better man with Hilary, because I'm not dragging her down with my problems at work. I'm talking to her about solutions, but also, about life beyond the arena. I'm not defined just by hockey anymore. It's not a realization that smacks me in the face. It's one that I can see now, looking back.

Warren 77 is a success. The thing I was learning about the bar business, though, was that buzz comes faster than profits, so you have to be prepared to hang on. At the moment, I was making about a teacher's salary from the place, and I could have lived on it if I took in roommates.

Being a professional athlete has a short shelf life, but if you think about exiting the game while you're still playing it, then you should be able to create opportunities off the ice for yourself. Then you can slide into them once you retire. And that's what I was doing. Given that Warren 77 was going strong, I wanted to maximize that buzz, and so I was starting a new bar and restaurant called Tiny's and the Bar Upstairs with some partners. John Tortorella got wind of it and called me into his office to ask me about Tiny's, which was two months away from opening.

I knew right away that the reason for our meeting was to scare me, because Tortorella somehow knew that Henrik Lundqvist was an investor (my guess is that John Rosasco, the head of Rangers PR, told him). Hank was in his only slump since the beginning of the 2009 season, and Tortorella was blaming me and the business for distracting him. He told me that he didn't want me opening this bar and that he didn't want Henrik Lundqvist to be part of it.

I was stunned. A coach was telling me that he didn't want me to do anything outside of his team. He was telling me not to have a personal life. He had no idea how much time I was spending on my private affairs, and if I wasn't playing, practicing, or training, then it was none of his business. He had moved from interfering with our endorsements during the season to trying to take total control of our off-ice time.

I've never walked out of a meeting with my head coach, but if I didn't leave the room I was going to end up in Rikers for choking this little shithead within an inch of his miserable life. If he really believed that Henrik was playing poorly because of Tiny's, then he knew nothing about his star player. Lundqvist was not working at Tiny's, he was investing in it. Players have slumps. Anyone who knows how to coach professional athletes would know how to deal with that.

I told Glen Sather about it, but he had nothing to say, really. He kept a poker face and wasn't going to play his hand, but all he had to do was watch a game—he didn't have to live through playing for a coach who responded to something he didn't like on the ice by kicking water bottles or throwing shit on the bench or tugging on a player's jersey and screaming at him and ripping him a new asshole.

I wasn't telling Slats anything he didn't already know. The question was: Who would go first? Me or Tortorella?

I got benched by Tortorella for five of our last twelve games as we fought for a playoff spot. One blogger who covers us said that I'd been thrown under the bus by Tortorella so often that I might as well buy the bus and drive it out of town. But of course, I couldn't leave of my own accord.

Hilary is as supportive as she can be for someone who's never really been in a situation like this before. And I'm doing a pretty good job of not letting it bother me when I come home, because I don't want it to poison our relationship, but I'm also starting to get used to it. It will not control my life because it will make us both crazy. And Hilary is sane. She loves me, I love her more each day, and I will keep playing my game. It's the one thing I can control on the ice.

We made it into the playoffs, with the lowest point total of any team that season—ninety-three. I was benched for Game 1 against Washington, which we lost in overtime, and then got back in for the final four. We won just one of them. It was going to be a long summer. Little did I know just how long.

———

In early May 2011, I became the first athlete in any of the four major league sports in North America to take a stand on a particular issue, and it was so radical that it surprised me by getting me attention everywhere, both good and bad. Brian Ellner, who was the senior strategist for the Human Rights Campaign's successful effort to win marriage equality in New York, contacted me through a mutual friend with a request. And so I did a public service announcement for him, in my Rangers jersey, in support of marriage equality. What I said on camera was this: "Committed couples should be able to marry the person they love. Join me in supporting marriage equality."

I did this because I was raised by Al and Marlene to treat everyone as I would like to be treated. I know, this was not always apparent on the ice, but as I said earlier, I was playing a villain in a kind of theater—I'm not actually a villain. It seemed a no-brainer that if I could marry whoever I wanted to marry, then everyone else should be able to do the same. At the time—and to this day—no NHL player has come out as gay, and I would stand next to that player as he told his teammates who he was, and help him should there be anyone who took issue with it.

In fact, no NHLer—nor anyone from any other sport—thanked me for doing it. No player said anything negative to me about it either, but fans certainly did. They would hold up signs in opposing rinks calling me a fag. The referees, and the NHL, ignored them. The word "fag" is part of NHL culture, and used as common slang. If a guy came into the dressing room wearing a paisley tie, someone would say, "That's a faggy tie." You heard it all the time.

Even so, I was just stunned that not one New York professional athlete had stepped up. Who the hell do they think our fans are in any of the sports? Straight white men? Our fan bases are as diverse as our community, though that's not something that really registers with hockey players. But shame on them for hiding in the ostrich culture of pro sports, and the idea that we'll somehow be run out of town if we actually tell the fans that we have lives just like they do—gay, straight, both. How will this repel people? And if it does, well, here's a chance to educate.

The Rangers were great about this. James Dolan, who takes major hits of criticism from the media, had been nothing but a stand-up guy to me all through my time with the Rangers. He had no hesitation in supporting me, and he let me wear the Rangers jersey in the ad. He signed off on it, and didn't feel the need to make a big thing about it, or even speak to me about it. In putting the Rangers colors out there in support of the rainbow colors, I saw that Jim Dolan also doesn't play by the old-boy rules laid out by NHL owners, and I was proud to be playing for him, however much longer that I lasted here.

On Saturday, May 14, 2011, at 2 P.M. I was at home with Hilary and my teammate Aaron Voros when my phone rang. It was the Rangers PR head John Rosasco calling, and he asked me if I was sitting down. My immediate thought was, "Where have I been traded?" Even with the dismal way our season and my season had ended, I wasn't ready to go. I felt a surge of anxiety in my gut.

I was right to feel anxious. The news was worse than I thought. Derek Boogaard was dead. He had overdosed and died in his sleep the night before.

I hadn't seen Derek in a while. At the end of February, he had just started skating to come back to join the team. One morning he showed up at the rink and was so loaded on Xanax and wine that he could barely stand, and yet there he was, out on the ice. I couldn't believe he'd actually made the drive to our practice rink in Tarrytown, given the state he was in.

I stormed into Glen's office and said, "Someone has to get him off the ice and send him to California."

Jim Schoenfeld went out and got him off the ice, and a couple of days later Boogey was on his way to the Canyon.

The last conversation I had with the Boogeyman was fresh in my mind, as he'd called me to ask for an introduction to any Los Angeles boxing coaches I knew, along with a good trainer who could help him work on his foot speed.

He also wanted some advice on his next couple months of life in rehab. NHL players have great health care coverage, probably the best health care coverage on the planet. Derek was in the league's substance abuse and behavioral health program, which was almost always required when a player had discipline issues or a problem not associated with hockey. The best part about the program is that everything is paid for—from your therapy, both mental and physical, to your yoga lessons, to any medical expenses, including rehab, which can cost up to $70,000 a week.

I told Derek to take full advantage of this, to stay out in sunny California for the entire off-season, to get healthy and train so that he'd be ready for camp in a few months. I think I was one of the few guys on the team he felt comfortable speaking with about his issues. I'd always told him never to hesitate in calling me anytime that he needed to talk, and I even gave him Hilary's cell phone number just in case he couldn't reach me.

I kept stressing how great an opportunity it was to be able to spend those months in California. I knew Derek had recently broken up with a girl he was dating and was trying to do the right thing and stay in Cali so that he could move on from a relationship that seemed a bit destructive. The combination of not playing the second half of the season, being cut loose from the team by Tortorella, and breaking up with his girlfriend put Derek in a bad place.

Derek had been given permission to leave rehab and fly home to Minnesota for his sister's college graduation. He relapsed into a night of drinking with his friends and brothers, and finished it off with some

Percocet. He never woke up. He was a week away from his twenty-ninth birthday.

We got word the next day that the funeral would be held on the following Saturday in Regina, Saskatchewan. The Rangers were sending the team plane. I was not the captain of the Rangers, but I was privy to the same type of information that the team leaders would receive because John Rosasco, the Rangers PR guy, told me when I was asking him about travel arrangements and who was going to go pay their respects to Boogey. By Wednesday, I noticed that the head count of Ranger players attending Derek's funeral was at six.

Six? I sat on the patio of Tiny's, shocked and angry. I lit a cigarette and hit Slats on my speed dial list. The boss answered with his signature "Helllllllll-Low?" I told Glen that I was upset because as of right now we had six Rangers confirmed to attend the funeral, and if this was how it shook out, it would be the most shameful thing to happen to the Ranger organization. He told me to call "Dru" (Chris Drury) and tell him that every Ranger player living in North America should be at that funeral on Saturday. Nobody stepped out of line with Slats, and if they did then he would simply make a few calls and you were ancient history.

The moment I realized Hilary would always be more important than hockey was a few minutes after the Rangers' PR man John Rosasco told me that John Tortorella wasn't going to attend Derek Boogaard's funeral. I was sick to my stomach, and she was there to console me and give me support, which helped stop me from doing something that could have landed me in prison. I have never felt more hatred toward someone in my life than I felt toward Tortorella at that moment. It was more of a shock than when I heard Derek had died. And it made me wonder: Who is going to be there at the end? There might be no one, and I didn't want that. I wanted it to be the woman standing beside me now, and onward through the flames ahead, because nothing mattered but love.

Tortorella's stated reason for missing the funeral was an inability to fly because of recent hip surgery. I can promise you right now that if I had been Tortorella and the doctors had told me not to fly, I would have taken a bus (which Mr. Dolan would have surely paid for) with whatever physiotherapist needed to make the trip to Regina—a thirty-hour drive from New York City. A coach not attending his player's funeral is unheard of. But maybe it's just as well he wasn't there, since in my opinion the appalling manner in which he'd treated Derek after he was injured had been a factor in Derek's decline and death.

The night before we flew to Saskatchewan, a bunch of Rangers came back to town, and we all went out to Roseland Ballroom. Not to drown our sorrows, but because there was a DJ playing, Armin van Buuren, who the guys liked and wanted to see. The next morning on the team plane some of the Rangers were still high on ecstasy. I didn't care. At least they were going to say goodbye to their teammate and if this is what it took, well, so be it.

There were forty Ranger players and personnel at Derek's funeral, but I know there would have been much fewer had I not called Slats and told him what was about to happen.

The day after Boogey died, Aaron Voros and I went and cleaned out his Manhattan apartment on 58th Street and 9th Avenue, which he had sublet from Voros. There were empty pill and wine bottles all over the place; it looked like a warehouse of booze and drugs. I was surprised when Voros told me the police had never talked to him.

Derek's parents donated his brain to science, and tests came back saying Boogaard had CTE—chronic traumatic encephalopathy—that was so bad his brain was in worse shape than that of Bob Probert, who had recently died at age forty-five. If Boogey had lived to middle age he would have had dementia. His parents also launched a lawsuit against the NHL, saying the league and its drug policies and its celebration of "enforcer" culture led to their son's death. The suit was dismissed in 2017, but Derek was still dead, far too young. The damage could not be undone.

The Rangers' training camp for the 2011–12 season was very different for me than the one ten years earlier, when I made the Red Wings and the NHL. This time I came into camp in the best shape of my life, and I was faster, too. I had taken up tennis over the summer as part of my training regime, and I found that I loved the game. It has a lot of similarities to hockey, in that you have to anticipate where the tennis ball is going to land in the court just like you have to anticipate where the puck is going to go on the ice.

Playing tennis in your head is like playing a virtual chess match, where every move you make is about the next move coming, and the beauty of it all is that you need to make the decision as you're moving, and growing tired. So you have to play smart, and the more you play the more you start to see patterns. Playing tennis is like solving one big geometry problem.

But I have another problem to solve, and it looks like it's beyond my control. I've never been concerned about starting training camp on the fourth line, but when camp starts and I'm on the fifth line, I know I'm done. Slowly but surely Tortorella has done to me what he's done to so many of my teammates—chipped away all meaning from me and my game.

But I get a chance at redemption. Or revenge. Or a bit of both. This year we're going to play our second half of training camp in Europe. We land in Prague, and after a quick drive to the team hotel, all the players are exiting the buses to a horde of fans wanting autographs and pictures. There are groupies there, too, who after taking a photo with you, hand you an envelope with a note inside about what exactly they'd like to do with you in bed. It's pretty brazen.

The crowds waiting for us are calling out for the attention of a trio of Rangers: the hometown hero, Marián Gaborík, King Henrik Lundqvist, and No. 16, which would be me. Although I was still very humbled by and appreciative of my fans, I had also grown numb to it because their cheering seemed to be pointing out the disaster that Tortorella was making of my career.

This time around I love it because the coaches will exit the bus last, so I get to walk by Tortorella and into a throng of screaming fans who want a piece of the team's two superstars and their now fifth-liner. It's gratifying to me because there's little else that's gratifying in my professional hockey life, and I've always been a fan of irony.

After beating Sparta in Prague, we move on to Sweden to play against Frolunda, Henrik Lundqvist's old club. I play very well on the fourth line (wow, a promotion!) with my centerman Kris Newbury, a career minor-leaguer who was a tough, hard-working player and who did the best with the skills he had.

I scored a goal in that game and also lost the bottom half of my two front teeth, courtesy of a cross-check to the face from a Swedish defenseman who definitely shit himself after I told him I was going to hit him into the next world before the game was over. By this point in my career, every hockey-playing pro knows that I mean it when I say that—you don't know how or when, but the hit will come.

I decided on a sneak attack, which started with a cross-body two-handed slash to this bug-eyed Swede's right knee, and quickly followed that with a left-handed open slap to the left side of his face—with my glove on, because I'm not a dirty player.

I got bounced, and as I skated to the dressing room for my early shower I noticed something that only someone who's done this more than 100 times before could notice: some of the fans were standing on their feet cheering, excited to see the Sean Avery shitshow in real life.

On the flight home to New York, not long before we landed, Jim Ramsay, the trainer for the Rangers, came back to my seat and said Coach Tortorella would like to speak with me. As I walked to the front of the plane, I really didn't believe I was about to be cut from the Rangers and sent to the AHL team in Hartford, but halfway through Tortorella telling me this piece of astonishing news, I started to laugh out loud. Then I stood up and just walked back to my seat.

In fact, Tortorella had shown his hand in Sweden when he said to the media, class guy that he is, "I think we have better players than Sean Avery, plain and simple."

I knew at that moment I wasn't going to quit because I was owed the last $4 million of my contract, and if I walked, I'd lose money. I also knew that I was going to turn their farm team into a disaster, and I was going to do it by not saying a single word.

Which wasn't strictly true, because when I arrived in Hartford I told the assistant coach I had an injured shoulder and couldn't play until the team doctor examined me. It turned into a two-week holiday, rehabbing my injury. It also gave me time to get to work setting up life after hockey, which was coming sooner than I expected. But then, as I suspected, it always does.

David Lipman had recently confirmed me as the talent for the upcoming advertising campaign for Hickey Freeman clothiers, for which he'd been hired to be the creative force. David is a famous New York advertising guru whose family has been in the business since the 1920s. He's somebody who I connected with on my New York circuit and who understands sports, fashion, and the arts as well as anybody. Working with David is like working with family crossed with working for a very smart guy who gets pop culture.

A week before I was sent down to Hartford, the Hickey Freeman shoot finally happened. This was my first real major advertising campaign, and not since Phil Esposito, Anders Hedberg, and Dave Maloney appeared in the Sasson jeans campaign in 1979–80 had an NHL hockey player graced the pages of *Vanity Fair* and *GQ* in a fashion campaign with a stylish brand.

All the marketing dollars the NHL throws at Sid the Kid and Alexander the Great couldn't land them an endorsement deal like this, and David Lipman had a great idea. He would get someone to follow me around for three or four days and shoot me reportage style. He knew an Italian photographer, Francesco Carrozzini, who happened to be the son of the editor of *Vogue Italia* and who would become like a brother to me. He shot me in the Hickey Freeman clothes as I went to the game, or to practice, or out to Warren 77. It was totally original compared to what I had done before in photo shoots, and a lot of fun.

My Life After Hockey had begun, even though I was still supposedly playing for Hartford.

At the end of every season, professional athletes have two realities: we're either celebrating a championship or we're saying, "Wait until next season." But eventually there comes a third reality called "Transition Season." You hang up your skates, and call it a day. There won't be another season. There's just the rest of your life. Even if you retire with $20 million in your bank account (and hardly anyone but a major-superstar-endorsement-deal-king does that), you still have to reckon with the fact that when next season starts, you'll be watching from the stands. Or on TV. Or in the worst-case scenario, closing your eyes and covering your ears, pretending that it's not happening without you.

But it is, and it will. So the question is: How do you make the transition from the game that defined your life to a life that will keep you moving forward and not wallowing in nostalgia for who you used to be?

I'd been thinking about this for a long time, and with my internship at *Vogue*, and my bars, I'd built up a range of experience in a variety of work situations, and now I needed to apply it.

For the next six months, I spent every spare moment I had beyond my life with Hilary beside David Lipman. I would drive back to New York after my mandatory time in Hartford right to David's office in the Meatpacking District just below 14th Street on the far west side of Manhattan and learn as much as I could about creating brands and selling them. I knew that it wasn't going to be long before I was heading to his office straight from home, and not from Hartford.

And if I needed any more irony in my life, it was Hartford. My alarm would go off at 5:30 A.M. in Manhattan and I would be in the car cruising up the West Side Highway by 6. I'd pull into the arena parking lot in Connecticut by 8 A.M., and then I'd sleep for half an hour before heading inside to hit my morning workout.

The interesting thing was that I was getting text messages from people who were watching the Rangers at home and could hear the crowd at MSG chanting my name. I've only heard a few players' names chanted like this, and now it was happening and I wasn't even in the building.

I played a couple of games for Hartford, finally, after basically telling them to blow me for two weeks because I knew the call from Glen was coming. I know, not great, but I was pissed off. I'd play hard in the first period until I scored or got an assist, and then I'd find a way to get kicked out of the game—jump someone, take a whack—and the team would need to kill a five-minute penalty. I wasn't trying to be a bad teammate, but rather to show how hurt and angry I was at being treated like this by a team I'd given everything to, a team I'd nearly died for. And yet here I was in Hartford, taking the place of some guy who really should have been in the AHL, all because John Tortorella didn't like me.

It's safe to say that I was probably the happiest guy on the planet when I got the call that I was going back up to New York; to make it even better, the Montreal Canadiens were at MSG the next night to give my return a real sense of occasion. I pulled my bag off the Hartford team bus and said goodbye to the assistant trainer who was standing beside Coach Ken. I told the trainer that I hoped I wouldn't ever again see this shit-dump city (he knew exactly what I was doing and didn't take it personally), and then I spent six hours driving back to New York in probably the biggest and worst snowstorm I've ever seen. I was going home to stay.

I played fifteen games for the Rangers that season, and we went 11–4 with me back in the lineup. On December 1, 2011, I scored my third goal in ten games, the winner in our 5–3 victory at Carolina. Usually after scoring a goal in an NHL game, no matter who it's against and regardless of whether you win or lose, you feel good (OK, it doesn't feel *as* good after a loss), and if your goal is the game winner, then you feel great.

Tonight I hit the showers in a hurry and send Hilary a text telling her that I'd be upstairs in the green room in five minutes and we could get back out into real life. I know the end is close because I know that Tortorella feels me picking up momentum and that he'll do everything he can to slow that down. At this pace I would have scored twenty goals, which would have made me the first player in NHL history to score twenty goals while averaging seven minutes of ice time a game. Which makes this all the more obvious.

And so it is. That was my last goal in the NHL, even though I didn't know it at the time.

I unofficially retired from the NHL on my friend Andy Cohen's Bravo TV show *Watch What Happens Live* on March 13. I'd been sent back to Hartford at the end of December because the thing Tortorella feared the most was me playing well, and I went because I wanted to get paid the rest of the money the team owed me, but I was done. I told Andy that I'd thrown my skates in the Hudson River (not quite true—too environmentally unfriendly, so I literally just hung them up). And the other truth was that the Rangers told me I didn't have to play anymore in Hartford once the March 1 trade deadline had passed.

I'd had a few conversations with my agent, Pat Morris, about a trade, and he made the usual agent noises about finding something out there. But I didn't have the energy to hold my own press conference close to the trade deadline in March so that I could explain the situation I was in and try to solicit my own trade. If I had faced the media, I would have said "I have lots left in the tank and I'm still the best in the world at what I do. But to continue my NHL career I need to be playing somewhere that John Tortorella is not the so-called coach."

I knew that New York wasn't going to trade me because they didn't want me to come back and play against them. Well, that's not quite true, because after I was sent down in training camp, I'd shut down a trade to Calgary that Pat had rustled up, believing that when I got called back to the Rangers I'd play so well that they wouldn't be able to send me down. I got the call and I came back and I scored more goals per game than in any stretch of my career. And now it was time to go.

I had, of course, prepared for this moment for quite a while, from learning various jobs to changing the way I traveled. When I went on vacation, I'd fly in economy class to harden myself for the real world. There was that time I flew twenty hours to New Zealand in coach, even though my salary was millions of dollars a year (though, as I've explained before, NHL players only take home a fraction of that).

Sure, people would say "Hey, look, Sean Avery is flying coach!," with some of them wanting to talk hockey and some just mocking me. But the thing many players fail to realize when they leave the game is that they've been living in a world that's only possible if you're fabulously wealthy. All the private jets, the five-star hotels, the catered gourmet meals, and the freebies in bars and restaurants, plus the crazy money for playing a game, can make you forget that you're really a guy from suburban Ontario and your parents are teachers. Flying twenty hours in coach sucks. But you need to remember that you're a normal human being before it's too late.

It's not just about the money. It's about keeping your expectations in check.

So now I was ready to leave the game that had given me so much (and vice versa, I think) to become a husband and a businessman. Sure, I could have waited until the following September came along and handpicked the team I wanted to step on the ice for, to start over in what would have been the prime of my career, but I was done with this shit. And no one tried to talk me out of it.

I was done with not being able to grow into the man I longed to be, a good man who prospered in all areas of my life. I wanted to listen to my music without being cast as a weirdo. I wanted to wear a dress shirt buttoned to the top with no tie. I wanted to be my own person and not a fucking robot answering to the whims of someone else I couldn't respect.

I was relieved, to be honest. I didn't have to deal with the bullshit anymore because now I didn't think doing so would change anything. Everyone from my parents to Hilary was fine with it. I mean, they realized that I was happy with my choice, and no one said I should go and play somewhere else. Partly because I don't think my friends, like Shanny or Cheli or Hully, really thought that I'd retired. I didn't have an official media event, and I didn't even fill out the paperwork. To be honest, I don't even know if I'm officially retired. Which pretty much sums it all up.

After my last season with the Rangers, we had a guys' trip to Miami—me, Mike Satsky (who owns the club Provocateur in the Meatpacking District), Aaron Voros, and Andy Cohen. I'd met Andy a few years earlier when I first went on his talk show. We'd met at a Christmas party, and it was the first time I had a connection with a gay man in a "bro" type of way and not a fashion type of way. Andy's from St. Louis, and he loves baseball, especially the Cardinals. And he's very manly. Most of his friends are straight. He's a straight man living in a gay man's body. He'd come to Rangers games and we'd hang out.

So on the Miami trip he'd hang with us at the pool by day, we'd go to dinner, and then we'd go to clubs and he'd go to gay bars. People started to see us together on social media, and then, later that summer, I went over to his house in Sag Harbor on the Fourth of July, and we took that picture of both of us with our shirts off, draped in the Stars and Stripes. We're both very comfortable with our sexuality and we find it funny that people think there's something going on between us. From that picture, some credible news source wrote that we were engaged, and it took off from there. No one ever called me to check it out. We played it up a bit. Our sarcasm on the topic was supposed to be our statement of clarity but it actually legitimized the story even more. It went away because I did the smartest thing I have ever done and I asked Hilary to marry me. Which, of course, is not why I did it. I wanted her to be my wife for better or worse, but I was going to make damn sure the "worse" would be negligible. We would have an epic and long life together.

We were going to go to Los Angeles for a week, and I had bought her a ring but was worried that I was going to lose it on the trip. So late at night, when we were getting ready for bed, I got down on one knee in the bathroom (I know, romantic spot) and asked her if she would make me the happiest man on earth by marrying me.

She said yes.

It was October 10, 2015, and one of those New York autumn days that they write songs about, with a flawless blue sky and as warm as late summer. But what made it completely perfect was the fact that it was my wedding day. Hilary and I were getting married at the Parrish Art Museum in Water Mill, New York, which is just up the road from Southampton, on Long Island. Hilary has a house there, and the gallery has been a home for art to this community for more than a century.

We make our vows in the new gallery, and then afterward, we have our dinner and dance with 100 friends and family members—with space heaters strategically positioned to ward off the October nighttime chill.

The paparazzi turned out, of course, parked a few hundred yards away and leaning on the fence separating a field from the Montauk Highway. Once the sun went down, they were out of luck.

Hilary wore a gorgeous white Carolina Herrera gown and diamond earrings. She could have worn workout sweats and still been the most beautiful woman in the room.

As I said my vows to love her, for better or worse, I knew that we'd already seen so much that was good, and together had stickhandled through the bad stuff with the Rangers. But it wasn't bad, really, as hockey had brought me to New York, and my hockey success and interest in the world beyond the rink had compelled me to open that bar that Hilary walked into. And the rest would be our history one day.

I wasn't nervous as the minister pronounced us "man and wife." I was emotional. In fact, I was experiencing the most intense feeling of happiness I had ever known. This was easily the best day of my life.

But there is more to come. I didn't convince Hilary to leave her life as a supermodel in New York and move with me to suburban Ontario, to a condo on a golf course, where I would spend my days meandering toward the nineteenth hole. No, I told her that I was going to be a Shakespearean actor on Broadway.

Seriously. This came about because my friend Peter Berg, who I first met all those years ago at my first Cheli Malibu beach party, put me in a movie he was directing, *Patriots Day*. It's about the Boston Marathon bombing, and I had a small role as a cop.

As soon as the cameras rolled, the clock turned back to when I was a kid, when I first knew that I wanted to keep replicating this feeling of exhilaration that came from hockey. I had found it again, and it was called acting. So I started taking acting lessons, and I've fallen in love with Shakespeare.

I never really studied him in school, because I wasn't in school all that much. I was trying to make the NHL. Now I'm making up for lost time. Shakespeare's great mind can get inside the heads of everyone from kings to killers, and that speaks to me. He even does trash talk. I mean, his line "Thou art the son and heir of a mongrel bitch" is something I could have used on Tortorella. "Thou art as fat as butter" was made for Marty Brodeur.

I was trying to get inside people's heads too, though in a much different way. Not saying I'm Shakespeare here, I'm just saying that he speaks to a world that includes me, and now I want to speak his words back to the world.

I had been acting all those seasons in the NHL, so it seems like a natural transition now.

And yes, there are people saying, "You can't do it, won't do it," and you'll recall my response to that when it happened to me as a little kid. I think I did a pretty good job of proving them wrong, and hearing it again now just motivates me.

I still want people to enjoy my performance, but now it will be in a different arena. You can even hate me, but that will be because of who I'm playing, and if I bring out emotion in you—love, hate, laughter—then I've succeeded. As Jacques says in *As You Like It*:

All the world's a stage,

And all the men and women merely players.

They have their exits and their entrances,

And one man in his time plays many parts.

ACKNOWLEDGMENTS

Al and Marlene Avery

Scott Avery

Jim Dolan

Barry Watkins

Glen Sather

Tom Renney

Dr. Andy Feldman

Jim Ramsay

Bill Durney

Cass Marques

Bruce Lifrieri

Chris and Tracee Chelios

Brenden Shanahan

Lawrence Leibel

Cody Leibel

Nicole Chabot

Peter Berg

David Rosenthal

Adam Campbell

David Lipman

Mattias Nordstrom

Rachel Hunter

Roly Evelyn

Kelly Kimball

Pat Minachia

Tom Sachs

Kris Draper

Brett and Darcie Hull

Shakespeare

Michael McKinley

Harry "Percy" Hotspur

Brad Norton

Laurel Canyon Country Store

Nick Garrison

NY Rangers season ticket holders

Madison Square Garden

The NHL

Neil Joynt

Larry Mavety

Scotty Bowman

David Vigliano

Steve Yzerman

John Lovell

Mike Babcock

Joe McDonnell

The girl named Hilary who walked into that bar on Warren Street and changed the course of my life forever . . . I love you.